GIRLS GUIDES

The Buzz on Beauty

A Girl's Guide to Looking and Feeling Your Best

Amy Gelman

the rosen publishing group's
rosen central
new york

For Sophie, my beautiful girl.

Published in 2000 by The Rosen Publishing Group, Inc.
29 East 21st Street, New York, NY 10010

Library of Congress Cataloging-in-Publication Data

Gelman, Amy, 1961–
     The buzz on beauty ; a girl's guide to looking and feeling your best / Amy Gelman
        p. cm. -- (Girls guides)
     Includes bibliographical references and index.
     Summary: Provides advice for preteen and teenage girls about finding their inner beauty as well as navigating the complex wold of hair, clothes, and makeup.
     ISBN 0-8239-2986-8
     1. Beauty, Personal Juvenile Literature 2. Teenage Girls—Health and hygiene Juvenile literature. 3. Skin—care and hygiene Juvenile literature. 4. Cosmetics Juvenile literature. [1. Beauty, Personal. 2. Girls—Health and hygiene. 3. Grooming.] I. Title. II. Series.
RA777.25.G44   1999   99-38938
646.7'046--dc21   CIP

Manufactured in the United States of America

ADN - 9473

Contents

About This Book

The middle school years are like a roller coaster—wild and scary but also fun and way cool. One minute you're way, way up there, and the next minute you're plunging down into the depths. Not surprisingly, sometimes you may find yourself feeling confused and lost. Not to worry, though. Just like on a roller-coaster ride, at the end of all this crazy middle school stuff, you'll be laughing and screaming and talking about how awesome it all was.

Right now, however, chances are your body is changing so much that it's barely recognizable, your old friends may not share your interests anymore, and your life at school is suddenly hugely complicated. And let's not even get into the whole boy issue. It's a wonder that you can still think straight at all.

Fortunately, reader dear, help is here. This book is your road map. It's also a treasure chest filled with ideas and advice. Armed with this book and with your own inner strength (trust us, you have plenty), you can safely, confidently navigate the twists and turns of your middle school years. It will be tough going, and sometimes you'll wonder if you'll ever get through it. But you—fabulous, powerful, unique you—are up to the task. This book is just a place to start.

The Truth About Beauty

"Real beauty comes from inside." You've heard that phrase so many times—from your parents, your teachers, or your favorite celebrities—that there's a distinct possibility that you'll gag if you hear it once more. Maybe it's true, but that doesn't help much when you feel as if the whole world is staring at the huge zit on your chin.

Society seems to care about the kind of beauty that shows on the outside. Everyone—from writers of fashion magazines to your crush—pays some attention to looks. And there does seem to be some (if not much) general agreement about what makes a person physically beautiful. So it can be hard to walk around feeling beautiful inside and out when there seem to be such high expectations of beauty to live up to.

Not only that, but you may not even recognize your own body from one week to the next, much less love what it looks like. You might be growing much faster than your gal pals (not to mention any of the boys you know). You might have to deal with zits, pubic hair, periods, underarm odor, and other little body delights for the first time. Puberty can hit you as rapidly and as hard as a truck. (By the way, you can count on this stuff working itself out eventually. But more on that later.)

In short, you may not always feel inclined to love the creature who has replaced the girl you saw in the mirror only, it seems, a few days ago. You'll most likely find it hard to see her—er, that is, you—as beautiful. But trust us. You are.

More important, you're beautiful because you're you. Y'know, you: the one who listened patiently to your best friend when she was all goofy over her latest crush. The one who called Grandpa on his birthday without anyone's having to remind you. The one with the hiccuping laugh who can beat your brother one-on-one in basketball. The one your family and friends love even if you drive them crazy sometimes.

All of this adds up to a person who is not exactly like any other on the planet. Therefore, you are special—and beautiful in a special way.

Outer Beauty

"That's all very well and good," you're thinking, "but all this stuff about inner beauty isn't going to help me decide what to wear to the party on Friday night, and it's not going to make my crush notice me. When do we get to the part about outer beauty?"

Well . . . although your inner beauty will do a lot more for you than any lipstick or new dress ever will, you can still pay attention to how you look on the outside. Throughout history people have tried to improve upon the faces and bodies that nature gave them. It seems to be almost as human as breathing.

Besides, wearing fashionable clothes and wearing makeup can be fun. You've known that since you were five years old and playing dress-up. Now, however, it's a lot more complicated than putting on your mother's dress and lipstick. You may be baffled by all the products out there that promise to make you beautiful. If you're confused, you're not alone. We're bombarded with so many messages about beauty—from advertisements and TV commercials; from friends; and from movies, magazines, and television—that it's easy to think you have to spend every penny of your allowance on the latest products just to keep up.

Relax. It's not really all that complicated. With a little practice and some help from this book, you can find ways to look good and have fun without making beauty a full-time obsession. After all, you have better things to do than agonize over the right shade of lipstick, don't you?

Beauty Buzz

In the United States, wearing makeup has not always been approved of. During the nineteenth century, especially, makeup was seen as a sign of vanity, a way of interfering with the way God had made a person look.

Makeup was referred to as paint, and the women who wore it in public sometimes were called painted ladies. Wearing paint was thought of as a moral weakness—a sign of a troubled mind or an unhealthy spirit.

Of course, even "respectable" women used products that made their skin a little whiter or their lips and cheeks slightly redder. But these products were more subtle and were simply supposed to enhance a woman's natural beauty.

In reality, makeup was often the cause of an unhealthy body. Both paint and the more accepted products contained stuff like mercury, arsenic, and lead—all of which are poisonous. A few women even died of poisoning after using these beauty treatments for too long. The U.S. government didn't begin regulating makeup safety until the late 1930s.

Looking Like You

"Be yourself" is another one of those lines that's supposed to be helpful.

"Just be yourself if you want guys to like you," say the advice columns in your favorite mags. That's usually on the page before the article that tells you that if you don't have this outfit or that lipstick, you might as well not bother to leave the house until next season.

"Be yourself, and you'll be happy," your parents say. Of course, it often seems as if what they mean is "Be yourself—the way we want you to be."

It's enough to make a girl wish that she could be somebody else for a while. But once again, it turns out that there is quite a bit of truth in what they're telling you.

You probably know someone, for instance, who acts completely different around certain people.

Maybe you have a friend who thinks that sports are really cool but pretends to hate them to go along with her new friends in the anti-jock club. It drives you crazy when she does this, doesn't it? Sure it does—because she's not being herself.

Maybe you're the one who does this. Maybe you're really smart but pretend to be ditzy and dim when you're around your crush. You probably don't feel too great when you catch yourself changing who you are to impress someone else. Imagine how much better it would be if you found yourself a honey who really likes the everyday version of you. Someone, in other words, who likes you when you're being yourself.

It's the same thing with beauty. If you're more of a T-shirts-and-jeans kind of gal, you're most likely going to feel awkward and uncomfortable forcing yourself to shop for the latest, trendiest clothes and slathering on gobs of makeup. On the other hand, maybe you love dressing up and wearing makeup, and you feel prettier whenever you do.

All that matters is what works for you. If you love hot pink lipstick, be sure to love it because it looks so striking against your skin, not because the girls at school tell you that it's the "in" color or because the fashion mags say that it will attract all the guys. (In six months, they'll tell you that no one would be caught dead wearing hot pink lipstick, and then what will you do with the ten tubes you've bought?) Make sure that you're the one who decides what counts as beautiful for you.

Who Am I?

Although your physical appearance doesn't determine your value as a person, it does tell the world something about you. Your style can send all sorts of messages, such as "I'm adventurous" (if you're wearing something loud or outrageous) or "I'm laid-back" (if you're wearing old, comfortable clothes).

So how are you supposed to figure out what your look is? This is where it gets fun, because the best way to find out what works on you is to experiment.

Maybe you already have favorite brands of clothing and favorite places to shop. Great, then you're well on your way to knowing what your look is. You can also just start from scratch. Fashion magazines can be a good place to begin discovering your look, as long as you don't take their word as law. (Their word will change in a few months anyway, so buying everything they tell you to would be impractical—and

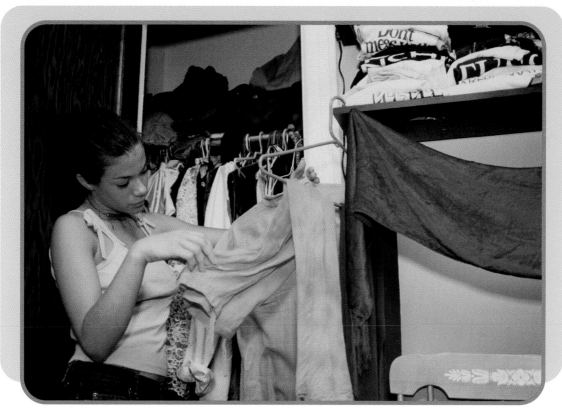

expensive.) Use magazines as guidebooks, nothing more.

Another clue to finding your style will come from look-ing around you at school or in your neighborhood. Is there a girl in your math class whose clothes you love? Ask her where she bought her outfit. She might think that it's a weird question, but then again, she might be so flattered that she tells you all of her shopping secrets. Maybe your older sister has a great look. Pick a day when you're getting along with her and ask if she'll give you a mini-makeover.

When you experiment with styles, you can try out differ-ent identities and messages until you find one—or several—that fit.

Trust Yourself

It's a good idea to take a close friend along when you go shopping to find your look. A friend will tell you when something looks good on you and when it doesn't. But don't let her taste override yours. If your friend loves delicate little floral prints, she may not like the bold colors that catch your eye. You should take her opinion into consideration before you buy, but ultimately trust your own taste.

Baa, Baa (A Word on the Sheep Mentality)

Maybe you think the clothes that most of your classmates wear are boring, and you can't stand the sheeplike way they all seem to dress alike, so you want to wear clothing that shows that you're different. If you want to wear outrageous clothes, go ahead, unless doing so will get you kicked out of school or home. Just be sure that you're dressing that way because you like the way it looks and

feels, and not because someone else tells you that you should.

On the other hand, sometimes conformity—wanting to be like the majority of other people—is exactly what draws us to particular types of clothes. Looking more or less the same as your friends or classmates can be a comfortable feeling. In middle school fitting in seems like a big deal, and you may not want to stand out too much. So if you're happier shopping at the same stores that your classmates go to, and you're satisfied with the way you look in the clothes you buy there, that's fine too. There are plenty of ways to express your individuality other than through your looks.

What's in a Label?

Clothing is also sometimes used as a status symbol, to show that the wearer is somehow important because he or she can afford a particular brand or product. The truth is that expensive clothes can be nice (although they're often no nicer than the ones without the fancy labels), but they're not any indication of a person's worth.

Never let anyone make you think that you're less important than he or she is just because that person wears more expensive clothes. If you can't afford designer labels but love the way they look, you can try to find less expensive versions at outlet and discount stores. These can be great places to shop, but remember that in the end, clothes are not magic objects that will make you into a better person. They're just pieces of fabric that cover you up and protect you from the weather. They can make you feel glamorous or trendy, but they won't change who you are.

Thrifty Shopping

If you're adventurous and/or budget-conscious, thrift stores can be fashion paradise. Depending on the store, you can find anything from 1940s glitz and glam to barely worn outfits from the latest hip designer, at prices that are often ridiculously low.

You have to be willing to wade through endless racks, bins, and piles of clothes, including some stuff that's so bizarre and ugly that you'll wonder how it ever could have been worn by anyone on this planet. But that's part of the fun. (And as a bonus, you might even come up with an outfit for next year's Halloween party.) Your efforts will be rewarded when you find that perfect little something for only $3.

Most cities and towns of any size have at least one thrift store, usually run by an organization like the Salvation Army or Goodwill. Other religious and charitable groups, such as City of Hope and the Society of St. Vincent de Paul, also run thrift shops in many cities.

COOL "QUOTES"

"What I have to say is far more important than how long my eyelashes are."
—Alanis Morissette

"Outside show is a poor substitute for inner worth."—Aesop

Beauty Basics

Oil-free. Pore-minimizing. Eye-enhancing. Ultimate finish. Powder perfect. What does all of this mean, and why should you care?

Those are all terms used to describe a few of the gazillion different kinds of makeup available at your local drugstore. Whether you care or not is up to you. But if you do, you don't need to be mystified. Makeup is much, much simpler than it seems.

A Long History

Makeup may seem like a modern invention, but the truth is that women have been decorating their faces for centuries. People around the world, from aristocratic women in northern India to members of ancient Native American groups, have put colored powders and paints, jewels (and here you thought that facial piercings were a new thing), and other decorations on their faces. These adornments have been used to show marital status, for religious reasons, to celebrate an occasion, or just to enhance a woman's looks.

Things to Consider

Talk to the 'Rents

Should you wear makeup? Before you decide, make sure that you have your parents' permission. Parents may have all sorts of reasons for not wanting you to wear makeup. Whether it's for religious reasons or simply because they don't want you to grow up too quickly, you should respect their rules.

You may be able to persuade your parents that makeup won't change the person you are inside and that you just want to have some fun with it. But if you can't, you'll just have to deal. When you're old enough to live on your own, you can make your own decisions about makeup. For now, you can still be beautiful without it. Makeup is just a tool, and it won't make you beautiful (or grown-up and sophisticated) the minute you put it on.

The same is true for piercings, tattoos, hair dyes, mehndi, and other body arts. If your parents don't want you to get your tongue pierced, it may be partly because they're creeped out by the way it looks. But they're also concerned about the health risks (like nasty, pus-filled infections) of putting holes in various delicate parts of your body. And they may have an idea that you'll be less enthusiastic about that piercing or tatt when you're their age than you are now. (After all, they're their age, and they're not enthusiastic at all, are they?) They may be more open to mehndi, because it's temporary, than to piercings or tattoos, which are fairly permanent. But they may not. In either case, you should respect their decision.

Again, you can always wait until you're old enough to live on your own. At that point you may feel completely different about the idea of body decoration any-way. Piercings and tattoos are trendy now, but do you really want to wear a ring in your eyebrow just because everyone else is doing it?

Think body piercing is a modern fad? Think again. For a brief period in the 1890s, breast piercing was all the rage. Fashionable women attached rings or small jewels to their nipples. Of course, the pierc-ings were buried under corsets and bras and frilly dresses.

$$$$$

Also remember that makeup can be expensive. You don't have to buy the most expensive brands or fill your makeup bag with new products every week; the makeup that you find at the drugstore is pretty much the same stuff they sell behind the fancy counters at the mall.

But even if you're a savvy shopper, lipstick and eye makeup and face makeup and even body makeup can start to add up—not to mention the brushes and sponges and

other equipment that you'll need to put all that stuff on. No one will blame you if you decide that you'd rather spend your money on books or CDs or presents for your friends.

If you want to try wearing makeup (and your parents are okay with your decision), what do you do next? As with clothes, the only way to find out what's right for you is to experiment. Here are a few basics to keep in mind as you explore.

The Basic Face

A building needs a foundation to stand on. And according to cosmetics manufacturers, so does your makeup. Foundation comes in liquid and powder forms and is generally used to even out the skin tone of your cheeks, forehead, chin, and nose. If you're concerned about covering up pimples or dark circles under your eyes, you can also use concealer.

Some women like to top their foundation off with powder—either the pressed kind, which you can put on with a sponge or pad, or loose powder, which is applied with a brush. (If you're the allergic type, you may find that loose powder makes you sneeze.)

Foundation Fundamentals:

- *Unless you want to look like the victim of a tanning booth accident or a really bad fright, look for foundation that is roughly the same color as your skin.*
- *Test foundation by putting on a little spot of the makeup at your jawline. (Use the tester, please. It's in the bottle marked "Tester.") You may have heard that you should test makeup using the back of your hand, but don't. The skin on your hands is usually darker than the skin on your face.*
- *Unless your skin is totally acne-free, you'll probably want to stick to oil-free foundations and powders, which are less likely to cause pimples.*

Those Lips, Those Eyes

There's all kinds of goop for enhancing your eyes: eye shadow, mascara, pencil liner, liquid liner, brow pencil. If the eyes are truly the windows of the soul, as people say they are, we apparently like our souls to have curtains, blinds, and shades.

Lips can also be dressed up with a range of products. If basic lipstick isn't enough for you, you can try lip liner, lip pencil, and lip gloss. They all do similar things, though. Many girls find that lipstick is all they really want to bother with. Lipsticks come in matte (non-shiny or "flat") and glossy (shiny).

The key word to remember when you're trying out eye makeup and lipstick is "subtlety." Being subtle means not being totally obvious. If you're going for a 1970s-retro look, for instance, heavy turquoise eye shadow is great, but otherwise you'll probably want to wear less garish colors. And black lipstick with thick raccoon-style eyeliner may look perfect at a goth party, but it's not going to work as well in gym class or at Grandma's birthday dinner.

Blush is another type of makeup that demands a light touch. You don't want to look as though your great-aunt just pinched your cheeks, after all. Blush should be applied with a brush, which makes it easier not to overdo it. Just pat and blend a little bit of blush onto the "apple" of your cheek (the part that sticks out farthest). Unless you want to look like a clown school dropout, be sure to choose a color that suits your skin. If you're dark-skinned, for example, peachy pinks aren't going to look as good as reddish brown shades.

Other Stuff

These days, nearly every company that makes cosmetics also has a line of skin care products. Do you really need facial wash, toner, astringent, night cream, day cream, or exfoliator? In most cases, no.

When you're an adult, you might find some of those products useful, but for now, plain old soap (or cleanser) and water should be enough to keep your skin looking its best. If you have acne—and most people your age have at least a little—don't look for miracle cures at the makeup counter. Instead try an acne fighter like benzoyl peroxide after you wash your face, or ask your dermatologist to recommend a product that will help.

Hate your freckles? Wish your skin was clear? Well, you could try a common skin treatment from early America: Apply the warm urine of a young boy to your face as a mask, and your skin will be pure as alabaster in no time.
(We don't recommend trying this, though we'd love to know if it works!)

Makeup Dos and Don'ts

 Apply makeup on clean, dry skin.

 Make sure that you remove all your makeup at night. Even though today's makeup is lighter and less greasy than ever, you don't want to sleep with it on your face. Eye makeup is easiest to remove with, uh, eye makeup remover (logically enough), but the rest should wash off with just soap or cleanser and water.

 If you wear contact lenses, ask your eye doctor if it's okay for you to wear makeup on your eyes. You may find it hard to wear eyeliner, especially the liquid kind.

 Don't stress about how much makeup to wear or even whether you should wear it at all. Maybe you're too busy to mess around with a lot of creams and powders, or maybe you prefer the way you look without any makeup on. Or you could be the sort of person who never leaves the house without putting on lipstick. Either way, decide what you like and don't like and go with it, and don't give it another thought. It's hard to be beautiful if you worry about it all the time.

Fun with Hair

Hair offers almost endless possibilities for changing your look. You can wear it curly one day and straight the next, put it in an updo or a french braid if your hair is long, spike it or slick it down if it's short, and—with all of the new temporary colors on store shelves—make yourself into a redhead (or bluehead or pinkhead, if you're so inclined) for a few days or a few weeks. You can even shave your head.

As with makeup, be sure you have your parents' okay before you do anything too daring (like coloring your hair or shaving it). If you're curious about coloring your hair, it's best to let a professional do your color the first time. If you like the results, you can ask him or her for advice on how to keep it up yourself. There are plenty of temporary and semipermanent dyes on the market that don't involve too many nasty, bad-smelling chemicals and don't last long enough for you to get sick of the way they look.

Whatever else you do with your hair, be sure to wash it regularly—every day or so if it's oily, every few days if it's dry—and keep it trimmed. Eating well (that means plenty of veggies) and keeping yourself healthy will also keep your hair looking great.

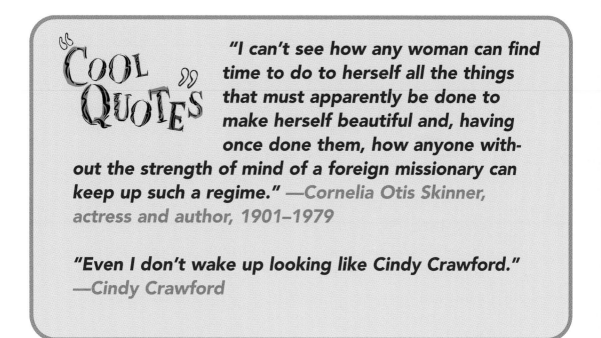

"Cool Quotes"

"I can't see how any woman can find time to do to herself all the things that must apparently be done to make herself beautiful and, having once done them, how anyone without the strength of mind of a foreign missionary can keep up such a regime." —Cornelia Otis Skinner, actress and author, 1901–1979

"Even I don't wake up looking like Cindy Crawford." —Cindy Crawford

Do the Clothes Make the Girl?

4

Clothes may be just the wrapping on the package, but they do make a statement about the person wearing them.

Wearing the "in" labels and styles can be a way to identify yourself with a particular group of people. Wearing clothes that are completely different from what's in style might be a way of saying, "I don't care what everyone else thinks—this is what I think looks good." Throwing on the first clothes you grab from your closet makes another kind of statement. That statement might be, "I'm not interested in clothes." But it can also tell people that you don't care enough about them to make yourself look good for them, or that you don't think highly enough of yourself to take care with your appearance.

Like it or not, people will get information about you from your clothes. So before you decide what to wear, think about the statement you want to make. Make sure that if your clothes are going to speak for you, they say what you want them to say.

No one can tell you how to dress (although your parents can stop you from wearing clothes they don't approve of), and no one should make you feel ashamed or uncool if you're wearing clothes that make you feel good about yourself. Whether you live for labels or you'd never dream of leaving the house in anything but basic black, you should wear whatever clothes are right for you.

Shopping Without Tears

Do you hate to shop? Do you start to hyperventilate and shake when you get within 500 yards of a mall? If so, you're not alone. Follow these easy tips for pain-free shopping:

- *Find your personal style. If you're still having trouble with this, reread chapter two or check some of the resources at the end of this book.*
- *Pick a store or two that carry the kind of clothes you like, and stick to them. You can always branch out if you discover a great new shop, but just wandering vaguely around the mall or department store will only make shopping take forever and be more stressful.*
- *Set a budget and make a list. (This will impress your parents.) Figure out what you need (or want) most, estimate how much it's going to cost, and put off buying any other items until you can afford them. That way, you're less likely to come home with a really expensive party dress you'll wear once when you really needed a new pair of school shoes.*

- Network. Where do your friends shop? How does that girl on the school bus manage to look so good on the same allowance that you get? Sharing ideas is a great way to make shopping easier.

- If you shop with a parent, try to decide in advance where you're going to go. This will avoid the possibility of Mom taking you to a store you hate. Also be prepared to compromise. If Mom and Dad are buying, it may not be reasonable to expect them to let you pick up a see-through lace crop top. Save your baby-sitting money and make that purchase another day. Let the parents buy you something more practical.

The Fashion Police

All sorts of rules exist about what people should and shouldn't wear. No one really knows who came up with these rules, but almost every-one knows at least a few of them: People with broad shoulders should never wear shoulder pads. If you're over-weight you should never wear bright colors or patterns. Horizontal stripes make you look wide.

Never wear white shoes after Labor Day. Don't wear plaids with stripes, or stripes with checks, or checks with plaids. Redheads shouldn't even consider wearing pink.

Should you commit all of these rules to memory and obey them faithfully? It's up to you. Some of the rules seem sorta strict. If you're a plus size but you like bright red and electric blue, and you feel comfortable with the way you look in these colors, go right ahead and wear them. If you love the way you look in white, don't avoid wearing it in the winter just because someone else made a rule about it. On the other hand, some of the rules are practical. Plaids just don't look all that great with stripes, in most cases.

Then there are the rules about flattering your figure. Those are the ones that say that pleated skirts don't look as good on people with rounded stomachs or wide hips as they do on other people, or that short girls shouldn't wear knee-length shirts because they make the legs look shorter. Do you have to follow these rules? Of course not; you can wear whatever you like (within reason). But again, think about the statement that your clothes make. If you wear clothes that are not flattering to your body, what statement are you making? Is this the message you want to send?

Beauty: Who Decides?

So what does it mean to be physically beautiful, anyway? Who decides what is or isn't beautiful?

It's true that although everyone probably defines beauty a little bit differently, society does seem to be in general agreement about what makes someone beautiful. But ideas of beauty change over time even within one society.

A History Lesson

Consider these "ideal" body types for American women in the twentieth century:

Early 1900s: The "hourglass" figure, with full breasts, round hips, and a teeny waist (often created with the use of breath-squeezing, flesh-smooshing corsets), was in fashion. The hourglass was replaced with the S-shaped figure, with the bust and butt sticking out (often with the help of padding).

1920s: The "flapper" look became popular. Women wore loose, almost shapeless dresses and showed more leg than they had in the past. The style favored thin women, and women who weren't naturally thin used bandages, corsets, and anything else they could find to flatten their fronts. (Ouch!)

1940s and 1950s: The fashionable figure was healthy-looking, strong, and fit, with plenty of curves.

1960s: Superthin models like Twiggy set the new standard for women's bodies. Thin has continued to be in, though in the 1980s and 1990s, fitness and strength have become as important as thinness.

As you can see, American women have had to deal with quite a range of "ideal" body types. The only thing that hasn't changed over time is how hard it is for girls and women with real bodies to look like an idealized type.

For some girls it's not just hard; it's impossible. If you come from a family of short, large-boned people and all the women in your family have big hips and breasts, you're not going to look like Kate Moss no matter what, even if you want to. And there isn't necessarily any reason you should want to. Instead, why not enjoy your curves and strength?

Think about this: In the United States, which has long been home to people from all kinds of different places, it doesn't make much sense to think that only a certain look or hair color or skin color makes someone beautiful.

Nowadays if you look carefully at a big enough selection of fashion magazines, you probably can find a range of skin and hair types and colors on display. A few magazines and catalogs show women with a variety of body types. That's a big change from even the recent past! Until the 1970s or so, most companies that sold clothes and beauty products showed white people of European ancestry almost exclusively in their advertisements. The models in fashion magazines were almost all white as well, with an occasional Asian or African American woman thrown in for an "exotic" touch. Some companies made beauty products especially for African American women, but these were kept separate on store shelves and weren't advertised in the same places as mainstream products.

Slowly the fashion and beauty industries and the media have begun to realize that many types of women buy their products. Their articles and advertisements have (finally) started to reflect this. Thumbs up to them!

Beauty Is Big Business

Still, change is slow. You may have trouble finding anyone who looks much like you in the pages of your favorite teen mag. Why is this?

There are a few reasons, but a major one is that beauty and fashion are businesses—multibillion-dollar businesses, in fact. The people who create makeup and clothes make their money in part by convincing you that you should look like the idealized beauties that they use to sell their products. If they told you that you were perfect just the way you are, and that the clothes you wore last year still look good on you, they wouldn't be able to sell you all those fabulous new styles and products every six months.

Editors of fashion magazines support this practice because otherwise they'd have nothing to write about. With all the messages out there telling you to wear this style and look like that model, it's hard not to believe that you are hopelessly, incurably flawed. But the next time you catch yourself feeling geeky and unattractive because you don't have the latest hip outfit or your size isn't small enough, remember who told you that you had to look that way, and why.

Beauty Bio

Madame C. J. Walker was the daughter of former slaves who became one of the most successful businesswomen of her time. Born Sarah Breedlove, she began her career in the early 1900s by selling Wonderful Hair Grower—which she had invented when her own hair began to thin—door-to-door. Before long she was the head of a huge, successful hair care products company with saleswomen all over the South and Midwest. Even after her death, in 1911, the Walker Company continued to thrive until the 1930s.

Beauty Inside and Out

Respect

6

Here's a beauty secret you may not know: One of the easiest ways to look good is to respect your body. You can't look good unless you feel good, and you can't feel good unless you treat your body with respect. That means giving your body what it needs. Sometimes what it needs is chocolate, and that's a need that should be listened to. But it also needs:

Plenty of sleep. Ask any supermodel: Sleep is a secret weapon for looking good. Getting those eight hours in will help keep your skin clear and your eyes free of dark circles. More important, you need sleep so that you have enough energy to hang out with your friends, read, play, and do all of the other things you love to do. When you spend time doing stuff you love, you feel good—and that's the only way to look good.

A healthy diet. Eating right doesn't mean eating just carrots and celery sticks. It means eating a variety of foods that you enjoy and making sure that you eat them all in moderation. You can eat junk food and still be beautiful, but if you eat nothing but junk food, your body won't get the nutrition it needs, so you'll be unhealthy—and unhealthy people are not beautiful.

Exercise. Your body was made to move, so go, girl! You don't have to go to aerobics class or do hundreds of push-ups a day. Just try to stay active as much as possible, whether by playing a sport, trying a fitness video, or going for a long walk. Exercise will help you feel good, will keep your body working right, and may even give you an attractive rosy glow. It can also help you lose weight, but that's not why you should do it. Even if you don't lose an ounce, exercising will make you look better because it will make you feel better.

R-E-S-P-E-C-T

Respecting your body also means not abusing it. That means staying away from drugs, which damage your body and your mind, and tobacco, which gives you death breath, stains your teeth and fingers, and—oh yeah—has more health risks associated with it than you can shake a cigarette at. And rumor has it that guys don't like to kiss girls who smoke.

It might sound as though respecting your body takes a lot of hard work, with all that exercising and eating right. But trust us, it's a whole lot easier to do healthy things that make you feel and look good than it is to make yourself look good when you're sleep deprived, starving, or a couch potato.

COOL QUOTES

"The real sin against life is to abuse and destroy beauty, even one's own— even more, one's own, for that has been put in our care, and we are responsible for its well-being."
—Katherine Anne Porter

Becoming Beautiful

By now you've probably got the idea: You can't be beautiful unless you accept yourself and love yourself as you are. All the makeup and fashionable clothes in the world won't make you pretty if you don't respect what's inside of you. Part of our physical appearance is mostly beyond our control, although makeup and clothing can be used to help us improve upon what nature has given us. But accepting and appreciating our looks as they are is an even better way to feel and look good.

Self-esteem means respecting, loving, and believing in yourself. If you don't have self-esteem, how can you expect anyone else to respect, love, or believe in you? That's true for looks too. If you think that you're not beautiful enough, you will convey that message to other people in the way you carry yourself, the way you present yourself to the outside world.

You can't just go out and buy self-esteem. So how do you get it? It's not always easy, but there are lots of ways it can be achieved. Try these on:

Make a list of everything you like about yourself. Include physical qualities if you want, but be sure to include some nonphysical stuff too. Try to be honest and not too critical. Keep that list with you or put it in your journal, and refer back to it every time you're feeling bad about yourself.

Avoid dwelling on the negative. It's like a disease that some girls have, the way they sit around and list all of their negative qualities. It can even get to be a competition: "My thighs are fat." "Oh, yeah? They're nowhere near as fat as mine." It's silly, and it's not very healthy either. The next time your friends start a self-criticism fest, suggest that you all talk about something else, preferably something positive.

Don't spend too much time comparing yourself to others, either people you know or idealized images in magazines and on television. You'll never be exactly like them, so you're bound to come up short in some of those comparisons. But the fact that you're not exactly like anyone else is something to be celebrated; it's what makes you—well—you.

Beauty Is as Beauty Does

Yes, it's another cliche to ponder. (This is the last one, we promise.) Like the others, this one has a solid basis in truth.

Think about it: When you first noticed your current crush, you probably weren't thinking about how funny or smart or sweet he is—because unless your crush is someone you've known for a long time, most likely you didn't have any idea whether he was a nice guy or a jerk. But if you get to know him and he turns out to be a jerk, you'll no longer care about his incredibly buff bod or beautiful green eyes or other physical features. People who are cruel, thoughtless, or rude aren't attractive, even if they look exactly like your favorite models or actors. People who are truly beautiful show their beauty through their actions as well as their faces.

Wanna be beautiful? Try letting some of your inner beauty show through. Organize a neighborhood cleanup, do the dishes when it's your brother's turn even if it's not a special occasion, or bring your friend some Ben and Jerry's when she's stuck baby-sitting. If that's too easy or if it's the kind of thing you do all the time anyway, try volunteering. Sign up to serve meals at a homeless shelter, clean the cages at the Humane Society, or stuff envelopes for your favorite cause.

Find as many ways as you can to make the world a more beautiful place, and all that beauty will reflect back on you. That's the best beauty secret there is.

"What is beautiful is good, and who is good will soon be beautiful." —Sappho

"That which is striking and beautiful is not always good; but that which is good is always beautiful." —Ninon De L'Enclos

"No woman can be handsome by the force of features alone, any more than she can be witty by only the help of speech." —Langston Hughes

It's a Girl's World:
helpful info

Alloy Online
http://www.alloyonline.com

American Cheerleader Magazine
http://www.americancheerleader.com
Resources and chat for cheerleaders.

Beautyhabit
http://www.beautyhabit.com

Chick Click
http://www.chickclick.com
A network of independent girl-powered "sites that don't fake it." Offers free e-mail addresses and lots of sassy content.

Cool Girls Japan
http://www.coolgirlsjapan.com
A look at the latest fashions, Tokyo style.

Cute Girls Unite!
http://www.kevamarie.com
Not as silly as it sounds.

Fashion Icon
http://www.fashionicon.com

Fashion Net
http://www.fashion.net

Girl Power
http://www.girlpower.com
A site that encourages and motivates young women to express themselves creatively, especially through writing.

Girl Power Campaign Home Page
http://www.health.org/gpower/index.htm
National public education campaign sponsored by the Department of Health and Human Services to help encourage and empower nine- to fourteen-year-old girls.

The Girl Scouts of America
http://www.girlscouts.org
Find out about troops in your area.

A Girl's World
http://www.agirlsworld.com/
A virtual clubhouse for girls, hosted by Amy, Geri, Rachel, and Tessa, that has over 60 interactive areas for hours of fun.

girls
http://www.workhouse.com/girls/girls.html
A look at girls in America at the turn of the twentieth century.

Grrl
http://www.grrl.com/main.html

Looks Aren't Everything
http://magazine.gurl.com/looks
Part of gURL, a fabulous on-line zine.

moXiegirl
http://www.mxgonline.com

Planet Girl
http://www.planetgirl.com

Teenvoice
http://www.teenvoice.com

By the Book: *further reading*

Banks, Tyra, and Vanessa T. Bush. *Tyra's Beauty Inside and Out.*
   New York: HarperCollins Publishers, 1998.

Dorling Kindersley staff. *Classic Makeup and Beauty.* New York:
   DK Publishing, 1998.

Fornay, Alfred. *The African American Woman's Guide to
   Successful Make-Up and Skin Care.* Phoenix, AZ: Amber
   Books, 1998.

Girl Games Staff. *Let's Talk About Me: A Girl's Personal, Private,
   and Portable Instruction Book for Life.* New York: Pocket
   Books, 1997.

Levchuck, Leslie, R.D. *Fuel Up: A Girl's Guide to Eating Well.*
   New York: Rosen Publishing Group, 1999.

Miklowitz, Gloria. *Stand Tall, Look Good.* New York: Bantam
   Doubleday Dell Books for Young Readers, 1992.

Moss, Miriam. *Street Fashion.* Parsippany, NJ: Silver Burdett
   Press, 1991.

Pratt, Jane. *Beyond Beauty: Girls Speak Out on Looks, Style, and
   Stereotypes.* New York: Callaway Editions, 1997.

Schwager, Tina, and Michele Schuerger. *The Right Moves: A
   Girl's Guide to Getting Fit and Feeling Good.* Minneapolis,
   MN: Free Spirit Publishing, 1997.

Shaw, Victoria. Body Talk: *A Girl's Guide to What's Happening to
   Your Body.* New York: Rosen Publishing Group, 1999.

Index

Credits

About the Author

Amy Gelman is an editor and writer. She loves lipstick, is indifferent to eye shadow, and has never quite figured out blush. She also enjoys thrift store shopping, reading, and music. She lives with her family in Brooklyn, New York.

Photo Credits

Cover photo by Thaddeus Hardin; pp.11, 26, 37, 39 by Scott Bauer; pp. 13, 16, 21, 25 by Brian Silak; p. 30 by Thaddeus Hardin.

Series Design

Laura Murawski

Layout

Oliver Rosenberg

Friday the Rabbi Slept Late, Saturday the Rabbi Went Hungry, Sunday the Rabbi Stayed Home, Monday the Rabbi Took Off ... and now Tuesday is school day for America's favorite rabbi (and most unorthodox detective).

Rabbi David Small has had it with the constant bickering of congregational life, so when offered the chance to teach a course in Jewish studies at Windemere Christian College, he grabs it. He should have quit while he was ahead. His encounter with Windemere makes a temple board meeting look mild in comparison

"Rabbi," according to the tradition, means "teacher"—but there's nothing traditional about the way Rabbi Small, trained in Talmudic scholarship and *pilpul* (Jewish hair-splitting logic), reacts to campus permissiveness, Women's Lib, even the noble profession of teaching (to a Jew a *melamed*, a teacher, is someone who's failed at everything else!).

One of the great appeals of Harry Kemelman's books is the way he weaves his views of Judaism into the plots (often in theological exchanges with Catholic Chief of Police, the popular Hugh Lanigan). As lecturer on Jewish Thought and Philosophy, the rabbi is free at last to present his ideas in full—to students who are indifferent to their religion at best (they enroll because it's a "gut" course), argumentative at worst ("Why *don't* Jews eat ham?" "Is God dead—true or false?").

At a student protest a bomb goes off ... a man is killed ... and it's up to Rabbi Small, who can see the *third* side of any question, to discover whether the kids are getting away with murder. ... Literally.

Tuesday
The
Rabbi
Saw Red

Tuesday
The
Rabbi
Saw Red

Harry
Kemelman

ARTHUR FIELDS BOOKS, INC.
NEW YORK

Published simultaneously in Canada by Clarke, Irwin & Company Limited, Toronto and Vancouver

To my grandsons,
Jonathon Dor Kemelman
and
Jared Daniel Rooks

Tuesday
The
Rabbi
Saw Red

I

"What do you mean you're not interested?" George Chernow, short, square, and now choleric, glared his indignation at his daughter. "I've been selling Lubovnik the Caterers insurance for years. The least you can do is let them bid on the job." In a voice loud enough to penetrate to his wife, who had retreated to the kitchen and intended to remain there, he continued. "One hand washes the other, don't it? I sell insurance and they sell catering. All right, you don't buy catering every year, but if I'm marrying off a daughter, so the next time I see Morris Lubovnik about his coverage and he asks me about the wedding, I'm supposed to say we didn't ask you to bid on account my daughter wasn't interested? And don't try to tell me I don't have to tell him," he added, and then answered: "A wedding is something you can keep secret?"

"Because I know the stuff he does, and I can't stand it." His daughter, Edie, turned her head aside and gave a stylized shudder. "Yech! The greasy chicken soup, the oily knishes, the chopped liver mold—"

"So pick something else. Talk it over with him. Let him show you some sample menus. At least he'll know we're not ignoring him."

"All right! All right! So I'll talk to him already," said Edie. "But I'm warning you, here and now, if he can't come up with the type food I want I'm not having him no matter how much insurance he buys from you. I didn't want this kind of wedding in the first place, and I can still go off somewhere and marry Roger quietly without all this fuss."

This last was the tactic she had employed from the beginning to bring her parents to heel. When she had first told them she was marrying Roger Fine, she said she wanted just a little

1

party, "you people and his folks and some of our personal friends, and that's it. None of this big shmeer with the wedding cake and the ringbearer and the ushers and the maids of honor."

But the little party had grown as they discussed it. "How can I marry off my daughter without inviting my Uncle Joshua who was practically a father to me after my own father died?"

"Then that means I'll have to invite my Aunt Rose who is as close to me as Joshua is to you," Mrs. Chernow pointed out. "And that means I'll have to invite the girls too, because they live in the same apartment house."

"But the girls are only second cousins to you."

"But I've been close to them all my life. Besides, Rose would drive down, so there'll be plenty of room in the car and the girls can help out with the driving. New York is a long way for Rose to drive alone."

Before they knew it, the guest list had swelled from Edie's original dozen to over a hundred. And with that many people you couldn't have just a quiet little dinner in a restaurant. It had to be in a hall, and catered. Which meant, of course, an orchestra and dancing because you couldn't have a hundred people, most of them strangers to each other, just wandering around until it was time to eat. And afterward you couldn't just send them home. Besides, what kind of wedding is it without dancing? And that meant a proper gown for the bride. "Everybody will come all dressed up, and you'll wear a tweed suit?"

So Edie went to New York because, as she explained it to Selma Rosencranz, her best friend, "There isn't a thing to be had in Boston, not one single solitary thing that is halfway decent."

This, her father at least, had difficulty in believing, especially after he got the bill. "In the whole city of Boston she couldn't find a dress?"

"You want her to look nice, don't you?" Mrs. Chernow demanded fiercely. "You got one child, and she's getting married. A once-in-a-lifetime thing, and you want to scrimp on it? She'll get up to dance with the groom, alone in the middle of the floor, everybody looking, and you want her to be wearing some old hand-me-down?"

"They'll dance? He can dance?" asked Mr. Chernow with feigned incredulity, thereby renewing the argument he had been having with his wife—never in the presence of their daughter, of course—ever since he learned he was about to acquire Roger Fine as a son-in-law: for the young man was slightly lame and walked with a cane. "I have one daughter, a good-looking girl, and young, and the best she can get is damaged goods?"

"He's a little incapacitated. So what? And it's from the war."

"It's not from the war. He got it *during* the war. It's a kind of arthritis. He told me so himself. He had a desk job in Saigon his whole duty."

"So what? Does it interfere with his work?"

Which touched still another sensitive spot with Chernow: Roger Fine was a teacher, and what kind of living can a teacher make?

"He's not just a teacher," Mrs. Chernow insisted. "He's a professor. Of English. In a college."

"Assistant professor."

"So assistant professor. What do you expect? He's a young man. It's his first job."

It wasn't only the young man's profession that irritated Chernow, however; it was his whole style and manner. He was so sure of himself, so positive in his opinions; and his opinions were not those of Chernow. He listened, when Chernow talked of politics, for example, as he might listen to the barber who was cutting his hair or the cab driver who was driving him to the airport—politely but without interest. Chernow suspected he was a radical. Who knows, maybe even a Communist.

Because his catering business was strictly kosher, Morris Lubovnik of "Lubovnik the Caterers—We Catered Your Mother's Wedding" kept his hat on as he perched on the edge of the sofa, his menus and price lists spread out on the large

3

square coffee table before him. Edie Chernow, her round little rump encased in tight black satin pants, sat at the other end of the sofa, one leg crossed under her, the other dangling over the edge of the sofa, pretending to listen. She had made up her mind as soon as he entered, the minute she saw the shapeless felt hat with the greasy headband, the beads of sweat on the forehead, the blue jowls, the hoarse rasping voice. Lubovnik glanced down at the floor as he talked, or at his papers on the table, careful never to look directly at her lest he appear to be staring at the skintight pants or at her breasts clearly outlined under her lowcut white nylon blouse. He cleared his throat. "It's not just a matter of business with me, Miss Chernow. I want only my customers should be satisfied. I want that weeks later they should be able to close their eyes and taste again the deliciousness of the knishes and the meatballs." He closed his eyes and smacked his lips.

"Now you can have either the roast beef or the roast chicken for the same price. With our customers we got two types: those who swear Lubovnik's roast beef is the best thing they ever tasted and those who say it's the roast chicken." He smiled broadly to indicate it was his little joke. "Now here," he dived into the briefcase resting on the floor and brought forth a small card, "here is something that's been very popular with our patrons the last few years. You send it out with the invitations and it lets the guest pick out ahead of time which he wants, the chicken dinner or the roast beef. In that way everybody is satisfied. Now here's a picture of a sweet table we catered a couple of months ago."

Edie finally managed to get rid of him, promising to study the sample menus he left with her. But even as she edged him to the door, he stopped several times to search in his brief case for photographs, letters from satisfied customers. "That reminds me, only last week . . ."

Totally different was the man from "Stillman's of Boston. Founded 1890." He was young for one thing, not more than thirty, and dressed modishly in gray flannel slacks with a slight flare and a tattersall-check sports jacket. And he was not pushy; quite the opposite in fact, he seemed reserved and some-

4

what doubtful. "We don't go in for ethnic foods, Miss Chernow. Those knishes and that stuffed derma are quite tasty, although a little on the heavy side for me, but we don't do them, I'm afraid. We favor bland hors d'oeuvres: tiny sandwiches of cucumber, salmon, or crabmeat salad, with perhaps fried shrimp with the drinks. We feel that the appetizer should stimulate and arouse the appetite, not kill it. You don't want the meal itself to be an anticlimax, do you?"

Edie agreed with him.

"As for the main dish, I think we offer greater latitude than most houses. In addition to the usual roast chicken and roast beef, we do a lot with fish and lobster, but the market is so uncertain these days that we've had to withdraw the lobster. Then we have beef stroganoff . . ."

Edie just loved beef stroganoff.

"We served it at a wedding at the big Reform temple in Boston, B'nai Jacob. They received all sorts of compliments on it."

Edie absolutely adored compliments.

Rabbi David Small opened the door and then stood aside for Edie and Mrs. Chernow to enter. Although the Chernows had been living in Barnard's Crossing for several years, it was the first time Edie had been close to the rabbi. On the rare occasions that she had gone to the temple, for half an hour or so on the High Holydays, he had been slouched in one of the thronelike chairs that flanked the Holy Ark or in the pulpit making a short announcement—she had never remained through the sermon—and she had been unimpressed. Nor did she see any reason for changing her opinion now. He was of medium height, but thin and pale. He held his head forward in a scholarly stoop and peered near-sightedly through thick-lensed glasses. She had also noted when they entered, because she had an eye for such things, that his shoes were dusty and that his tie, inexpertly knotted, was slightly askew.

"Isn't the groom coming?" the rabbi asked.

"Oh, Roger couldn't get away," said Edie.

"He's a professor in a college in Boston," explained her mother. "He has classes."

"Ah well, it's no great matter," said the rabbi. "Once the principals are gathered together under the *chupah,* the canopy, that is, I will give you the necessary instructions."

"Is there any special rule about who goes up first?" asked Mrs. Chernow.

"No, Mrs. Chernow, you can arrange that pretty much as you like, as long as the bride comes last, usually on the arm of her father. Sometimes the groom enters from the side, either alone or with his parents; but he can walk down the center aisle if you prefer it that way. You can arrange a procession of the groom, his parents, the best man, perhaps with the maid of honor, then the mother of the bride, and finally the bride on her father's arm. In general, the tendency is to keep the bride's party separate from the groom's until they meet under the canopy, and even there I usually arrange them on either side with the bride's people on her side and the groom's on his." He smiled. "How you get there isn't as important as what happens after you arrive. I read the *ketubah,* that is the marriage contract, which the groom has signed previously, and of course the license as well. I recite the blessings, or you may have the cantor chant them. Then the bride and the groom sip from the same cup of wine. If you are going to wear a long veil, Miss Chernow, your maid of honor usually lifts it so that you can drink. Then the groom repeats after me, word by word, a short statement in Hebrew to the effect that you sanctify him by the ring which he places on your finger in accordance with the laws of Moses and Israel. The wine is sipped once again, and then the groom breaks a glass which is placed under his foot."

"Is that necessary, breaking the glass?" asked Edie.

The rabbi looked his surprise. "Do you object to it?"

"Well, it seems so silly, so—so primitive."

He nodded. "It's a tradition that may very well go back to primitive times. It's certainly an ancient tradition, so old in fact that the reason for it is lost in antiquity. Of course, there are conjectures, the most common being that it reminds us of

6

the destruction of the temple. Or that it suggests that even in the midst of happiness and joy there is sadness. Frankly, I find neither explanation particularly convincing. I prefer to regard it as symbolizing that just as the glass out of which the bride and groom have drunk together is now broken, so can no one partake of the new unit thus formed. Let's just say it's a tradition, as sensible as wearing the wedding ring on the left hand rather than the right. But it's a tradition that has characterized Jewish weddings for centuries, so we keep it up." He turned to Mrs. Chernow. "I can tell you one purpose it serves, and that very nicely: it's a dramatic climax for the ceremony. The groom breaks the glass and everyone says *Mazel Tov*, Good Luck, and the groom kisses the bride and it's over. You're married."

"It's only that the boy is lame," said Mrs. Chernow.

"Oh?" said the rabbi. "And you think he might be unable to crush the glass with his foot?"

"Oh Ma! Of course he can," Edie snapped crossly.

"Well, then," said the rabbi hastily, "there's no problem." He hurried on. "Then everyone goes downstairs to the vestry, this time bride and groom first, of course, followed by the rest of the *chupah* group. I suppose you'll have snacks and drinks before dinner, and you can set up a receiving line there. By the time everyone has passed through, the Lubovnik people will have everything in order and open the doors of the larger vestry room, which serves as a signal that dinner is served. You can rely on them to coordinate the times properly. They're quite adept at it. They've had a lot of experience."

"Oh, but we're not using Lubovnik Caterers," said Edie.

"No?"

"We're using Stillman's of Boston."

"I don't believe I've heard of them. Are they new?"

Edie laughed gaily. "Hardly, Rabbi. They've been in business for a long time. Surely you know Stillman's restaurant in Boston?"

"Oh yes, I've heard of *them*. But I was under the impression that it was not a Jewish restaurant, certainly not a kosher restaurant."

7

"Well, of course they're not, Rabbi—"

"Then they can't serve in our temple, Miss Chernow. Our kitchen is kosher."

"But that's ridiculous," cried Edie. "I've already arranged it."

"Then you'll have to unarrange it," said the rabbi quietly.

"And lose the money we paid on deposit?" demanded Mrs. Chernow indignantly.

The rabbi's fingers tapped a quiet tattoo on the desk. Then he said, "It's no worse than the money you've lost on your temple dues the last few years."

"Temple dues? What do you mean?"

"Because if in the several years you've been here you haven't found out the principles on which our temple operates, I'd say all the money you paid in annual dues was wasted."

Roger Fine, slim and tanned, sat with his long legs outstretched in the Chernow living room, moodily tapping the side of his shoe with his cane as he listened to Edie's account of her meeting with the rabbi. Her voice choking with indignation, she said, ". . . and the man had the nerve, the unmitigated gall to tell us to our faces that the money we had spent in joining the temple and the dues my father pays each year were just wasted. I've been on the phone all afternoon calling every place within twenty miles to see if we could rent it for that night, but they're all taken. And even if they weren't, most of them do their own catering. And then there's the problem of sending out notices of the new location and finding another rabbi. I even thought maybe we should just slip off to some justice of the peace. Oh, Roger, I'm so upset."

Roger Fine knew he should take her in his arms and soothe her, but he remained silent and continued to stare down at his shoe. Finally he said, "I'm sure my folks wouldn't feel we were really married with a justice of the peace." He worked his cane in circles on the carpet. "They're coming out from Akron for the wedding. I'm hoping you'll like them when you meet them, and that they'll like you. I'm hoping they hit it off with your folks, too. Of course they're a little older than your

8

folks and kind of old fashioned. They go to an Orthodox synagogue and my mother keeps kosher at home. I don't think they'd eat this beef stroganoff you were planning to have, but it's just possible they might make a bluff at it because they'd be sitting at the head table and wouldn't want to spoil their son's wedding. More likely though, they'd just eat rolls and butter and the salad and the fruit cup. They wouldn't make a scene because they're not that sort. But how do you suppose I'd feel?"

The story got out of course. On Sunday, as the members of the board of directors waited around in the temple corridor for their meeting to begin, they discussed it. Typical was Norman Phillips' comment. "Just like our rabbi." He tapped his head with a forefinger. "No smarts. He's supposed to be an educated man, and I guess he is since he's a rabbi, but smarts he sure hasn't got."

"Well, for God's sakes, Norm, what could he do? You know our house rules call for strictly kosher catering in the temple. And as I understand it, if you use non-kosher type food, then all the dishes and pots and pans are automatically non-kosher. Then the next wedding or bar mitzvah that comes along, you want us to go out and buy a whole new set of dishes? So it isn't as though you could make an exception that one time. You use non-kosher type food in the kitchen, and zip, that's it. The kitchen is non-kosher from then on. And even if you could make an exception, why should we do it for Chernow?"

"Who's saying we should make exceptions? I'm only talking about the way the rabbi handled it. We got a house committee, haven't we? Nate Marcus is chairman, right?"

"Yeah. So?"

"So if our rabbi had any smarts he would have said—and he changed his voice to simulate the rabbi's—'you understand, Miss Chernow, that all matters governing the use of the facilities require the approval of the house committee, which the chairman is Nathanial Marcus, I believe. This applies to any caterer which has not used our facilities heretofore. Our house rules require that he receive the prior approval of our house committee. If you like, I'll phone Mr. Marcus and arrange for an appointment for you.' "

"So Nate would have had to turn her down, wouldn't he?"

"But that's just the point. Nate is not a salaried employee who may need a member's vote someday. This way the rabbi made enemies of the Chernows, and the last thing the rabbi needs in this congregation is another enemy."

Because the weather was mild, frail old Jacob Wasserman, the first president of the temple, had ventured forth to attend the board meeting. He had been brought by his good friend Al Becker, and though they were standing apart from the others, they could not help overhearing.

"I don't set much store by a loudmouth like Norm Phillips," Becker commented in a low rumble, "but I think he's got a point. Why does the rabbi always have to stick his neck out?"

Wasserman smiled. "What's a rabbi, Becker? A rabbi is a teacher. In the old country when I went to school, the teacher was the boss—not like here. Sometimes, if you were maybe fresh, or if you said something stupid, you'd get a slap from the teacher. Believe me, many times I got slapped when I was a boy." His smile broadened with reminiscence. "But the mistakes you got slapped for, Becker, you didn't make them again."

"Maybe. But you know what I think? I think the rabbi doesn't give a damn anymore."

Wasserman nodded sadly. "Maybe that, too."

2

The call came in mid-September, right after the High Holydays, and was totally unexpected. When the voice on the phone introduced itself as Bertram Lamden, Rabbi Small did not immediately connect him with Rabbi Lamden, the swarthy, bewhiskered young man who was the Hillel director at the University of Massachusetts and whom he had first met at the Greater Boston Rabbinical Council meeting a few weeks earlier.

"I've been giving a course in Jewish Thought and Philosophy at Windemere College in the city for the last few years," Lamden said, "but I won't be able to do it again this term. I took the liberty of recommending you in my place."

"How did you happen to think of me?" asked Rabbi Small.

A short laugh. "Well, to tell the truth, Rabbi, because the dean of the college happens to live in your town. Do you know her by any chance? Millicent Hanbury?"

"It's a local name, I believe. There's a Hanbury Street downtown."

"Right. Now the course is three hours a week; it's in Boston, in the Fenway, less than an hour's drive for you, and it pays thirty-five hundred dollars. Why don't you give her a call?"

Rabbi Small asked how they happened to be offering a course in Jewish philosophy.

Lamden laughed. "Oh, they get a lot of Jewish kids from around here and from the New York-New Jersey area. Windemere's a fallback school, but they maintain decent academic standards."

"She's *the* dean, the dean of faculty?"

"That's right. It used to be a woman's college. You know, one of those ladies' seminaries that flourished in New England around the turn of the century. It's been co-ed for the last ten years or so, but it's still two-thirds women. Look, why don't you talk to her? You're not committed in any way."

"Ladies' seminary," "New England," "Dean," "turn of the century" had evoked in his mind an image of Millicent Hanbury as a tall, gaunt spinster with carefully coiffed gray hair and pince-nez on a gold chain. After hearing her low contralto over the phone when he called to make an appointment, he revised his estimate of her age downward and pictured

11

her as trim, businesslike, a modern woman who favored conservative, basic suits.

It was a pleasant day, so although the address she had given him was some distance away, he decided to walk. As he approached the old rambling house with its turrets and gables and useless porches, all decorated with the fret-saw work of a century earlier, and saw the overgrown bushes, the cracked concrete path leading to the heavy oak front door badly in need of a coat of varnish, he revised his estimate of her age upward again. So he was totally unprepared for the extremely attractive woman, no more than in her early thirties, who answered the door and extended her hand in a firm handshake.

She was tall, slim, and her short dark hair was carefully tousled, as styled by a hairdresser. Her fine gray eyes were candid as she explained, "Frankly, we're in something of a pickle, Rabbi. The course has been taught by Rabbi Lamden for the last three years on an annual contract. We just assumed he'd be back again this year. And then he told us he was leading a group to Israel. Oh, I'm not blaming him," she hastened to add. "We should have contacted him earlier. I suppose it's really my fault."

She motioned him to a chair. On another was the knitting she had dropped when she answered the door. She began to put it away, but he said, "You don't have to stop on my account."

"Oh, you're sure you don't mind?"

"I like to see women knitting. My mother is a great one for it."

"It's not as common as it used to be, I'm afraid." She sat down with the knitting in her lap, and to the pleasant accompaniment of clicking needles she explained, "Christmas presents for nephews and nieces. I start early enough, but I always seem to be rushed toward the end. I keep three or four projects going all the time. I have a separate bag for each wherever I'm apt to be sitting, and I work at the one that's available whenever I have a free moment. A gift is so much more appreciated if it's the work of your own hands. Don't you agree?"

As she knitted, she told him about the school. The enrollment was just under two thousand with a pupil-teacher ratio of twelve to one. "That doesn't mean, of course, that our classes average twelve pupils, because several of our teachers are on leave each year and quite a few teach only one course. The course in Jewish Philosophy usually runs between twenty-five and thirty students. Do you think that's a lot? Some of the younger men feel put upon if their classes run over twenty. On the other hand, since we have unlimited cuts, you never get the full enrollment at any one class."

"It's three hours a week?"

"That's right, Rabbi Small. Mondays and Wednesdays at nine, Fridays at one. I'm sorry about the Friday hour. We only have a couple of classes scheduled for Friday afternoon, but we're awfully tight for space and I'm afraid your class has to be one of them."

"What's so bad about Friday afternoon?"

"Oh you know." She looked up from the knitting. "People like to leave for an early weekend. Certainly students tend to cut class more on Fridays."

"I don't mind Friday afternoon as long as I'm through by two o'clock," he said. "Any later would be a problem, because the Sabbath comes early in the winter."

"Of course." She nodded to show she understood. "Then we can expect to have you with us this year, Rabbi?"

"Well, I'll have to notify the board of directors of the temple." He saw that she seemed a bit disappointed, and he smiled. "It's just a formality, but I do have to tell them. Of course, if they raised serious objections . . ."

"How soon can you give me a definite answer?"

"They meet Sunday morning. I could let you know that evening."

"Good. Then if everything is all right, you could come in Monday for the faculty meeting and meet President Macomber and I'll get you squared away on all the forms you have to fill out."

Not until he left, about an hour later, did he realize that she had not asked to see his academic resumé, although

13

Rabbi Lamden probably had given her some idea of the academic background required for the rabbinate. Nor had she discussed the scope of the course or how he planned to teach it, but then she probably did not feel qualified. On the other hand, he had not asked her a number of questions. He grinned. Perhaps he was as anxious to come as they were to have him.

A passing police car hooted and then drew up beside him. The square red face of Hugh Lanigan, Barnard's Crossing's chief of police, leaned out of the window and hailed him. "You want a ride home, Rabbi?" When the rabbi climbed in, he said, "I saw you coming out of the Hanbury house. You trying to convert Millie?"

"Oh, you know her?"

"How many times must I tell you that I know or know of everyone in town?" said the chief. "It's part of my job. But the Hanburys are an old Barnard's Crossing family and Millie I can remember from the day she was born."

"She seems a very attractive young woman. I was wondering why she'd want to live in an old ark of a house all by herself."

"And you came to ask her?"

The rabbi smiled. "Oh no. That was just a little private thought I had."

"Well, maybe I can clear it up for you. She lives there because she was born there. It's the Hanbury house and she's a Hanbury. It's a—well—it's a matter of pride."

"What's pride got to do with it?"

"It's a matter of how you're brought up," the chief said, slowing down for a delivery boy on a bicycle. "The Hanburys have been important people in these parts since Colonial times. Josiah Hanbury was captain of the town company of militiamen, as a matter of fact. You'll find his name on a bronze plaque in the Town Hall. He had his own boat and was a privateer during the Revolutionary War." Lanigan laughed. "For privateer read pirate and you won't be far wrong, I guess. At least there was money in it. And afterward the Hanburys were in whaling, and after that in the molasses-rum-slave traffic. And Hanbury Shipping Lines did right well during World War I. These days they still operate as Hanbury Shipping but they no longer have any ships. It's an insurance and factoring business now, and their stock is quoted on the New York Stock Exchange. The office is in Boston, of course. It's too big an operation to remain here in Barnard's Crossing. All the Hanburys had, and still have, money. All except Arnold Hanbury, Millie's father. His branch of the family never did too well and never had much luck either. But still he was a Hanbury, and no one was allowed to forget it.

"That house there, Rabbi. It practically bankrupted him when he built it, but of course he had to have a big house because he was a Hanbury. And Millie, she couldn't play with her rich cousins and their friends—they had ponies and sail-boats when they were kids growing up and later on, their own cars and trips to Europe, and she couldn't afford any of that. Even so, she wasn't permitted to play with the ordinary kids in town. Because she was a Hanbury."

"But surely at school she'd meet—"

Lanigan shook his head vigorously. "You still don't understand about the Hanburys. Her cousins all went to private schools and she had to go to the public school because Arnold Hanbury couldn't afford anything else. But they wouldn't let her associate with the common folk. They had this old woman that worked for them for little more than board and lodging —Nancy—Nancy something—it'll come to me. Anyway, one of her duties was to wait for Millie at the school gate and hustle her home as soon as school let out."

"What about college?"

"Not even there. She went to a school in Boston and commuted from here. It was an all-girls' school, too, where they teach physical education—you know, to be a gym teacher. Now, if a girl wants to latch onto a man she's got to go where men are available, right? Lots of men. And I don't suppose being a graduate of a physical education school helps either. It might even scare a man off. You know, a fellow makes a pass at a girl, he figures the worst that can happen, he'll get his face slapped. But if she's a physical education type, he could wind up with his jaw broken." He laughed coarsely. "I'd worry about it myself. The two lady gym teachers at the high school aren't married either."

"It's surprising that she got to be dean if all she had was a Phys. Ed. degree," the rabbi remarked.

"Why, what's a dean supposed to do?"

"Well, the dean is head of the faculty," said the rabbi, "and usually a scholar of some distinction."

"Could be you're a little out of date, Rabbi. I know the dean at the community college in Lynn. He used to be the manual training teacher and coach of the football team right here in the high school half a dozen years ago. I gather that these days what they want is some forceful executive type who can keep the kids in line."

As they drove along, the rabbi told him of Dean Hanbury's offer.

"Are you going to take it?"

"I think so. It will be an interesting change."

"How does Miriam feel about it?"

"I haven't talked to her about it yet."

The rabbi encountered little difficulty when he made his announcement. Of course, it would not have been a Temple Board meeting without some questions.

"What if there's a funeral, God forbid, on one of the days you're teaching, Rabbi?"

"I'll merely notify my class I will be unable to meet them."

"How about the *minyan*, Rabbi? Does this mean you won't be able to make it on the days you teach?"

"I might not. But of course, my role as rabbi does not include being the permanent tenth man at the daily *minyan*. It seems to get along very nicely without me when I can't make it now."

After he had left and they were making their way to their cars in the parking lot, they voiced their real feelings.

"I notice the rabbi kept talking about Windemere College,

but the full name is Windemere Christian College. Maybe I'm old-fashioned, but to me it's kind of funny a rabbi should teach in a Christian college."

"That don't mean anything these days. They got boys going to girls' schools, girls going to boys' schools. And Jewish kids going even to Catholic schools."

"Yeah, but that it should be Christian right in the name! I wouldn't mind if it were something like Notre Dame, for instance."

"Notre Dame! You know what that means? It means 'Our Lady.' And you know who's the Lady they're referring to?"

"So? What I mean is you can't tell from just the name. Besides, Mary was a Jewish girl, wasn't she?"

They laughed. Then someone raised another objection: "What bothers me is the way he told us. He just announces he's taking a teaching job. He doesn't ask us. He just tells us."

"You think he's getting paid for it?"

"You kidding? Did you ever hear of a rabbi taking a job for nothing?"

"Well, all I can say is he's supposed to be working here full-time. So if he's getting paid, then bigod he ought to turn that money over to our treasury, same as if some engineer over at the GE works out some invention, he owes it to GE."

"Yeah, that'll be the day."

"Well, I think somebody ought to ask him."

"All right, I'll appoint you a committee of one."

"I don't mean me. But the president ought to, or the treasurer."

"Hell, they do it all the time. When they go off someplace to give a lecture, do they turn the money in? And some of these hot-shot rabbis they do more talking outside the temple than in it."

"Some of the rabbi's sermons, I wouldn't mind if they were outside, to tell the truth."

They guffawed.

"It's not like it's someplace like Harvard or M. I. T.," said Norman Phillips, who was in the advertising business. "That would give the temple some prestige. But Windemere?" He emphasized his disparagement by swinging an imaginary golf club in a long approach shot to the green. Although in his mid-forties, Norm was with it in the matter of clothes: two-tone fancy shoes, wide flared trousers worn low on the hips and supported by a heavy leather belt with a massive brass buckle. His long hair was not cut by a barber but shaped by a hair stylist. His opinions carried a certain weight with the other members of the board who assumed he knew what the young people of the community were thinking.

"What's wrong with Windemere?" demanded Malcolm Selzer belligerently. "My Abner goes there and he says it's a damn good school. He ought to know because his first year he was at Harvard and he likes Windemere better." Malcolm Selzer was definitely not with it clothes-wise. In the refrigerator business where you had to push heavy models around the sales floor, or even lend a hand to the boys loading the truck, it was hard enough just to keep your clothes clean and pressed.

"Wasn't your Abner's name in the paper the time they had the bombing there? I seem to remember him giving out some kind of statement from the student organization."

Malcolm Selzer nodded proudly. "That's right. He had nothing to do with it, of course, but he's a big shot in the student organization, meets with committees from the faculty and the administration. The kids these days, they're involved; not like in our time."

Miriam, the rabbi's wife, also had questions. She was tiny with a mass of blonde hair that seemed to overbalance her. She had wide blue eyes that gave her face a schoolgirl ingenuousness, but there was determination in the set of the mouth and in the small rounded chin. "Are you going to have any trouble with the board over this, David?"

"No, I don't think so. None that I can't handle."

"But won't it mean a lot of extra work?"

"Not really. Maybe some quiz papers to correct every now and then. Preparing my lectures won't take much time."

She asked whether he was really keen on it, or was it just the money.

"Well, the extra money can be useful. It makes another trip to Israel possible."

"And a new rug for the living room?" she asked slyly.

He laughed. "And a new rug for the living room," he agreed.

"Well, it will be a change of pace for you, I suppose. It's just that . . ." she hesitated.

"What?"

"Well, knowing you, I know it's not the money at all. It's the teaching you're interested in, isn't it?"

"So?"

"So I just hope you won't be disappointed. Colleges and college students have changed a lot since you were in school, you know."

"Oh, I don't think so," he said confidently, "not really."

3

Dean Hanbury swung her car sharply into an alley, drove down the narrow, muddy passageway behind two rows of apartment houses, made another sharp turn, and brought the car to rest against the wire-netting shielding some cellar windows.

"This is the school parking lot?" the rabbi asked in surprise. Dean Hanbury had suggested he ride with her to learn the way to the school.

"This is *my* parking spot," she said, pointing to a small wooden sign that said "Dean Hanbury." "At least it's been mine since we took over this apartment building a couple of years ago. I like it because on rainy days I can go through the back door and come out right across the street from the administration building."

They mounted the granite steps of the administration building, whose sandstone and red brick gave it an institutional look. All the other buildings resembled apartment houses. "This is the one and original building of the school," she explained. "After we grew, we built on some vacant land and then over the years gradually acquired the apartment buildings between."

"These are all student dormitories?" he asked.

"Oh no, we remodeled them just as we're planning to do with the one across the way. There are still a couple of tenants on the top floor who've left but still have some of their furniture there. And oh yes, Professor Hendryx has an apartment on the first floor. But that was because when he joined us from down South, he just didn't have a place to live."

She led him up wide stairs flanked by a massive mahogany balustrade. "You'll be sharing an office with him, by the way. The poor man doesn't know it yet, but I can't think of any other place to put you. Professor Hendryx is acting head of the English Department. I think you'll like him. He's originally from Barnard's Crossing, too. So you'll have something in common."

She unlocked her office. "My secretary has the week off between trimesters," she explained. "The place is like a morgue right now, but once classes start this building—the whole area —is simply mobbed. You'll be lucky to find a parking spot. That's important to remember, because your class is required to wait only eight minutes after the hour for you to appear. And believe me, come in after the eight minutes and they're gone."

She shook her head. "I don't understand it. They don't go anyplace in particular; like as not they're sitting on the front steps, but they won't remain in the classroom even if they see you coming along the street. There's a kind of impatience among young people these days, although things have quieted down considerably in the last year or so. The change in the draft law probably had a great deal to do with it. We still get student agitation from time to time, of course, but nothing compared to '68 and '69. Although there was a bombing last year. I'm sure you read about it in the papers."

"Yes, I remember."

"Our students weren't responsible, I'm sure," she said quickly. "The police are fairly certain it was the work of outsiders—the Weathervane organization probably. Of course, some of our students could be members. Well, if you'll excuse me, I'll see to the mail. But first let's see if President Macomber is free."

She spoke into the phone. "Ella? Dean Hanbury. Has President Macomber come in yet? Oh, I see. Well, I'm in my office with Rabbi Small. You'll let me know, won't you?"

She hung up. "He's busy at the moment," she said.

There was a knock on the half-open door, and a workman with a tool kit stuck his head in. "Professor Hendryx's office?"

"No," said Dean Hanbury. "It adjoins this one. I'm sure he's not in yet, though."

"That's all right, ma'am. I can start here. The order calls for cutting into your line." The man ran his eyes expertly along the telephone wire above the molding of the chair rail. It fed over the frame of the closet door, then along the picture molding. "You say his office is right on line with this one?"

"Yes—" A bump sounded from the other side of the wall. "Oh, he must have come in, after all," she said. "Come along, Rabbi, I'll introduce you."

They went down one corridor and then another and she stopped in front of a door whose upper panel of translucent glass had a long diagonal crack. "We'll have to replace that," said the dean mechanically, as though she had said it many times before.

She knocked, and Professor Hendryx let them in. He was of medium height with a van dyke beard that emphasized a full sensuous underlip. A pipe jutted out of one corner of his mouth. His eyes were dark and appeared even darker behind tinted glasses in heavy tortoiseshell frames. He was wearing slacks and a tweed sport coat with leather patches on the elbows. His shirt was open at the collar. He wore a silk kerchief, knotted with fastidious negligence around his throat.

The rabbi estimated he was a little older than himself, perhaps thirty-eight, even forty.

The dean introduced the two men and then said, "I'm afraid you and the rabbi will have to double up, John. There's no other place in the building. Mr. Raferty can put in another desk."

"Where?" asked Hendryx, surprised and annoyed. "It's almost impossible to move about in this cubbyhole as it is. If you put another desk in there'll be no room between them. Will we climb over them to sit down?"

"I was thinking of a smaller desk, John."

"I don't really need a desk," said the rabbi quickly. "Just a place to leave my hat and coat, and perhaps a text or two."

"Well, that's all right then," she remarked brightly. "I'll leave you two to get better acquainted."

Hendryx circled the desk and pulled out his swivel chair so savagely that it banged against the rear wall, incidentally explaining for the rabbi how the Dean had known he was in his office. Finding Hendryx's annoyance embarrassing, since he was the innocent cause of it, David Small looked around the dusty shelves lining the rear wall, the lower ones filled with stacks of bluebooks yellow with age. "It *is* rather confined," he remarked.

"It's little more than a damn closet, Rabbi, although it's better than the intolerable clack of the English office on the first floor where I spent two years. Actually, this was a storeroom for freshman themes and exams and old library books. It's pretty bleak, but I hope to bring over some more of my things and fix it up a little when I get a chance. That print"—pointing to a large framed drawing of medieval London—"is mine, and so is that bust of Homer"—nodding to a large plaster cast on the top shelf immediately above him. He tilted back in his chair and stretched out his legs so that he was almost lying down, in what the rabbi would come to know as a characteristic pose.

Fishing in his pocket, he brought forth a tiny brass figurine with which he tamped down the tobacco in his pipe. He puffed gently during the operation, and when his pipe was drawing satisfactorily again, he returned the tamper to his pocket.

"So you're the new instructor in Jewish Thought and Philosophy," he said. "I knew your predecessor, Rabbi Lamden. According to one of my students who took his course, he used the time to give little lectures on morality. Believe me, it was a most satisfactory arrangement all around. As far as the students were concerned, it was an easy three credits. As far as Lamden was concerned, it was a pleasant few hours a week for which he got some extra money. And I suppose he could always salve his conscience with the thought that he was returning his students to the religion of their forefathers."

"I see."

"Of course, the administration stood to gain from the course," said Hendryx. "As you know, the official title of the school is Windemere Christian College. The catalogue and the bulletin we send out to prospective students are careful to explain the school is completely non-denominational, and that's the actual truth. I'm sure the trustees—one of whom is the insurance tycoon Marcus Levine, one of your kind, I presume, judging by the name—would be happy to drop the 'Christian,' but it would involve all sorts of legal complications. Now we get quite a few Jewish students, not only from around here but also from the New York-New Jersey area. It's a fallback school, you see, and their parents are apt to jib at sending them to a school clearly labeled Christian. So it helps if there's a course in Jewish Thought and Philosophy, taught by a real honest-to-goodness rabbi." He grinned broadly. "From their point of view, you're a kind of Judas sheep, I suppose."

"You don't like Jews, do you?" asked David Small curiously.

"How can you say so, Rabbi? Some of my best friends are Jews." He smiled sardonically. "I know you people consider that the stock rationalization tag of the anti-semite, but I suspect that in a way it's true. You people are just the opposite of the Irish in that respect. The individual Jews one knows

23

are dedicated, idealistic, selfless; and yet one is convinced that all the rest one does not know are cunning, grasping, and crassly materialistic. The Irish on the other hand, are supposed to be gay, quixotically gallant, unworldly, even though the Irishmen of one's acquaintance might be drunken, quarrelsome blackguards whose word no sensible person would accept." He smiled, showing even white teeth. "No, I don't consider myself the least bit anti-semitic, but I guess I'm rather outspoken, and when a thought occurs to me I don't hesitate to say it. You might call me a sort of devil's advocate."

"Some of my best friends are devil's advocates," said the rabbi.

There was a knock on the door. Hendryx jerked to a sitting position and circled the desk to admit a man carrying a short aluminum ladder. It was the telephone serviceman.

"I'm here to install the phone," he said. "Where do you want it? On the desk?"

"Right."

Resting his ladder against the shelves, the serviceman began measuring the wall with a folding rule. He moved his ladder behind the swivel chair and climbed to the top shelf. He grasped the plaster bust with both hands as if to remove it, and then finding it too heavy to lift easily, he slid it along the shelf.

"Hey, what the hell do you think you're doing with that statue?" demanded Hendryx. "I want it right there."

"I'll put it back, don't worry," the man said. "The wire has to come through behind it so I can run it down to the desk."

"Well, see that you do."

The man drilled the hole and then left to return to the dean's office. Hendryx felt it necessary to explain his show of temper. "I was given that bust by the first class I ever taught. It isn't anything you can pack easily—it must weigh fifty or sixty pounds—but I've lugged it around with me from job to job for the last dozen years."

The rabbi nodded sympathetically, although he suspected the outburst at the serviceman was caused by Hendryx's earlier displeasure on learning he would have to share his office.

Another knock; this time it was Dean Hanbury. "We can go up to see President Macomber now," she said.

President Macomber was a tall, gray-haired man, dressed in slacks, sportshirt, and nylon windbreaker. A bag of golf clubs lay on the floor in one corner of his office. "I just played nine holes," he said to explain his costume. "Do you play golf, Rabbi?"

"No, I'm afraid not."

"Pity. You have a parish, or . . . ?"

"I have a congregation in Barnard's Crossing."

"Of course," he nodded enthusiastically. "You're from Dean Hanbury's hometown. Well, I imagine it's like being minister of a church or pastor of a parish. I mean, you've probably got a board of vestrymen you've got to get along with."

"We have a board of directors."

"That's what I mean. And I'm sure you'd find it a lot easier to work with that board if you played golf. You can come to an understanding on a golf course a lot easier than sitting across a table decked out in a tie and business suit. A college president these days is a combination salesman and public relations man; and take it from me, there's nothing like a golf course to transact business. Think about it. Well, Rabbi. I'm happy you were able to join us."

He extended his hand to signify the meeting was over.

"What do you hear from Betty?" the dean asked.

President Macomber smiled. "She's almost completed her residence requirement." He shook his head in amusement. "Sorry, Rabbi, but it's hard to break the habit of academic lingo. My daughter is in Reno," he explained to the rabbi, "getting a divorce."

"Oh, I'm sorry," said the rabbi.

"No need to be. It's one of those things. You people believe in divorce, don't you?"

"Oh yes, as a cure for an impossible marriage," said the rabbi.

"Well, that's what this was." And to Dean Hanbury, "If

25

everything goes according to Hoyle, she'll be back here as Betty Macomber again by next week."

"Oh, that's nice," said Millicent Hanbury.

"Well, again, Rabbi, we're happy to have you with us, and if you have any problems, don't hesitate to come and see me."

Rabbi Small returned to his office for his hat and coat, and finding Professor Hendryx busy with grade lists and uncommunicative, he wandered down to the first floor of the building to wait for the faculty meeting to begin. It was scheduled for eleven o'clock and by half-past ten the teachers began to arrive. The rabbi killed time, idly looking at the commemorative tablets, dingy oil paintings, and yellowing portrait photographs of earlier presidents and deans—women in stiff lace collars and oval pince-nez, just as he had originally pictured Dean Hanbury—that lined the walls of the marble-floored, rotunda-like foyer. Faculty members greeted each other, with someone occasionally looking at him curiously, but no one came over.

Then he heard his name called. Turning, he saw the tall figure of Roger Fine advancing toward him. "I thought it was you," Fine said, "but I couldn't imagine what you were doing here."

"I'm going to be teaching here," said the rabbi, pleased to see a familiar face. "I'm giving the course in Jewish Thought and Philosophy."

"I've only been here since last February myself," said Fine, "but wasn't there another rabbi listed in the catalogue?"

"Yes, Rabbi Lamden."

"Oh, you take turns at the course?"

Rabbi Small laughed. "No, he couldn't give it this year and they asked me to fill in."

"Well, that's great," said the young man. "Maybe we could arrange to drive in together if our hours correspond. You been assigned an office yet?"

"The dean arranged for me to share an office with a Professor Hendryx."

"No kidding?" He began to laugh.

"Did I say something funny?"

Instead of answering, Fine hailed a fat young man who was passing. "Hey, Slim, come here a minute. I want you to meet Rabbi Small, the man that married me."

The young man extended a hand. "And you're checking up on him, Rabbi?"

"Slim Marantz is also in the English Department," he said to David Small. "The rabbi is teaching the course in Jewish Philosophy, Slim, and Millie just assigned him to the same office with Hendryx."

"You're kidding." And Marantz began to laugh.

"And you thought Millie had no sense of humor," said Fine.

The rabbi looked questioningly from one grinning young man to the other. Fine proceeded to explain. "John Hendryx has been clamoring for a private office ever since he arrived at Windemere a couple of years ago."

Marantz amplified: "He objected to the loud, friendly chaos of the English office."

"Not conducive to concentration," mimicked Fine.

"And totally inimical to his fine, high pronunciamentos on all subjects philosophical, psychological, sociological—"

"And racial, especially Jewish racial," added Fine.

"Right. So when he was made acting head of the department early in the summer session, he demanded a private office and Millie Hanbury managed to find him an oversized closet on the second floor. A poor thing, but his own."

"His very words," explained Fine with relish. "Needless to say, there was no great mourning in the English office when he moved. No one got up a petition begging him to reconsider; no black-bordered resolution of regret was passed."

"If truth be told," said Marantz, "while there was no dancing between or on the desks, there was quiet rejoicing, more in keeping with the grove of academe."

"And now you tell me, Rabbi, that Millie has put you in with him," said Fine. "Do you wonder we find it amusing?"

"And a rabbi at that," said Marantz, shaking his head in wonder.

"What's my being a rabbi got to do with it?" asked David Small.

"Because he's an anti-semitic sonofabitch," said Fine. "Oh,

not the Elders of Zion type; more like 'some of my best friends are Jewish.'"

"He told me so this morning," the rabbi admitted.

"Aha!"

"But, I didn't find it offensive. Besides, I don't expect to be using the office much. I doubt we'll be seeing much of each other."

"Don't get me wrong, Rabbi," said Marantz, "he's polite enough. My desk was beside his in the English office for the couple of years that he was there, and I never got into a hassle with him. On the other hand, Fine here has a quick fuse. I'll bet it's as much on your account, Roger, that he wanted out of the English office. Unless, he wanted a private place where he could make out with a chick."

"So he could lecture her on Chaucerian rhyme schemes?" laughed Fine.

"It's hard telling with those dark glasses he always wears, but I seem to have detected a random glint of interest when a good-looking coed passed by." His face split in a wide grin. "Hey, you don't suppose it's Millie he's got a thing for and that's why he moved up to the second floor?"

"Now that would really be something," said Fine with a chortle and then cut it off. "Cool it," he said. "Here she comes."

Dean Hanbury walked toward them purposively. "There you are, Rabbi. I wanted to make sure you knew where to go for the faculty meeting. Welcome back, Dr. Marantz, Professor Fine."

4

President Macomber's normally cheerful countenance was somber as he listened.

"There's no question about it," the dean said. "Two quizzes

were given in that Miss Dunlop's section and she failed both of them—badly. The final was the departmental exam, the same exam for all seven sections, and consisted of a hundred questions—"

"A hundred?"

"That's right. It was an objective test—short, two- or three-word answers. Each of the section men submitted ten questions and Professor Hendryx added thirty of his own. No one else saw those thirty questions except Professor Fine, who was given the job of mimeographing the exam."

"Professor Hendryx's secretary?" suggested the president.

"He doesn't have one. Besides, Professor Hendryx assured me he had typed the stencil himself."

"All right."

"Kathy Dunlop got an A in the exam, and it averaged out with the two quizzes to give her a C-minus in the course."

"She could have studied hard and boned up for it, you know," the president observed.

"Professor Hendryx checked with Mr. Bailen, her instructor. The girl answered every single question correctly. Mr. Bailen said he couldn't have done it himself. Eighty-five right is an A; one hundred is unheard of. The way these objective tests work, no one is expected to get all the answers correct."

"All right," said Macomber. "But why assume Professor Fine is to blame? The girl could have got it from a discarded sheet in the wastepaper basket, or from one of the janitors."

Dean Hanbury shook her head. "Professor Fine was instructed to take a reading on the automatic counter before and after running off the stencil. The difference between the two numbers was one hundred and fifty-three, and that was the exact number of copies he turned in to Professor Hendryx."

"I see. Did you talk to Professor Fine?"

"No. I didn't think it advisable until I had discussed it with you. I might mention that, according to Professor Hendryx, on several occasions Professor Fine has remarked that examinations were a lot of nonsense."

"With that attitude I imagine Professor Fine is quite popular with his students," said Macomber wryly.

"I believe he is," she admitted, "and with the younger members of the faculty as well. He's quite outspoken and is regarded as concerned. That's the term they use nowadays—concerned. He was the leader in the movement to recruit black students, and even organized a tutoring service for them among the younger members of the faculty. He wrote the article in *The Windrift* that I showed you, if you remember."

"Oh yes. The red-headed chap? Walks with a cane?"

"That's the one. He came at mid-years on a one-year contract, so if you decide to drop him there should be no problem with the AAUP."

"Well now," said Macomber, "let's not be hasty. Just because he has no tenure and no legal right to a hearing, doesn't mean it wouldn't cause a lot of trouble if we failed to grant him one. You yourself say he's popular with students and faculty. This is just the sort of thing that could be blown up into a student protest. I'm sure I don't have to tell you, Millicent, that's the last thing we need now with school opening in a couple of days."

"But a member of the faculty helped a student to cheat! Do you have any idea what could happen if that got out?"

"Oh, I don't think that's likely. Not if Professor Fine is approached in the proper manner. Suppose we play it this way. . . ."

Seated in the visitor's chair, Roger Fine appeared completely at ease except for his whitened knuckles on the hand gripping his cane. "You realize, Miss Hanbury," he said, "that you have no real proof."

"Do you deny it?"

"I neither deny nor affirm it," he said negligently. "I don't think I'm required to answer at all."

Dean Hanbury tapped her desk with her fingertips as she gathered her thoughts. Finally she said, "I have not spoken to Miss Dunlop—as yet. I feel certain that if told she must substantiate her phenomenal grade in the final by taking another exam, she will admit everything." She looked away and then added, "I understand she has a small scholarship from some religious group in Kansas where her father is a minister."

"What do you want, Dean Hanbury?"

"Well," said the dean, noting the change in tone, "we don't want a scandal, and we don't want another confrontation with the students."

"In other words, you'd like me to resign quietly."

"No."

"No?"

"Since the semester has already started," said the dean, "I suspect that some of your more concerned friends among the student body and the faculty would realize that your resignation probably had been requested and might initiate the inquiries and possible actions we're trying to avoid."

"Then what exactly are you recommending, Dean Hanbury?"

Millicent Hanbury, feeling in control now, picked up her yarn and resumed knitting. "You were hired on a one-year contract which expires at the end of this semester," she said. "We would be happy to have you fulfill your contract, but on the mutual understanding it will not be renewed."

"What's the catch?"

"No catch, Professor Fine. But to insure that you leave quietly at the end of the semester, I'm asking you to sign this paper, which is your admission that you showed the Dunlop girl an advance copy of the exam. I will put it in my safe in a sealed envelope, and that will be the end of it."

The room was silent except for the click of the knitting needles. "How do you mean the end of it?"

"Just that," she said. "We are willing to let the matter rest if you are. When you have fulfilled your contract, you will leave Windemere and the envelope will be destroyed or returned to you."

"And how about my getting another job?"

"We won't interfere in any way," she assured him.

"Let me get this straight, Miss Hanbury," he said. "If I sign that paper, you put it away and say nothing. You don't mention it if I apply for another job someplace else, and they write you for reference?"

"We will make no mention of what is in that paper. We'll handle it as a matter of form and transmit whatever ratings you've been given without comment. I believe Professor Bowdoin gave you a rating before he retired?"

"Superior."

"And your student rating?"

"Also Superior. But how about Hendryx?"

"He's only acting head of your department and so would not be asked to rate you," she said.

"All right. Give me the paper. I'll sign." He switched his cane to his left hand and reached into his breast pocket for a pen. He glanced at the single typed paragraph and was about to sign when a thought occurred to him. "How about Miss Dunlop?"

The dean laughed shortly. "Oh, we're not greatly concerned about *her*. Dunlop barely passed even with that A on the final. And judging by the rest of her grades, I doubt the girl will stay the distance."

Ever since the death of his wife three years earlier, President Macomber had been a lonely man, rattling around the large President's House, ministered to by his efficient but dull housekeeper, Mrs. Childs. Outwardly he appeared to maintain an active social life, going out two or three nights a week to meetings, conferences, official dinners. Once a year he was 'at home' to the faculty, serving sherry, crackers and cheese, coffee and cake, under the supervision of Mrs. Childs and a crew from the school cafeteria. And once a year, he gave dinner to the board of trustees, a dinner served by outside caterers, much to the annoyance of the estimable Mrs. Childs who regarded it as a reflection on her.

On those evenings when he stayed home, he read the newspapers after dinner, watched TV or read a book. At ten, Mrs. Childs appeared with tea which she set down on the table beside his easy chair, wished him goodnight, and went off to her own quarters off the kitchen. He usually puttered around until the eleven o'clock newscast and then himself went to bed.

Just before the fall term Macomber's daughter Betty called from Reno to announce the glad tidings that her divorce had been granted and that she was taking the next plane out. He indulged in pleasant daydreams that now things would be different. He would now have someone to talk to at breakfast and dinner. Perhaps he might even play hookey some afternoon and sneak in a round of golf. They were both avid golfers.

She would be his official hostess, and once again he could hold those purely social parties, not connected with business, that he had missed so much since his wife's death. Of course Betty was still young, thirty-five, and after a while she would develop her own circle of friends, young people with interests different from his. But not for a while yet. She would want some peace and quiet after her unfortunate marriage.

It did not work out that way. She arrived early in the evening. Her plane had been delayed on the ground and then was locked into a holding pattern for almost an hour before it could land. The gaiety in her voice when she had called him from Reno was gone; she was tired and peevish.

"That awful plane!" she exclaimed by way of greeting. "I thought I'd have time to lie down for a while, and now I barely have time to shower and change."

"You don't have to change on my account, dear," said her father. "Mrs. Childs has prepared a quiet little meal. I can't

33

tell you how I've been looking forward to the chance to talk and catch up on things."

She was contrite. "Oh, I am sorry, Dad, but I'm due at the Sorenson's for dinner. They're having a few people over. It's a kind of freedom party for me—you know, celebrating my divorce. And Gretchen said she had this fascinating man she wanted me to meet."

Nor did it change with time. He saw as little of her as when she had been married and living in the suburbs. She went out almost every night, and even when they had dinner together she always seemed rushed.

"Look, Betty," he remonstrated, "must you go out again tonight?"

"Oh, I really have to, Dad. I promised."

"But you've been out every single night this week."

"Dad, I'm thirty-five—"

"I know that. I'm not trying to play the stern *pater-familias,* but—"

"You've been a dear, Dad, but you must understand that I have no intention of remaining single for the rest of my life. I mean to get married, and just because I'm thirty-five I can't waste any time."

He was old-fashioned, and the bluntness with which she stated her position embarrassed him a little. "Well, naturally, I want you to get married, Betty. I realize I'm probably being selfish," he went on, "but I rather hoped that we could have some evenings together, just the two of us. You know, the president of a college, like the president of anything, is a kind of lonely figure. He has to make all sorts of decisions, and almost anyone he turns to for advice, or just to talk out some problem, has an axe to grind."

She laughed. "Poor Dad. All right, tomorrow I'll stay home and—Oh, no, tomorrow I can't or Thursday either. Perhaps Friday?"

The weekend was out of the question, of course, because then she went upcountry to New Hampshire where her son, Billy, was at school.

6

Monday was registration day, classes began Tuesday; so Wednesday morning was the first session of Philosophy 268, Jewish Thought and Philosophy; Mon. & Wed. at 9:00, Fri. at 1:00, Admin. Building, Room 22; three credits.

By a quarter to nine they began to drift in—the freshmen checking the number on the door against the number they had copied down on their program cards, the upperclassmen gravitating to one corner.

"Hey, Harvey boy!" A tall, willowy youth in yellow plaid slacks, crimson shirt, and a yellow silk kerchief fastened around his neck appeared in the doorway and was instantly hailed by the group in the corner. "How they hanging?"

"You taking this course?"

Harvey glanced around the room to see if there were any attractive new girls, then sauntered over. "You bet I'm taking this course." Harvey Shacter perched his elegantly clad bottom on the arm of the chair occupied by Lillian Dushkin. "Can't you just see Uncle Harvey turning down a gift of three credits? You know Cy Berenson? He took it last year and didn't even take the final. The rabbi let him write a five-hundred-word paper and gave him a B."

"Yeah, but Berenson used to wear a yarmelkeh all the time," said Henry Luftig, a short, thin, intense young man with a high bony forehead ending in a cap of jet black hair. "The rabbi probably figured he knew the stuff anyway."

"Yarmelkeh? Oh, you mean that black beanie? Okay, if it will guarantee a B I'll wear a yarmelkeh."

"That will be the day," Lillian Dushkin giggled. "Come to think of it, you might look cute."

"Hey, Lil," said Aaron Mazonson. "I heard this Rabbi Lamden was a regular swinger. All a chick has to do is sit in the front row and give him an eyeful and she's practically guaranteed an A."

A sophomore nearby joined in. "It's not Rabbi Lamden this year, it's a different guy."

"Where'd you hear that?"

"When I registered for the course. My adviser told me when he initialed my program."

"Well, it says Rabbi Lamden in the catalogue."

"Yeah, well, that's because it was a last minute change."

"Great!" exclaimed Shacter in disgust. "That's just what I need. My one pipe course, and they get a new guy who will probably want to show how tough he is."

"So we'll set him straight," said Luftig, grinning.

Shacter considered, and then he, too, grinned. "Yeah, that's the idea. We'll set him straight."

The street was lined with cars, and the broad granite steps of the administration building were so crowded with students that Rabbi Small had to zig-zag his way to the doors. Inside the enclosed area of the Marble, the marble-tiled rotunda, students were swarming about while others were manning tables behind signs: "Support Your School—Buy a Sports Card, Admission to All Athletic Events," "Subscribe to *The Windrift*, Your Own Magazine," "Sign up for the Dramatic Club," "Concerned? Join the Democratic Party," "Concerned Students Join SDS," "Hear the Truth—Join the Socialist Study Group."

"Hey! You a freshman? Then you'll want to go to all the games. Sign up here."

"Sandra! Coming out for dramatics again this year?"

"Get your free copy of *The Windrift*."

The rabbi managed the stairs leading to his office without either buying, pledging, or signing anything. Pleased and excited by the unaccustomed activity, he stopped to catch his breath before entering his class.

There were twenty-eight students present; his class list, sent to him a few days before, showed thirty. He mounted the platform and wrote on the blackboard: "Rabbi David Small, Jewish Thought and Philosophy." And then announced: "I am Rabbi Small. I will be giving this course instead of Rabbi Lamden who is listed in the catalogue."

Harvey Shacter winked at Lillian Dushkin and raised his hand lazily. The rabbi nodded.

"What do we call you? Professor or Doctor?"

"Or Rabbi?" from Henry Luftig.

"Or David?" asked Lillian sweetly.

"I am neither a doctor nor a professor. Rabbi will do perfectly well." He gave Miss Dushkin a sharp look and went on, "This is a one-semester course, and the subject is a large one. The most we can hope for is to get some understanding of the basic principles of our religion and how they developed. For you to derive any benefit from the course, however, you'll have to do a great deal of reading. I shall suggest books from time to time, and within the next couple of weeks or so I hope to have a mimeographed reading list to distribute to you."

"Will that be required reading?" asked a shocked Harvey Shacter.

"Some of it will be required, and some will be collateral reading. We will start by reading the Five Books of Moses, the Torah, on which our religion is based. I'll expect you to finish it in the next two or three weeks and then we'll have an hour exam."

"But that's an awful lot," Shacter protested.

"Not really. I don't expect you to study it intensively at first. Read it as you would a novel." He held up a copy of the Old Testament that he had brought with him. "Let's see, in this text it runs about two hundred and fifty pages. It's good large type. I'd say it's about the length of a short novel. I shouldn't think that would be too much for college students."

"What text do we use?"

"Is it on sale in the bookstore?"

"Any special translation?"

"Can we use the original?" This last from Mazonson.

"By all means, if you can," said the rabbi with a smile. "For the rest of you, any English text will do. If it's not on sale in the bookstore, you should have no trouble getting a copy. I would appreciate it if you did not leave it until the last few days before the exam. If you begin your reading immediately you can have a better understanding of the material as I deal with it in my lectures—"

"This is going to be a lecture course?" Henry Luftig seemed aghast.

"What else did you have in mind?" asked the rabbi dryly.

"Well, I thought it was going to be a—you know, like a discussion course."

"But how can you discuss something you don't know?"

"Oh, well, like general principles. I mean everybody knows something about religion."

"Are you sure, Mr.—er—?" the rabbi began gently.

"Luftig. Hank Luftig."

"Are you sure, Mr. Luftig? I'll grant that most people have some general ideas, but often they're much too general. Religion can be regarded as an overall blueprint for our thinking and our basic attitude toward life. Now the Jewish religion differs widely from the prevailing Christian religion, but at some points the differences involve subtle fine distinctions."

"So that's why we ought to have discussions, Rabbi," Shacter offered.

The rabbi considered and then shook his head. "You mean that by combining your ignorance, you'll be able to achieve knowledge?"

"Well . . ."

"No, no. Let's proceed in the traditional way. When you have some knowledge, then perhaps we can discuss its interpretation." Procedural matters over, he launched into his introductory remarks. "Now one immediate difference between Judaism and many other religions is that we're not bound by an official creed. With us, it's largely an accident of birth. If you're born a Jew, you're a Jew, at least until you officially convert to some other religion. An atheist who was born a Jew is therefore a Jew. And conversely, someone who was not born a Jew but follows all our traditional practices and shares our traditional beliefs would still not be considered a Jew if he had not officially converted to Judaism."

He smiled. "And I might add for the benefit of any ardent exponent of Women's Liberation who may be among us that by rabbinic law, only one born of a Jewish mother—note, mother, not father—is a Jew."

"Who you kidding, Rabbi?"

He was startled by the interruption from an attractive girl in the first row.

"I don't understand, Miss—er—"

"Goldstein. And that's *Ms*. Goldstein."

"I beg your pardon, Ms. Goldstein," said the rabbi gravely. "I should have known."

"I mean isn't that just a line Jewish male chauvinists hand women nowadays to hide their second class status?" She went on. "Women are brainwashed into thinking they're more important because they're the ones who decide whether the kid belongs to the Jewish race or nation or whatever it is. Terrific! When actually wasn't it because with Jews a persecuted minority everywhere, there was greater certainty if you traced descent from the mother?"

"Oh, I see what you mean. Yes, I imagine that could be the rationale," he admitted.

A frosty smile flitted across her face. "And isn't it true that women have no place in the Jewish religion down to the present day? In some synagogues they even hide them behind a curtain up in the balcony."

"That's only in strictly Orthodox congregations."

"In our synagogue they sit on one side," Lillian Dushkin said.

"And they're not allowed to take part in the service," Ms. Goldstein added.

"That's not true," said the rabbi. "The service is a recitation of a series of prayers. Women who attend the service recite the prayers along with the men."

"Big deal," said Lillian Dushkin. "They're never called up to read or anything."

"They are, in Reform temples," the rabbi corrected her.

"I know for a fact that the husband can divorce the wife by just sending her a letter," said Mark Leventhal, not because he had any great sympathy for the women but because they appeared to have their teacher at a disadvantage. "And she can't divorce him at all."

"And if her husband dies, she has to marry her brother-in-law," said Mazonson, for the same reason.

The rabbi held up both hands to bring them to order. "This is a very good example," he said, "of the danger of discussions based on ignorance and limited knowledge."

They quieted down.

"In the first place," he went on, "our religion is not ceremonial like the Catholic religion, for example, which requires a consecrated holy place, the church, to conduct its business. The center of our religious practise is more the home than the synagogue. And in the home, the woman certainly shares in whatever ceremonial there is. She prepares the house for the Sabbath, and it is she who blesses the Sabbath candles."

Ms. Goldstein whispered something to the girl in the next seat. She laughed.

"We are not immune to the influences around us," said the rabbi, raising his voice slightly. "All through recorded history, society has been patriarchal, but the Ten Commandments call for honoring thy father and mother, and father and mother is the way we normally refer to them, rather than by that weak collective—parents. Even in biblical times a Jewish woman could not be forced to marry against her choice. The penalty for adultery was death, but both parties were equally punished. When a woman married she retained title to her property, and when she was divorced, she not only took it with her but also received a large sum which was stipulated in advance in the marriage contract in the event of a divorce."

"But a man could divorce his wife anytime he wanted to," said Leventhal, "and she couldn't ever."

"No. The mechanics of the transaction called for the husband to give the divorce and the wife to receive it. But he has to go to a rabbinical court and convince them before they will give him a *get*, a bill of divorcement. The wife can do the same.

40

The difference is that the rabbinical court then orders the husband to give the divorce."

"What if he don't want to?"

"Then the rabbis can apply whatever sanctions they have. In modern Israel, they put him in jail until he agrees. I might add that even by contemporary standards, the grounds for divorce were quite liberal, more so than they are in most Western countries today. There was divorce by mutual consent, for example. The woman could also claim a divorce if her husband was physically repulsive to her or if he failed in his duty toward her which was laid down as the basis for married life. 'Let a man honor his wife more than himself, and love her as he loves himself.' No, Ms. Goldstein, I see nothing in the divorce laws that would suggest second class status for women."

"How about a widow having to marry her brother-in-law?" demanded Mazonson.

"Or the other way around?" said the rabbi with a smile. "It's all in how you look at it."

"I don't get it."

"You evidently don't know what the law was or its purpose, for that matter. The law called for the widow and her brother-in-law to marry only if she were childless. But the obligation was on both of them and the purpose, according to the Bible, was that she might have a child who would be named after her dead husband, 'so that his name should not be lost to Israel.'"

"Well, I heard—"

"Why would—"

"It seems to me—"

"How about Golda Meir?"

The rabbi rapped his knuckles against the lectern for quiet.

"So why do they keep us separated in the synagogue?" asked Miss Dushkin.

"Certainly not because they regard women as inferior," he said with a smile. "It goes back to primitive times when in many religions a service that included both sexes ended in an orgy, was arranged for that purpose, in fact, since it had to

41

do with fertility rites. In more recent times, it was felt that the natural attraction of the sexes would interfere with the concentration on prayer." He spread his hands and added wryly, "How long ago was it that coeducation was disparaged on the grounds that boys and girls sitting in the same classroom would be unable to keep their minds on their studies? But look here," he went on, "you're all making the mistake of forming your opinions on isolated bits of information or misinformation instead of on your own experience. Think about your own families and then ask yourself if the women, your mothers and grandmothers, your aunts, are registered as inferiors by their husbands or their families."

As they trooped out at the end of the class, Harvey Shacter turned to Henry Luftig. "I thought you were going to set him straight."

Luftig shook his head. "I don't know. I thought we had him on the ropes in the opening rounds, but he came back strong. He might turn out to be one tough baby."

7

"How did it go?" Miriam asked when he returned Wednesday morning.

"It was nice," he said, and then smiled. "I enjoyed it. I really enjoyed it tremendously. I've been thinking of it all the way home, Miriam, and I've concluded there are few quiet pleasures in this life to compare with that of imparting knowledge to a receptive listener. I remember noticing it the last time we had trouble with the heating system. As the plumber explained to me how the system worked and what was wrong, you could see he was enjoying himself."

"Why not? He was getting about nine dollars an hour for it," she remarked.

But the rabbi refused to be dampened. "I'm sure it wasn't that. It's a sense of superiority. You're bound to get a lift to the ego from dispensing information about anything you know better than others. And when that knowledge can change a person's way of living, his life-style, it's even more satisfying. It's quite something this—this ego trip, I think the students call it."

"I'm not sure they consider it a particularly nice thing, David. I think they use the term disparagingly."

"Really? Well, that just shows how little they know. I suppose it's part of the Anglo-Saxon ethic. In sports, for example, the champion is taught to attribute his success to his trainer or his teammates or to luck, to anything except his own superiority. It's so obviously false. No one believes it, but the tradition continues. All I can say is that I frankly enjoyed my first lecture."

"So I see," she said. "And it's done wonders for your modesty."

"I was only trying to answer your question," he said stiffly, and then they looked at each other and both smiled.

But Miriam was anxious to pursue it. "But lecturing is nothing new to you. You give a sermon, which is a lecture of sorts, every Friday night and on all the holidays."

"No," he said, "sermons are different. They involve moralizing, which, come to think of it, is just what they said Rabbi Lamden used to deliver when he ran the course. Besides, the people who hear my sermons are the people who pay my salary, and I always have the feeling they're judging me to see if they're getting their money's worth."

She was amused. "Oh David, I don't know where you get that idea."

"Besides, their minds are all fixed, their thought patterns crystallized. Nothing I say is apt to influence them. But these young people in school, they're not frozen, they're not afraid to express their ideas. Mostly they're wrong, of course, but they hold them tenaciously and are ready to argue them. There was a girl today, obviously Women's Lib, who tried to heckle me—"

43

"That I would have liked to see," laughed Miriam.

The rabbi laughed, too. "She wasn't bad, at that."

He looked forward eagerly to his next lecture on Friday. The street was practically empty when he pulled up in front of the administration building, and for a moment he wondered if perhaps his watch was slow; but as he strode down the corridor he could hear voices from his classroom. As he pushed open the door, he thought he must have made some mistake. Only a scattering of students was present. Then he had the sickening feeling that he had misjudged their reaction to his first lecture. He forced a smile. "The class seems to have shrunk."

Several of the students smiled back and one volunteered, "Most of the kids cut on Fridays to get a head start."

"A head start? A head start for what?"

"Oh, you know, for the weekend."

"I see." He understood now why the Dean had been apologetic about scheduling his course for Friday afternoon. He was nonplused, not sure how to proceed. Should he go ahead with the material he had prepared or devote the hour to reviewing his last lecture so that the absentees would not fall behind? He decided to deliver the lecture, but it was not the same. He could not help feel indignant, and he was sure the students were aware of it and took a perverse pleasure in his discomfiture.

At last the class was over, but his annoyance lasted all the way home. Fortunately, Miriam was busy preparing for the Sabbath, so there was no time to discuss it.

The following Monday he had full attendance again: twenty-eight. On Wednesday, too; but on Friday there were even less than the previous week: only ten. And so it continued: good attendance on Mondays and Wednesdays, a mere handful on Fridays.

When after a month they had finished the Pentateuch, he announced a quiz—for Friday. It was a declaration of war on his part.

"Are we going to be responsible for all the names? You know, so-and-so begat so-and-so?"

"No, but I will expect you to know certain genealogical material. Certainly, you ought to know the names of Adam's children, or Abraham's."

"Couldn't we have the test on Monday?"

"Do you think you will be luckier then?"

"No, but we could have the weekend to prepare for it."

"Look at it this way. Now you can have the whole weekend to recover."

He stopped off at his office on Friday, and Professor Hendryx, seeing the bluebooks, looked up in surprise. "You enjoy giving quizzes, Rabbi?"

"Not particularly. Why?"

"Because anyone quizzing on Friday has to quiz twice," said Hendryx.

"I don't understand."

"Simply that you have to prepare not only the original, and then read the bluebooks and make all those comments in red in the margin and grade them, but the make-up as well. You can't expect more than half your class to turn up on a Friday."

"Oh, I think they'll all be there today," said the rabbi confidently. "I gave them plenty of notice and impressed on them this was an hour exam and important to their grades."

But he arrived at the classroom to find only fifteen students. He spent the hour walking about the room as the students wrote. As each finished, he would hand in his paper and hurry out of the room. Long before the bell rang the rabbi found himself alone.

He graded the papers over the weekend and returned them on Monday. There was an immediate reaction.

"You said we wouldn't be responsible for the begats."

"Benjamin is hardly just one of the begats. Benjamin is an important part of the Joseph story."

"How much will this count toward the final grade?"

"It depends on how many hour exams I decide to give."

"Will they all be given on Fridays?"

"I can't say. Probably."

"Gee, that's not fair."

"Why not?"

"Well—a lot of us—I know I can't get here Fridays."

This was it. He said coolly, "I'm afraid I don't understand. The Friday session is a regular class hour. If it conflicted with some other course, you shouldn't have arranged to take this one."

"It's not that it conflicts—"

"Yes?"

"Well, I drive back to New Jersey weekends and I've got to get an early start."

The rabbi shrugged his shoulders. "I don't know the answer to that."

He opened his text to indicate that he considered discussion closed, but the atmosphere was charged. The students, even those who had taken the examination, were sullen. His lecture suffered as a result, and for the first time he dismissed them before the hour.

When he returned to his office, he found Hendryx stretched out in his usual reclining posture, puffing gently on his pipe.

"How's it going, Rabbi?"

"Well, I'm not sure." In the few weeks that he had been teaching, he had seen Hendryx less than a half dozen times, and then usually for only a few minutes before or after class. "I get about twenty-six in my class. Actually the official class list shows thirty, but twenty-eight is the most that have appeared at any one time."

"That's not bad," said Hendryx. "In fact, darn good where students are allowed unlimited cuts."

"Well, I'm not dissatisfied with the attendance on Mondays and Wednesdays, but on Friday afternoons I'm lucky if I get a dozen."

"At one o'clock? On Friday? I'm surprised you're getting that many."

"But why?" the rabbi insisted. "I can understand that one or two might have a trip planned for the weekend and want to make an early start—"

46

"They've all got plans for the weekend, Rabbi. If it's a girl, she's been invited to another college for the football game on Saturday. If she attends your class, she finishes at two and can't start much before three, so she'll get wherever she's going too late for all the fun on Friday. And young people nowadays can't afford to miss any fun. It's a kind of commitment, even a kind of religion, you might say."

"You mean that all those absent have weekend dates?"

"No, not all," said Hendryx. "Some stay away so that their friends will *think* they've got a date. Some figure they might as well make it a long weekend. Some—although personally I doubt it—use the time to study for other courses, supposedly the rationale behind unlimited cuts: they're supposed to be mature enough to organize their own time."

"And what am I supposed to do on Fridays when less than half my class shows up?"

"Well," said Hendryx, drawing on his pipe, "that's a good question. There aren't too many courses given Friday afternoon. Joe Browder has a geology class at one over in the Blythe Building. Off-hand I don't know any other. By noon the place is deserted. Even the cafeteria is closed. Haven't you noticed?"

"But what am I supposed to do?" the rabbi persisted. "Not give the lecture?"

"I've known instructors to do just that. Not that they openly cancel out, but every other week or so they announce they'll be unable to meet with the class." He looked at the rabbi, a faint derisive smile on his face. "But I guess you wouldn't do that, would you?"

"No, I don't feel as though I could," he said.

"So what have you been doing?"

"So far, I've treated it as just another hour and given my regular lecture. Last week, as you know, I gave a quiz."

"I meant to ask you about that," said Hendryx. "How many showed up?"

"Only fifteen."

Hendryx chuckled. "Well, well, well. Only fifteen, eh? And

47

for an hour exam? You handed back the books today? Tell me, how did your class react?"

"That's what bothers me," confessed the rabbi. "Many of them seemed resentful and some appeared actually indignant, as though I had been unfair."

Hendryx nodded. "You know why they acted indignant, Rabbi? Because they *were* indignant. And they were indignant because you *were* unfair, at least according to their lights. You see, yours is traditionally a snap course. That's why so many elected it. So why get yourself in a sweat, Rabbi, trying to change it? Why not do as the rest of us do and go along with things as they are?"

"Because I'm a rabbi," he said, and then added with obvious disparagement, "not a teacher."

Hendryx laughed uproariously in acknowledgment of the thrust. "But Rabbi, I thought that's what a rabbi was. Isn't that what the word means—teacher?"

"Not that kind. A rabbi is one who is learned in the law by which we are expected to order our lives. His major traditional function is to judge, but he also expounds the law on occasion for the benefit of his congregation and community. The kind of teacher you have in mind, the kind that coaxes the young and immature to learn, a teacher of children—that's something else. Him, we call a *melamed*, and the term has a derogatory connotation."

"Derogatory?"

"That's right. You see, since Jews have had practically one hundred percent literacy for centuries," the rabbi said, enjoying this, "anyone can teach. Naturally, the social prestige or the financial reward for doing what everyone else can do is not great. So the *melamed* was usually someone who had failed at everything else and finally had to fall back on teaching children to make a living."

"And you feel that by going easy with your class, you will be a *melamed?*" Hendryx asked, interested in spite of himself. "Is that it?"

"Oh, I'm not so much concerned about my status as I am about their attitude. We Jews expect to tease and coax children to learn. That's why when a child starts school we give him cake and honey so he will associate learning with something sweet and desirable. But I don't feel I should have to continue the treatment with adults. Of course, not all adults want to become scholars, but those who do and come to college should have an adult attitude toward instruction. I shouldn't have to tease and coax them to learn."

"You don't," said Hendryx. "And neither do the rest of us. We give our lectures. Those who want to come, come; and those who don't, stay away."

"And those who decide to stay away—do they pass?"

"Well, of course—"

"But that's cheating!" he exclaimed.

"I'm afraid I don't follow you, Rabbi."

"Let me put it this way," said David Small, searching for an analogy. "Traditionally, the way you become a rabbi is to present yourself to a rabbi for examination. If you pass his examination, he gives you what we call *smicha,* a seal of approval, ordination. Of course some rabbis were harder, more exacting, in their examination than others because they were themselves more subtle in their thinking and even more knowledgeable. But I expect they were all honest in their decisions, because in designating the candidate a rabbi they were certifying him capable of sitting in judgment throughout the Jewish world.

"Now the degree granted here also has value and meaning throughout the world and the authority to grant it was conferred by the state, as I understand it. The college system calls for the candidate to accumulate credits toward the degree by sitting under a number of instructors and then satisfying them that he has properly completed their courses of instruction. I am being paid to pass on some small part of the total. So if I don't do my work thoroughly, I'm acting dishonestly. I'm cheating."

"Cheating whom?"

"Cheating everyone who assumes the degree indicates · a body of knowledge has been successfully assimilated."

"You mean you are planning to flunk students who cut their Friday classes?"

"Those who don't take the exams, or fail in them."

"Very interesting. Ve–ry interesting," said Hendryx. "In a little while we're supposed to submit to the dean's office the names of all students who are failing at mid-semester. Do you intend to submit such a list?"

"If that's the system, of course I shall comply. Don't you?"

"Well, the last few years, I haven't bothered with it much. As a matter of fact, last year I didn't flunk anyone in any of my classes. But I expect you're planning to."

"If they do not pass the examinations, I will give a failure mark of course."

"Well, all I can say, Rabbi, is that you're going to have a very interesting year."

8

The college bulletin appeared at the end of October following the semi-annual meeting of the trustees of Windemere Christian College. It was studied not only for what it included but for what it omitted. Thus, while it announced that Associate Professor Clyde had been appointed to full professor, the fact drew little interest; everyone knew that President Macomber was recommending him for the promotion and the trustees always followed the president's recommendations.

On the other hand, considerable attention was paid to the omission of any mention of the appointment of a permanent head of the English department. Clearly, this suggested that Professor Hendryx, the acting head, was only on temporary assignment until the administration could find a more suitable candidate.

This delighted a considerable number of older members of the department and most of the younger, in sharp contrast to their reaction to another omission in the bulletin—the reappointment of Assistant Professor Roger Fine. Fine was well-liked by most faculty members, but even those who did not hold him in high regard were displeased, since the reason was assumed to be purely political.

Albert Herzog, a young instructor in anthropology who was also an officer of the teachers' union, sought out Fine. "Hey Rog, what's this I hear about you being dropped at mid years?"

"I'm not being dropped. That's when my contract runs out."

"What's that got to do with it? The job is there. They'll have to get someone to replace you. As a matter of fact, I happen to know they're planning to hire two men on your end of the ranking scale, instructors or assistant professors."

"That may be," said Fine, "but I was hired last February on a one-year contract, or two semesters. They let me teach summer session as well, so that's three semesters. I don't see that I've got any kick coming."

"Well, a regular contract is normally renewed from year to year. Macomber doesn't have anything against you, does he?"

"Oh no," said Fine quickly.

"Then that can mean only one thing—that you're being fired for your political activity. And if so, the union is not going to stand for it. We'll demand a hearing."

"Come on, Al, climb down," said Fine. "The union's contract with the school specifically permits the president to drop a man without a hearing as long as he's not on tenure."

"Only if it's *not* for a political reason!" said Herzog, jabbing a bony finger to drive home the point. "He can fire you because he doesn't like the way you comb your hair, but he can't fire you for writing that article in *The Windrift* or for your support of the blacks. That's political, and that's specifically ruled out under contract. Same with the AAUP. No, this is a clear case, and we'll get to work on it."

"Please, Al, do me a favor. Mind your own business. I don't want to get into a fight with the administration." He put a hand on his shoulder.

Herzog shrugged him off. "I don't understand you. If there was one guy on this faculty I could count on to fight for his

51

rights, it was you. That's been the trouble with teachers all along; they think they'll get better treatment if they lie down and let administrations walk all over them. But you'll find that practically every time the union puts up a fight on this kind of matter, it wins. I'm going to call a meeting of the executive—"

"No."

"Look, Fine, it's not just you. If the administration can fire a fully qualified guy and hire somebody else to take his place, what in hell happens to the seniority rule? Answer me that?"

"Screw the seniority rule. I'm asking you as a personal favor, Al. I just don't want to get into a hassle with anybody now." He lowered his voice. "You see, Edie is pregnant. I don't want her upset."

"Hey, that's wonderful!" exclaimed Herzog. "Congratulations! All right Rog, I get the picture. I'll talk it over with the guys and tell them what you said. We'll do what's right."

But the next day there was a new table set up on the Marble with a large poster with a picture of an outsize baseball bat: "SIGN FOR FINE! HE WENT TO BAT FOR YOU —NOW GO TO BAT FOR HIM!"

Seated behind the table, urging passersby to sign the petition, was Nicholas Ekkedaminopoulos, called Ekko by all who knew him, even his instructors. He was older than his classmates, having already served in the Army, and he stood out from among the other students because he was clean-shaven —not only his swarthy face but his entire head. As he explained, "My old man is bald, my uncle is bald. And now I'm getting bald. It runs in the family. My old man, he combs the few hairs he's got on the side across the top and plasters them down. My uncle, he's a swinger with a pretty wife, so he spends a fortune on all kinds of treatments and oils and grease —and he's still bald. But me, I figure why fight it? So I shaved it all off."

Roger Fine knew him well; they were the same age and had both served in Vietnam. They had become close friends. They worked together on recruiting black students, and Fine had invited him to Barnard's Crossing during the summer.

Walking across the Marble, he saw the sign and hurried over to the table. "What the hell is going on, Ekko?" he demanded. "Who put you up to this?"

"Now, Rog, it was officially decided by the Student Activists."

"Don't give me any of that official crap, Ekko. You know goddam well that the Student Activists are just the half dozen of you on the executive committee. I want to know who put you up to this. Was it Al Herzog?"

"That windbag? Jesus no." Ekko lowered his voice. "Things are getting tough, Rog. Three years ago when I was a freshman, get up a petition for anything you can think of and before lunch was over you'd have five hundred signatures. They wouldn't even look what they're signing. But here we been sitting since the beginning of school trying to line up some support for our program and we're lucky if we got fifty signatures. They got all sorts of copouts. The coed dorm? Chicks say they can't put their name down, because it's like advertising they're an easy lay. Or even voluntary exams. You'd think anyone would go for that, but no, they say if they got to take exams why shouldn't everyone? Then the administration goes and shafts you. So we figured here's a great opportunity. You've got lots of friends in school and we could get lots of signatures. So at the same time they're signing the petition for you we thought—what the hell—we'll get them to sign the S.A. Resolution, too. And it worked!" he said triumphantly. "I been sitting here only a couple of hours and already I got thirty signatures on your petition, and six of them signed the resolution."

Fine shook his head in exasperation. "Did it ever occur to you to ask me before you got up this petition? Did it ever occur to you that it might interfere with my own plans?"

"Jeez, Roger, we thought you'd be pleased. Besides, if we didn't do it, the SDS would. Maybe even the Weathervane crazies. You'd rather have us doing it than them, wouldn't you?"

"Well, I don't like it, Ekko. I want it stopped."

"OK, if that's the way you want it. Excuse me a minute—"
He grabbed a student who was with a girl. "Hey Bongo, come
on sign a petition for Professor Fine!"

Roger Fine hurried away.

9

"What have you got against John Hendryx, Dad?" asked
Betty Macomber. It was Mrs. Childs' night off, and Betty was
clearing the dinner dishes while he glanced through the evening paper.

"Hendryx? Oh, the new man in English?"

"New! He's been here two and a half years."

"Really. It just shows how time flies. Why, I have nothing
against him."

"Then why hasn't he been appointed chairman of the department? Why is he only acting chairman?"

President Macomber put his paper aside and looked up at
his daughter. She was tall and blonde; "My Viking Princess"
he had been fond of calling her when she was a little girl. Although her face showed planes of maturity, it was unlined
and still attractive. "It's regulations," he began. "A chairman
of a department is required to have tenure, and that takes a
minimum of three years. Hendryx hasn't been with us that
long. So naturally he can only be acting chairman."

"But in the past people have been made chairman of their
departments without tenure," she persisted. "You told me
yourself that Professor Malkowitz was made chairman of the
Math Department the day he was hired."

"Malkowitz was a special case. He wouldn't have come to
Windemere otherwise, and we were very anxious to get him.
The trustees had to grant him tenure by special vote."

She put aside the bread tray and salad bowl she was carrying and sat on the hassock at his feet. "Well, why can't you do the same thing for Professor Hendryx?"

He leaned back in his chair and smiled. "Professor Malkowitz has a national reputation. He's an extremely capable man."

"And you have doubts about Professor Hendryx's ability?"

There was no doubt about the challenge in her voice. He tried to blunt it with a light answer. "Well, one thing I can say about him. He certainly knows how to enlist female support." He smiled. "For months now Millicent Hanbury has been after me about him, and now you. I can understand her attitude. They're old friends, I gather, or at least they both come from the same hometown. But you, I didn't think you even knew him."

"I met him the day I got back. He was at the Sorensons' party."

"Oh?"

"And I've seen quite a bit of him since," she added offhandedly.

But he wasn't fooled. "He complained about his treatment here?"

"No, it wasn't that," she said. "But when I happened to refer to him as chairman of the English Department, he made a point of correcting me and explained he was only acting chairman." She paused. "If you know anything against him, Father, I'd like to hear it."

Realizing that her interest was more than impersonal concern for a faculty member, he began cautiously. "He has a good degree. Harvard, I think. And I understand he's published some. But when you've been at this game as long as I have, you get a kind of feeling about faculty people. In the last ten years, before coming here, he's had three different jobs. And why would he come here at all? We're a small college, not too well known. With that kind of background he should have been able to wangle a job at one of the prestige colleges by this time."

"Your precious Malkowitz came here."

"Ah, but we went after him and made it worth his while.

Professor Hendryx, on the other hand, came to *us*, and at mid-years."

"Maybe he prefers a small college. A lot of men do."

He nodded. "But his last job was at a small college—Jeremiah Logan College in Tennessee. Why didn't he stay there?"

"Just because it's in Tennessee, I suppose. Any New Englander is apt to feel like a fish out of water in a small Southern town."

"True," he acknowledged, "and it's what I thought until I bumped into the chancellor of Jeremiah Logan at the College Presidents Association meeting last year. I mentioned Hendryx. Now you know, these days an administrator, any employer for that matter, has to be very careful of what he says about a former employee. You can be sued if you say something you know perfectly well but can't prove. That's why we don't pay too much attention to the run-of-the-mill recommendation. Well, this man from Jeremiah Logan was even more cautious than most, but I was able to gather that Hendryx had been in some trouble down there—about a girl, one of the coeds."

"I know all about that," she said calmly. "She was a cheap little whore, the original sweetheart of Sigma Chi—and all the other fraternities."

"He told you all this? Why?"

"Because we're interested in each other," she said, getting to her feet.

"Betty, the man called him an over-sexed—"

"Well, I could do with a little of that after Malcolm."

"Betty!"

"Look Dad, I might as well tell you. John and I are going to get married."

He stared at her.

"Don't look so shocked. And I'm not going to be put off just because a man of forty is not celibate. Now, aren't you going to wish me good luck?"

"But with a coed!"

"Big enough, old enough. You don't suppose your coeds here at Windemere are all innocent virgins, do you?"

56

"No, of course not," he said. "But I still cannot approve of male members of the faculty—well—having relations—that is, taking advantage of their position to—why—seduce female members of the student body." He started again. "Look Betty, I'm as modern about these things as any man my age can be. But it's not right for a faculty member—I mean, just from the point of view of fairness, because he can take advantage of his position. If nothing else, think what it indicates of his character."

"Fairness! Character!" She gave a hard laugh. "Dad, let me clue you in on the facts of life in the seventies. Sex is a woman's business; it's her specialty, her field of concentration. If any affairs are going on at Windemere between faculty and student, and I'm sure there are, believe me, it's something that the girl has initiated and is managing. And she'll usually be the one who terminates it when she finds someone else or has decided she's had enough. Now this affair of John's down at Logan, and others he's probably had at the other places he taught, well, he might think they were his doing but you can bet that in each case it was the girl's."

"Betty, are *you* having an affair with him?"

"Dad, you are sweet. No, I'm not, but it's just because it hasn't developed that way—not yet, anyway. Have I shocked you?" She looked at him in amusement.

"Do you love this man, Betty?"

"I'm not a teenager with a crush, if that's what you mean. I find him attractive. He's good-looking and intelligent."

"But you've only just met him. You don't really know him."

"Yes, and I practically grew up with Malcolm and see what happened," she said. "I've known John for almost two months now. It's long enough."

"Just because you made a mistake once—"

"I'm thirty-five and John is forty. Our backgrounds are similar. He comes of an old New England family, and he's unattached. He's the most eligible man around. If I wait, I'll end up marrying some widower with a couple of kids who's looking for a housekeeper to work without pay—if I'm lucky. As for any affairs he's had with some silly little coeds, well, if he hadn't had any, then I'd have cause to worry. What else can a bachelor professor in a small college town do? Would you rather have him make time with the wives of his colleagues?"

"Most men marry."

"Then he wouldn't be available to me. Look Dad, I'm going to marry him. Right now we're keeping it quiet because he has some silly idea people won't understand, but make up your mind to it. Don't worry, Dad," she hugged him impulsively, "I know you'll like him once you get to know him better."

"Has Billy met him yet?" he said.

"As a matter of fact, we're driving up to see him Saturday morning. I'm sure he and Billy will get along fine."

"And what about your plans for the future?"

"That depends on you," she said. "John would like to stay on here, but he considers his present position as acting chairman demeaning. When the last bulletin passed him over, he was going to resign, but I persuaded him to wait. If he does decide to leave, we could live for a while on the little money Mother left me while he looks around for another job. I suggested it, but he's too proud to accept it. But if he's given tenure and appointed permanent chairman, we could get married right away, and then we'd go on living here."

"But that has to be by a vote of the trustees."

"Have they ever turned down a single recommendation of yours?"

"No–o."

"Please, Dad!"

She looked as anxious as a child. And what did he really know to Hendryx's discredit? Still, it went against the grain to use the authority of his position in a purely family matter. On the other hand, Betty wasn't the only one. Dean Hanbury had urged him to make the promotion, so it probably would work to the benefit of the department and the school. "Well, perhaps I'll talk to Dean Hanbury," he said tentatively.

She knew she had won. "Oh thanks, Dad." She gave him another kiss. "When will you see her?"

He thumbed through his pocket diary. "Let's see, tomorrow is Friday. I don't have anything on for the morning." He made a note. "Friday the thirteenth. You superstitious?" He smiled at her. "I'll see her tomorrow morning."

She blew him a kiss and then hurried up the stairs. "I've got to change."

"I thought you were going to stay in tonight. . . ."

"Oh, but I want to tell John the good news."

10

They couldn't use Abner Selzer's place because his roommate had the flu, and Yance Allworth and Mike O'Brien both lived at home. So they had agreed to meet at Judy Ballentine's pad even though it was way to hell and gone on the other side of town, in the West End. At least, they would not be disturbed. Besides, since this Judy was shacking up with Ekko, two of the five were already there. She lived three flights up in a tenement house that real estate gougers had prettied up with tiled shower stalls and cabinet kitchenettes and a few sticks of furniture so that they could charge an arm and a leg to students, nurses, and interns at the Mass General Hospital, who couldn't find anyplace else.

Ekko appropriated the one chair. It was a wing-back job whose fabric was not only faded but marred by cigarette burns caused by the carelessness, if not actual vandalism, of the previous tenants who resented the inflated rent they had to pay. "Just pin on a couple of lace doilies and it'll look like new," the renting agent had said.

Judy, although a senior, looked like a young girl. Not only was she tiny, but her face had a childlike expression with a small rosebud mouth and large innocent dark eyes. She sat on the floor, her head against Ekko's knee, flicking her cigarette in the general direction of the ashtray on the floor. With her other hand she massaged his calf under his trouser leg.

On the ratty sofa with sagging springs sat Mike O'Brien who worked part time in a bank and so wore a regular suit and a white shirt and even a tie for God's sakes; his fat little fingers were intertwined on his lap.

Yance Allworth lay on the floor, his handsome Afro resting on a cushion he had pulled off the sofa. He was wearing fringed pants of purple leather and a pink silk shirt that contrasted dramatically with his dark black skin. His eyes were closed and he appeared to be asleep as Abner Selzer, bearded and with hair nearly down to his shoulders, reported on his conversation with the dean.

"I arranged it for half-past two today because—" He broke off. "Jeez Judy, do you have to feel him up while we're having a meeting?"

"Screw you," she said amiably.

"Get on with it," said Ekko, patting her head like a dog's.

"—because that's when Millie Hanbury suggested," he concluded.

"Screw Millie Hanbury," said Allworth through half closed lips.

"Maybe I wouldn't mind," said Selzer. "She's got some build."

"You'd mind, all right," said Judy. "She's a dyke."

"How do you know?" asked O'Brien, interested.

"It stands to reason," Judy said. "She was a Phys. Ed. major in college. All those Phys. Ed. types are. What I'd like to know is why we got to meet her at half-past two on a Friday."

"Friday the thirteenth," Yance Allworth murmured.

"Because Friday the place is like a ghost town. There won't be anyone around. Just us."

"So what kind of pressure can we bring with just the five of us?"

"More than if we held the meeting Monday morning as you suggested, Judy," Selzer retorted. "Then we could get maybe fifty kids, seventy-five at the most. And Hanbury would take one look, see we could only scare up a handful, and know right away she held all the cards."

"How do you know we'd only get fifty?" asked O'Brien.

"Because that's the name of the game nowadays," said Selzer. "You know how many signatures we got to our petition? With Fine as a drawing card? A hundred and nineteen. That's all we could get in a whole week, one hundred and nineteen lousy signatures. So when Hanbury suggested Friday afternoon, I snapped it up because that way we don't show our weakness."

"I bet if we'd joined with the Weathervanes, we'd have got a hell of a lot more," said O'Brien.

"Screw the Weathervanes," Allworth murmured.

"You and me both," said Ekko. "That's a freaked out bunch of crazies that I wouldn't join on a streetcar in a rush hour."

"They're real revolutionaries," O'Brien insisted.

"They're real zombies, is what they are," said Ekko. "You say, half-past two, Abner? Okay, so it's half-past two. Did you tell her why we wanted to see her?"

"No, but she knows we're pushing for Fine naturally because of the sign on the Marble."

"I told you Roger asked us to lay off," said Ekko.

"Screw Roger Fine," said Allworth.

"Right," Selzer agreed. "We aren't doing this for Fine. He's just an example. We're interested in like a principle."

"That's right, Ekko," said Judy. "If they're going to drop any teacher that sides with us, where in hell we going to get faculty support?"

They argued back and forth, getting nowhere, until it was time to split. Ekko saw them out, but on the landing he took Selzer aside.

"I didn't want to say it in front of the others, but Roger is pretty upset about the petition and even more about our meeting with Millie. You see, he's already resigned."

"Resigned? What the hell—"

"He had to," said Ekko. "He says they had him over a barrel and made him write out a letter of resignation. Millie's got it in her safe right this minute. I wasn't supposed to tell anybody, but with the meeting today I figured we ought to go kind of easy—you know, keep it like general—so we shouldn't end up with egg all over our face."

"Yeah." Already the wheels were spinning as Selzer began revising his strategy. Then he shook his head. "I don't know. Maybe we ought to let her spring it on us, and then just tell her we know but feel he was forced into it."

"I still think—"

Selzer felt his leadership questioned. "Look, you want to handle it, Ekko?"

"No, I just don't want to see Rog get the short end of the stick."

"Don't worry. All along, the best I ever figured was a draw."

"How do you mean?"

"We'd lose on Fine, but we'd get a promise on somebody else."

"Yeah. Well, keep it in mind." Ekko turned, then said: "Say, does anybody else know about this meeting?"

"I didn't tell anybody. Why?"

"Well, I wouldn't want any of those crazy Weathervanes to come pushing in. Then the dean would use that as an excuse to lower the boom on Roger."

"Who would tell them?"

"Well, Mike is always talking about how the Weathervanes would do this and the Weathervanes would do that, and I've seen him with that Aggie broad."

Selzer considered and then shook his head. "Nah, Mike's all right. He just talks. It makes up for the square clothes he has to wear at the bank." He laughed and clumped down the stairs to catch up with the others.

They separated at the Charles Street train station, Yance and Abner taking the stairs to the overhead while O'Brien continued into the city. After a block or so, Mike stopped at a drugstore pay phone and, carefully closing the door of the booth, dialed a number. The phone rang half a dozen times before it was answered. "Yeah?"

"Is Aggie there?" asked O'Brien.

"Aggie who?"

"Just Aggie. Just see if Aggie's there."

He waited and then another voice, a woman's voice, said, "Hi, lover."

II

Rabbi Small did not look forward to meeting his last class of the week, but each Friday he would hope that this time there would be a normal complement. And each time he would be disappointed.

He could not avoid the feeling of resentment, even though he knew it was irrational; and this Friday, the thirteenth, was no different: a dozen students were present and he was annoyed. He closed the door behind him, and without a word of greeting, mounted the platform.

Nodding briefly, he turned his back to write the assignment on the blackboard and when he turned around he received a profound shock: half the class was gone! Then he saw that they had not left the room but were sitting on the floor in the aisles.

He was not in the mood for joking; he never was on a Friday. "Will you please come to order," he called.

There was no response. Those still in their chairs looked down at their open notebooks, reluctant to meet his eye.

"Please take your seats."

No movement.

"I cannot give my lecture while you are sitting on the floor."

"Why not?" It was Harry Luftig, who asked from the floor, not impertinently—politely, in fact.

For a moment the rabbi was uncertain what to say. Then he had an idea. "To sit on the floor is a sign of mourning with us Jews," he said. "The devout sit on the floor during the seven-

63

day mourning period. We also do it on the Ninth of Av, the day of the destruction of the temple. In the synagogues we sit on the floor or on low stools and recite from the Book of Lamentations. But now it is Friday afternoon and the Sabbath is approaching. Mourning is explicitly forbidden on the Sabbath."

Of course Sabbath was still hours away, but he peered down at them through his thick glasses to see if they would accept his explanation as a face-saving way of giving up their little joke. He thought one of them was about to rise, but he only shifted position on the floor.

Suddenly he was angry—and hurt. These were not children. Why should he have to put up with it? Without another word, he picked up his books and left the room.

He strode resolutely down the corridor, his footsteps echoing hollowly in the silent building. His face was grim as he came to his office and, unlocking the door, went in.

He was surprised, not too pleasantly, to find Professor Hendryx tilted back in his swivel chair, talking on the phone.

He waved his free hand at the rabbi, said goodby into the instrument, and jerked himself to a sitting position to set it on its cradle.

He glanced at his watch. "Quarter-past one. Don't you have a class?"

The rabbi pulled up the visitor's chair and sat down across the desk. "That's right. I walked out on them."

Hendryx grinned. "What happened? They try to give you the business?"

"I don't know what they were trying," said the rabbi, indignation creeping into his voice, "but whatever it was, I didn't regard their behavior as conducive to teaching."

"What did they do?"

The rabbi told him, concluding, "And once having gone out on a limb by giving it a certain religious significance, I had no other alternative."

"But they didn't buy it."

"I'm afraid not. No one on the floor budged."

"So you walked out."

The rabbi nodded. "I couldn't think what else to do."

"You weren't here yesterday, were you, Rabbi?" Hendryx asked with seeming irrelevance.

"No. I just come for my classes. What happened yesterday?"

Professor Hendryx drew his pipe from his pocket and filled it from a canister on the desk. "Well, it really began Wednesday." He scratched a large wooden match into flame on the underside of the desk and held it to his pipe. He puffed on it gently, then went on. "On Wednesday the newspapers reported a visit made by the Citizens Committee on Penal Reform to Norfolk Reformatory for Boys. They found the usual deplorable conditions: overcrowding, broken windows, toilets that don't flush, cockroaches in the kitchen. And they were given the usual excuses by the warden: lack of funds, lack of trained personnel, divided authority. But there was something new since their last visit. There were no chairs in the recreation room and the inmates had to sit on the floor. The warden explained that he had ordered the chairs removed because they had been used for rioting in the rec room the week before. Most of the committee refused to buy it. They pointed out that the floor was uncarpeted and was cold and drafty, that the health of the little bastards was being jeopardized, and all the rest. Didn't you read about it?"

"Yes, but what's it got to do with my class?"

"I'm coming to that." He puffed on his pipe. "President Macomber is a member of that committee, and he was one of the few who not only did not protest but even supported the warden. So the next day—yesterday, this is—our students, the more involved among them at least, decided to sit out the week on the floor in all classes in protest against their president."

"They did it in your classes? What did you do?"

"Oh, I paid no attention to them," said Hendryx. "I just went right ahead with my lecture. Some of the instructors made some sarcastic remarks, but nothing much happened." He laughed. "Ted Singer—you know, sociology—said that since it

65

was a topsy-turvy world perhaps they ought to go all the way and stand on their heads. And one girl took him up on it for the rest of the period. A good ten minutes, he said. She's into yoga, I suppose." He smiled and showed a mouthful of even white teeth. "Her skirt flopped over, of course, but Singer reported that unfortunately she was wearing these pantyhose they wear nowadays so there was nothing to see."

The rabbi suspected that the story had been colored to get a rise out of him. Because he was a rabbi, he supposed, his colleague frequently made suggestive remarks to see if he could shock him. "Are you sure it's only for this week?"

"That's my understanding. Why?"

"Because if it continues, I won't stand for it."

Hendryx looked at him in surprise. "Why not? Why should you care?"

"Well, I do." Glancing at his watch, he said, "I better go see the dean."

Hendryx stared. "Whatever for?"

"Well, I walked out on my class."

"Look Rabbi, let me tell you the facts of academic life. The dean doesn't give a damn if you walk out on a class occasionally, or even if you meet with them at all. What you do in your classroom is your business. Last year, Professor Tremayne announced a three-week reading period in the middle of February and took off for Florida. Of course, Tremayne is the kind of teacher who may provide greater benefit to his students by his absence than his presence."

"Nevertheless, I think I'll tell her about it anyway. Besides, I've got to turn in my mid-semester failure notices."

Hendryx whistled. "You mean you're really sending out flunk notices after all I told you?"

"But last week I received a notice that the lists were due Monday, the sixteenth."

"Rabbi, Rabbi," said Hendryx, "when was the last time you had any connection with a college?"

"I've lectured to Hillel groups."

"No, I mean a real connection."

66

"Not since I was a student, I suppose, fifteen or sixteen years ago. Why?"

"Because in the last sixteen years—hell, in the last six—things have changed. Where have you been? Don't you read the papers?"

"But the students—"

"Students!" Hendryx said scornfully. "What in the world do you think college cares about students? The primary purpose of college nowadays is to support the faculty, presumably a society of learned men, in some degree of comfort and security. It's society's way of subsidizing such worthwhile pursuits as research and the growth of knowledge. Society has the uneasy feeling that it's important for someone to care about such irrelevancies as the source of Shakespeare's plots, or whether the gentleman above me"—nodding to the bust of Homer on the shelf above his head—"was responsible for the Homeric poems or if he was just one of a committee, or the influence of the Flemish weavers on the economy of England during the Middle Ages, or the effect of gamma rays on the development of spirogyra.

"We're set apart in the grove of academe to fritter away our lives while the rest of the world goes about its proper business of making money or children or war or disease or pollution, or whatever the hell they're into. As for the students, they can look over our shoulders if they like and learn something. Or they can pay their tuition fees which help support us and hang around here for four years having fun. Personally, I don't give a damn which they do, as long as they don't interfere with my quite comfortable life, thank you."

He drew deeply on his pipe and, removing it from his mouth, blew the smoke in the rabbi's direction.

"And you don't feel you owe the students anything?" the rabbi asked quietly.

"Not a damn thing. They're just one of the hazards of the game, like a sandtrap on a golf course. As a matter of fact, we do do something for them. After four years, they are given that degree you were talking about which entitles them to apply for certain jobs. Or to go on to a higher degree which they can cash into money by becoming doctors, lawyers, account- ants. Not the fairest arrangement from the point of view of those who can't afford college, but quite normal in this imper- fect world. Hell, is it any different in the tight trades where you have to serve a useless apprenticeship before you can join the union?" He shook his head, as if answering his own question. "The only trouble comes when the students catch on, as they have in recent years, and kick up a fuss or stage a dem- onstration as your class did today."

"But if the college is for the faculty, and the student is here merely to mark time, why should you care what he does?"

Hendryx smiled. "Actually, I don't. Not unless it kills the goose that laid the golden egg. And that's what's been happen- ing the last few years. The student sensed he was being had. Of course he'd known all along that what he was getting here wasn't worth what he was paying. I once figured out it costs him about ten dollars per lecture. God, my lectures aren't worth that. Are yours? How smart does a student have to be to figure it out for himself? Still, he went along because he had to have the degree to get any sort of a job or train for any sort of profession. But then they rang in the war on him, and it struck him as a bit much: this degree we were giving him turned out to be just a ticket, sometimes one way, to Vietnam. So he rebelled."

"It also gave him a four-year moratorium from the war," observed the rabbi.

"Yes, it did, but that's human nature. Things have quieted down a lot in the last year or two, what with the change in the draft law and winding down the war, and the students have quieted down correspondingly. But they acquired the habit of protest, even violence, and that we can't have. There was a bombing here, you know."

"Yes, I read about it of course, but that was last year."

"You never know," said Hendryx. "Take this very afternoon. The dean is seeing a committee on the Roger Fine business. Maybe, probably, all they'll do is talk. Nevertheless, she thought it advisable to call me and tell me to stand by."

"Because you're head of the English Department?"

"I'm only acting head. No, she wants me around in case there's trouble."

"Trouble?" The rabbi considered. "I've seen their poster on the Marble, of course. Professor Fine must be popular with the students for them to get up a petition for him."

Hendryx shrugged. "Maybe. On the other hand, students, some of them anyway, will take any opportunity to pick a fight. I don't know how popular Roger Fine is. He's a good-looking fellow, so I suppose the girls go for him. That red hair—" He broke off. "Somehow I don't think of red hair in connection with your people. Do you suppose there was some hanky-panky between his mother or grandmother and some Russian or Polish soldier?"

"If so," said the rabbi quietly, "it was probably involuntary, during a pogrom. But actually there is a genetic strain of red hair among our people. King David was supposed to be red-haired."

"Really? Well anyway, a handsome young professor is always popular with the women. Even though he is a cripple."

"Would that make a difference?" the rabbi asked.

"Oh, I'm not saying he's so crippled he's repulsive. He walks with a cane and in a curious sort of way, that may even make him more attractive. Like a modern Lord Byron. He looks a little like him, come to think of it, with that lock of hair falling over his forehead." He chuckled. "A red-headed Byron. A minor physical disability sometimes can be quite an asset. Look at the Hathaway shirt guy, or your own General Moshe Dayan, for that matter."

"Why aren't they rehiring him?" said the rabbi, to get back to the point.

"Well, that's just it. They don't have to give any reason. Maybe Prex or the dean spotted him walking down the corridor with his fly open, or maybe even goosing one of the coeds. How would I know? It could be anything."

The rabbi went down the corridor toward the dean's office, but just as he reached it he saw her door close. He hesitated a moment, and then, remembering the pending committee meeting, decided not to disturb her.

On his way out of the empty building, he noticed the large English office on the first floor was lit. He looked in and saw Professor Roger Fine sitting alone at his desk, abstracted.

He called to him. "Can I give you a lift back to Barnard's Crossing?"

Startled, Fine looked up. "Oh hello, Rabbi. No, I've got my car here. Thanks just the same. I—I'm waiting for a phone call."

As he let himself out the front door, the rabbi wondered if the poor fellow really was waiting for a phone call, or whether he was waiting for the results of the committee meeting that could decide his fate.

Although it was well into autumn, the weather was mild and balmy, and David Small rode with the window down. He was beginning to relax and enjoy the drive when he passed a couple of students sitting on the sidewalk and they reminded him of what had happened earlier in his classroom. He tried to put it out of his mind by concentrating on the approaching Sabbath when one should be at peace with the world. He pictured Miriam setting the table, laying out the twisted Sabbath loaves and the *kiddush* wine.

He visualized his arrival and her greeting: *"Shabbat Shalom,* David," and then the inevitable, "And how did it go today?"

And he would answer, "Well, it was—you see, the other day President Macomber went to visit the Boys' Reformatory as a member of some special citizens' committee, and . . ." It just wouldn't do. He could not minimize the fiasco. If he tried, she would sense that he was holding something back and it would be even worse.

Up ahead he saw a roadside cafeteria and pulled in. He badly wanted a cup of coffee.

12

"What's with the brief case?" Abner asked Ekko as they met in front of the administration building. "What's in it?"

"Nothing," said Ekko, "but I figured it would look business-like. After all, we're going like to a conference."

Abner looked at him doubtfully and then said: "Well, there won't be any conference if we don't get there. Let's go."

Upstairs Dean Hanbury pulled up some chairs in front of her desk and locked the office safe. Adjusting the venetian blind against the sun, she returned to her desk and began to knit placidly, waiting for the student delegation to arrive. Promptly at half-past two they entered, Judy Ballantine and Abner Selzer first, followed by Ekko, with his dispatch case, which he placed conspicuously on his lap.

The dean smiled graciously and continued to knit while the students shot glances at each other, uncertain how to begin. They felt somehow they had been put on the defensive even before the conference had begun.

Ekko cleared his throat. "Look here, Miss Hanbury—"

"Cool it, Ekko," Selzer ordered curtly. Then he said, "We're here on what we consider important business, Dean Hanbury."

She inclined her head to denote agreement.

"Well, with you knitting, it kind of throws us off, if you see what I mean. It's like you don't consider this very important."

"Oh, I'm sorry, Mr. Selzer. It's a habit with me. I'm afraid I knit even at faculty meetings."

She placed her knitting in the plastic bag at her feet. "There now, is that better? What can I do for you?"

"Well, first we'd like to take up the matter of Professor Roger Fine," said Judy.

"You say, 'first.' Are there other things?"

71

"There are other things," said Selzer.

"Well, why don't you tell me what they are. Perhaps there are some on which we are in substantial agreement and we can settle those at once."

"We'd rather take them up one at a time, Miss Hanbury," said Abner.

She shrugged.

"We'd like to begin with the matter of Roger Fine."

"Very well. But first let me ask just what your position is in the matter. Has he asked you to represent him?"

"We are representing him."

"But has he requested that you do so? Because if he has, if you are acting as his official representative, then I think you should have a written authorization from him to that effect."

"We don't have any written authorization, Miss Hanbury," said Selzer easily, "but he knows of our interest in the matter. I guess everyone does since we've been circulating a petition on his behalf."

"And did he authorize that? And how many signatures did you get, Mr. Selzer?"

"We got plenty, Miss Hanbury."

"May I see the petition?" She eyed the case on Ekko's lap. "Do you have it there?"

"We didn't bring it," said Abner.

"But why not? You circulate a petition and get signatures. I assume the petition was addressed to the administration. I can't understand why you would circulate a petition and then not bring it. Wasn't that the purpose of this meeting, or at least one of the purposes—to formally present the petition so that the administration could consider it and act on it?"

"Let's say it wasn't really a petition. Let's say it was a resolution. A petition means that we'd be asking for something. We're not really asking."

"Then what?"

"We're demanding."

There were nods of agreement.

Dean Hanbury considered. Then she nodded. "Very well, what is ıt that you're demanding? And in whose name? Is this a demand merely of this committee, or do you claim to represent the entire student body?"

"You're damn right, we represent the student body," O'Brien exploded.

Selzer gave him a withering glance.

"If you represent the student body, Mr. Selzer," she went on, "then more than ever I must see the petition or the resolution, or whatever you call it. I must have some assurance that you represent more than fifty percent, a majority, of the student body. If you are making a demand, the normal procedure, in the absence of a vote, would be to count the signatures and then look them over to make sure there are no duplicates and that all signers are bona fide students of the school."

"Look, Miss Hanbury," said Selzer, "you're just fencing. Let's put it this way: we represent the *concerned* students of Windemere. And it doesn't really matter whether we are authorized representatives of Roger Fine or not. Because the issue is more important than a particular person. The issue is whether the administration has the right to fire a member of the faculty because it doesn't like his political opinions. Now that's the issue and it's the only issue."

"Oh, I thought you had a number of issues."

"I mean that's the only issue in this particular case."

"That's a legitimate issue, Mr. Selzer, and I'm frank to admit that it is important enough to justify any member of the school raising the question—if it were true. But I'm afraid you've been misled. Professor Fine was not fired, in the first place. He was hired for a definite period, and at the end of this semester his contract expires. That's all there is to it. When you engage an electrician, say, to install a fixture, you pay him when he's done; then he leaves. I'm sure you wouldn't expect that just because he has installed one fixture he is now entitled to do all the electrical work in the house. I'm sure Professor Fine realized the conditions of his employment, and his political opinions had nothing to do with it. If he had been dropped before he had completed his contract, then you might have a case, but he is teaching now and will continue to teach,

I trust, until the end of the term in accordance with his contract."

"Why wasn't he reappointed then?" demanded Selzer.

"Because he wasn't hired with that in mind. He was hired to fill a temporary need. And for a specific period."

"But you are going to hire another instructor for the English department. As a matter of fact, we have it on good authority that you intend to hire two new men."

"That may be," said Dean Hanbury. "It's a matter for the president to decide, and I can't speak for him. I doubt if he has even made up his mind yet. But that does not affect the situation with Professor Fine. There is nothing to prevent him from making formal application for the job, in which case his candidacy would be considered along with all others who apply and no doubt his experience here last year would be one of the points considered."

"And what of his radicalism?" exploded Judy Ballantine.

"I don't know anything about his politics," replied Dean Hanbury. "He has never discussed them with me, or with the president, to my knowledge."

"How about his article in *The Windrift* on Vietnam and the Army?"

"I don't recall it, Miss Ballantine. I don't believe I read it." She swiveled her chair around and gazed out the window at the street below.

This was more than Judy could take. She jumped to her feet. "That's a crock of shit and you know it. Everybody in school read that article and everybody talked about it."

The dean did not answer. Instead, she rose and went to the door. "You'll have to excuse me," she said, and walked out, closing the door behind her.

They looked at each other uncertainly. Selzer turned on Judy. "You asshole," he said.

"Now, Abner, Judy didn't mean anything," said Ekko. "Hanbury probably just went to the can."

"Or maybe to see Prex," suggested O'Brien. "She'll be back."

"Maybe she just wants to let on she's sore. Then when she comes back, we feel funny and don't push so hard."

They discussed it, wandering around the room, looking at the pictures on the wall, pecking at the keys of the typewriter while waiting for her to return.

"If she was just going to walk out on us," said Judy after awhile, "wouldn't she have told us to leave?"

Ekko still thought she'd gone to the can.

"Well, maybe," said Selzer, "but if so, she's been there a long time now. It's at least ten or fifteen minutes."

"Well, women are that way," said Ekko.

"How about you?" demanded Judy. "You can tie up the john for an hour."

Ekko grinned.

Selzer came to a decision. "Look Judy, you go down to the women's john and see if she's there. Yance, you go up to the president's office. Me and Mike, we'll check around the other rooms."

"How about me?" asked Ekko.

"Somebody's got to stay here in case she comes back."

Alone in the office, Ekko sat down in the dean's swivel chair, teetered back and forth, and then hoisted his feet onto the desk. While he would have preferred that someone besides Judy had disrupted the meeting, he was not sorry it was over. Obviously, Selzer had forgotten he was supposed to play down the Fine issue. The dean was one shrewd cookie, and he was sure that if the meeting had continued she would have led them on and then sprung Fine's letter on them. It would get all over the school, and his friend Fine would really be hurt.

They began to drift back into the office, one by one. Finally, Selzer appeared. "I checked every goddam room, corridor, telephone booth from the top floor clear down to the basement. She's gone."

They looked at each other.

"What do we do now?"

13

Millicent Hanbury, outwardly cool and unruffled, pressed down the release bar on the front door of the administration building and let herself out. Outside, she hesitated and glanced up at the window of her office, then hurried across the deserted street to where her car was parked.

When she pulled into her driveway and glanced at her watch, she realized how fast she had been driving; she'd made it from school to her house in just thirty-five minutes, her best time yet.

Closing the door behind her, she leaned against it for a moment as if to reassure herself she was within the sanctuary of her own four walls. But only for a moment. She went to the phone.

"Barnard's Crossing Police Department, Sergeant Leffler," came the response from the other end.

"This is Millicent Hanbury, Sergeant, at 48 Oak Street."

"Yes, I know the address, Miss Hanbury."

"I've just returned home and I found a window in my living room open. I'm sure I closed it when I left."

"Was anything taken, Miss Hanbury? Does it look as though the place has been ransacked?"

"No," she said. "Everything seems to be in order, but I haven't gone through the rest of the house yet."

"Well, don't. I'll have somebody there right away. Just wait there. Or better, wait outside. The cruising car will be around any minute."

When the cruising car arrived, Officer Keenan accompanied

her from room to room while his fellow officer remained at the wheel. "Everything look all right to you, Miss Hanbury? Nothing missing?"

He examined the open window from the inside and the outside. "There's nothing that looks like a jimmy mark on the sash," he said. "And of course there wouldn't be any footprints on this concrete path. Was the window locked, Miss Hanbury?"

"I'm quite sure it was."

"Well, it's no big job to open a window with one of these old-fashioned latches. You can do it easy enough with a piece of plastic or one of these thin metal rulers. You ought to get the new type of latch for these windows on the first floor, Miss Hanbury."

From the cruising car came a loud, insistent honking. Keenan ran outside and came hurrying back. "Say, Miss Hanbury, a call just came in to the station. There was an explosion in your school. A bomb, they think. They want you back in Boston right away. We can drive you if you like."

"Oh David! I was going to call, but I didn't know where. I was so worried. Thank God you're safe!" Bursting into tears, Miriam threw herself in his arms.

"What's the matter?" He held her away and looked at her. "Pull yourself together, Miriam. I know I'm late, but I only stopped for a cup of coffee."

"Then you don't know?" she cried. "You weren't there when it happened?"

"Don't know what?" He was getting exasperated. "When what happened?"

"The explosion! There's been an explosion in your school, in the administration building."

"What kind of explosion? When did it happen? Make sense, Miriam."

"A bomb! They're sure it was a bomb," she said, taking out a handkerchief to dry her eyes. "I was watching 'Way of Life' and they interrupted the program with a news flash, only about fifteen minutes ago. They said no one appeared to be hurt, but with you not home yet . . ."

He put his arms around her and soothed her.

"You always get home around three," she said against his chest, "and here it was almost half-past. I tried to tell myself you sometimes get involved in something and lose all track of time."

"That's about what happened," he admitted sheepishly. "I started to read a book over my coffee and just didn't notice."

"Yes, of course," she said. "It doesn't matter. Nothing matters except that you're all right."

"I'm fine," he said. "I'm only sorry I made you worry. But I still don't understand it. A bombing? You sure they didn't say anything more?"

"No, that's all. It was a news flash. But maybe you could call someone. Lanigan? Wouldn't he know what happened?"

"No, it's something for the Boston police." He was very disturbed of course, but did not want to show it for fear of upsetting her further. "We'll get more details on the evening broadcast, I'm sure. In the meantime, the Sabbath is approaching."

While she made ready, he showered and changed, and then played for a while with his children Jonathan and Hepzibah. He did not want to leave Miriam alone, so he decided not to go to the temple for the afternoon *Mincha* service. By the time he had finished it was time for the news.

They sat together on the sofa, his arm around her, watching the picture in front of them. "Tonight's lead story," the announcer said. "At 3:05 this afternoon a bomb was exploded in the administration building of Windemere Christian College in Boston's Fenway. Police from Station 15 responded within minutes and the fire apparatus from the Boylston Street station immediately after. The explosion occurred in the dean's office and damage was minor, according to Inspector Frank Laplace of the Fire Department.

"The building was presumed empty since no classes are scheduled at that time on Fridays. However, Lieutenant Hawkins of Station 15 instituted an intensive search of the

78

premises and found the body of a man in one of the locked offices. He was identified by Mr. Laferty, the custodian of the building, as Professor John Hendryx. For a statement from Lieutenant Hawkins, we switch you now . . ."

14

Sitting on the bed, she watched him gather his few possessions together and stuff them into the duffle bag. They had not quarreled, he had not appeared angry. But then of course he never got angry; that's what she liked about him. He had merely announced he had to be pushing along and then resurrected his duffle bag from the depths of the closet.

If they had one rule, tacitly agreed on, it was that each was free to come and go as he pleased; should either of them decide to leave for any reason there would be no recriminations. But still she felt an explanation was—not due her, but, but— well yes, dammit, due her. However, she molded her voice so that it showed no hint of hurt, only normal curiosity: "Anything happen, Ekko?"

"The goddam school blows up and she asks if anything happened. One minute the place is peaceful like a morgue. Then Boom! It's a regular Fourth of July carnival with cops and fire engines, even the guy with the popcorn cart."

"Oh that! I meant between us. Are you sore because I sounded off at the meeting?"

"Nah," he said. "She was just looking for an out. If it hadn't been that, it would've been something else."

"So then why are you splitting?"

He threw more things into the bag. "Because they'll be coming after us, baby. They'll get hold of Hanbury and she'll tell them about the meeting and how she walked out and left us behind. And she'll give them our names and they'll pick us up. Then they'll start questioning and they'll find out I was in Nam, and in Ordnance, and next thing you know I'm in the slammer."

"But they haven't got anything on you."

"They don't need anything to start pushing, baby. When I got out of the Army, I made up my mind I wasn't ever going to let anyone push me around again so long as I could help it."

"But if you split now, won't that be suspicious?" she said. "Then they'll be sure you did it."

"They can think what they want, so long as I'm not around."

She was silent, trying to understand why he would invite suspicion by running away. Hesitantly, she asked: "Did—did you do it, Ekko?"

He snorted. "Why would I blow up the goddam school? For Roger Fine?"

"Then who did?"

"Probably those goddam Weathervane crazies. Same as last time. They're stoned out of their heads most of the time. They must have found out about our meeting somehow. They see Hanbury leave. Then fifteen minutes later they see us leave. So they get a clear road. Blooey: the Fourth of July!"

She looked at him. "How did you know they did it last time?"

"I just know." He continued with his packing.

"They could catch you tomorrow," she said.

"Sure, and I could be run over by a car and dead tomorrow. In the meantime, I'll be free."

In a quiet voice: "Are you coming back?"

"Sure, after things cool down. The college won't push this —bad publicity. Like the last time, the computer was wrecked and they gave out to the papers it was only minor damage. Same way now. The college won't press, and after a while the pigs will have to drop it. Then I'll come back."

"But you've paid for your tuition."

"Half a semester. So I've had half a semester. Big deal; the stuff is a lot of crap anyway. Maybe I'll get me a job as a carpenter like my old man. There, when you do some work, you can at least see something for it. Yeah, maybe that's what I'll do. Carpentering. Ten bucks an hour some places." He pulled the cords and closed the mouth of the bag.

"But you won't get the chance," she appealed to him. "Once they start looking, they won't let up till they find you. They got your picture in the school files and with that bald head they won't have any trouble finding you."

"Oh yeah? Turn around for a minute."

She did so, doubtfully.

"All right, now you can look."

She could scarcely recognize him. He was wearing a wig of thick black hair and the whole cast of his face was transformed by a Mongol moustache.

"How do you like it?"

"Crazy!"

He slung the bag over his shoulder. "I got a friend out in the western part of the state. I can hole up with him for a couple of days. Then there's a guy I know in Ohio who's running some kind of dope rehabilitation center. I bet I could stay with him for a month and nobody would even notice me. Don't worry about me." He hesitated then said, "Well, so long. Be seeing you."

"You going just like that, Ekko?"

He looked at her narrowly and said, "Okay, I guess it won't do no harm to start a little later."

Later, as she lay in his arms, she murmured, "I'm afraid, Ekko."

"What of?"

"Oh, what they'll do when they arrest me."

"You got no call to be afraid," he said. "Your old man will hire some high-power lawyer, and they'll treat you with kid gloves. It's just slobs like me that got to worry. They take it out double on me because they can't touch you."

"I'm afraid for you."

"Don't worry. They won't find me in a million years."

15

"Anything?"

Detective Sergeant Schroeder of Homicide was slim and boyish, and his dark crewcut showed no touch of gray for all his fifty years. He looked half that age, until you were close enough to see the wrinkling around the eyes and the well-defined musculature of the face. He stood in the doorway of the dean's office and watched the two men from the Bomb Squad carefully sweep up fragments from the floor.

One of the men looked up. "Low grade bomb." He straightened and pointed to the safe. "She was planted under there."

"You think maybe they wanted to bust it open?"

"They'd never do it that way. Looks as though it sprung the door though. They might need a can opener to get it open now."

"How come the window in this office is still intact where the other one shattered?" the sergeant asked.

"Well, Sarge, the force of the explosion wasn't strong enough to blow out this window, especially since the safe took most of the blast. But the jarring was severe enough to rattle any that happened to be loose."

"The janitor said the window in the other office was badly cracked," the precinct lieutenant offered.

"Well, that would do it all right," said the bomb expert.

Sergeant Schroeder went down the corridor to Hendryx's office where police photographers were taking pictures of the room from various angles. He stopped to look at the empty frame in the door. "Lucky that glass shattered," he said, "or it could've been Monday before he was found."

"That's right," the lieutenant agreed. "I sent a couple of men to look through the building, and naturally they wouldn't bother with offices that were locked. But with the glass shattered, my man could get in and he saw these feet sticking out from under the desk like they are now. It's plain what happened. The prof was sitting behind his desk, reading maybe. The bomb goes off, and this plaster cast—must weigh a good fifty, sixty pounds—topples off the shelf and comes crashing down on his head. It crushes the skull and he slides off the chair under the desk."

"What was he doing here?" asked the sergeant. "I thought you said everybody clears out Friday afternoons."

"The janitor says he lives—lived—right across the street, so he popped back and forth from his apartment to his office from time to time."

They were joined by a young man who introduced himself as Dr. Lagrange.

"You the medical examiner? Where's Doc Slocumbe?"

"He was tied up."

"I've never worked with you, I don't think," said Schroeder doubtfully.

The doctor smiled. "I don't see how you could have. I'm new."

"Okay, Doc, the boys are about through. He's all yours."

They returned to the dean's office. The Bomb Squad had finished and left; the photographers had done the room earlier. Schroeder sat down at the dean's desk and asked to see the janitor.

Pat Laferty was a small man of sixty, clean and neat in a business suit with a gray shirt and black plastic bow tie. He smiled ingratiatingly at the man behind the desk.

"What time do you close up here, Pat?" asked the sergeant.

"Well, that depends. If there's nothing doing, no special meeting or anything, around five."

"Fridays too?"

"Fridays a little earlier, maybe around four."

"And before you close, you go around to see that everyone is out of the building?"

"Well, not exactly. I take a look-see to make sure lights are out, no faucets running. That can waste a lot of water, you know."

"Now today, what time did you lock up?"

"Well, I didn't. The dean was having a meeting with some students at half-past two, so I decided to wait until it broke up."

"So anybody could have come in up to four o'clock?"

"Oh, sure."

"You mean anyone can walk right into this building?"

"Until I lock up—but what good would it do them? All the offices are locked. The classrooms aren't but what's there to take? Chalk?"

"Guess you're right," said Schroeder. "Now, you say this Professor Hendryx lives right across the street?"

"That's right," said Laferty. "That building right across the street. He's got the first floor apartment, the one with the curtains. You can see it from here."

Schroeder swung his chair around. "Seems to be the only one with curtains. The place looks empty. How come?"

Laferty explained the arrangement with Professor Hendryx. "It was good for both parties: it gave him a handy place to live nearby; and for the school, it was like having a watchman in the building. You know, kids see an empty building and first thing you know, they're breaking in and messing things up."

"All right. We got your address?"

"I gave it to the lieutenant."

A policeman put his head in the door. "That lady dean is here now, Sarge."

16

He picked the Albany bus because it was the first scheduled out of the terminal. Ekko took a window seat four rows back and watched as the passengers entered, speculating who would sit beside him. An attractive girl with long blonde hair got on and he looked at her with interest, but she passed him by. He turned and saw she had chosen to sit beside another woman.

A fat old woman carrying a bulging mesh bag was helped aboard by the driver and waddled down the aisle. Luckily, she too, passed by. But almost immediately after he felt the slight jar of someone plumping down beside him.

It was a middle-aged man with a square face capped by thick black hair. He wore eyeglasses with heavy frames of black plastic, above which black eyebrows all but met at the bridge of the nose. In the lapel of his dark gray suit there was a Kiwanis button. The man smiled and looked at his watch, a small square of gold much too delicate for his thick, hairy wrist. "We should be rolling pretty soon," he said.

"Yeah, I guess so."

Apparently the man was determined to make conversation. "I went into the cafeteria for a cup of coffee and a doughnut, but Lord! the service is so slow, I decided to pass it up. I didn't want to miss the bus."

"It is kind of slow sometimes."

"I like to travel by bus," the other went on. "Get a chance to see the countryside."

"You won't see much this trip," said Ekko. "Not at night."

"No, I suppose not, but even so, I like it a lot better than going by plane. You traveling all the way to Albany?"

"If I don't decide to get off before."

The man raised his black eyebrows. "You mean you don't know where you're going? You just came for the ride?"

Ekko shrugged. "I felt like taking a ride on a bus. This bus was scheduled to go, so I bought a ticket and got on board."

The other laughed a deep bass gurgle of a laugh.

"What's so funny?"

"You young people. . . . You're wonderful! You felt like taking a ride on a bus, so you . . ." He could not stop chuckling. "Tell me, why a bus?"

Ekko grinned. He warmed to this open admiration. The man

was such a complete square, a regular nine-to-fiver, probably with a fat wife and an acne-faced teen-aged daughter they were worried might go too far with some boy. He expanded. "It's like this: you're walking along the street"—he remembered his duffle bag in the rack above—"say, like you're taking laundry to the laundromat and you decide you're fed up. You suddenly get the idea you can't stand the rat race. Understand?"

The man nodded.

"So you just like decide you want a little change."

"I get it. And because you happened to be in Park Square, you took a bus."

"That's right," said Ekko grinning.

"And if you happened to be down by South Station, you'd take a train? Or in East Boston, a plane?"

Ekko looked at him suspiciously, but his face was bland and guileless. He shook his head. "Naw, I don't care much for trains or planes, but I like to ride on buses, especially at night. On a bus it's dark at night. They turn the lights off so the driver can see the road. Things can happen in the dark."

"What kinds of things?"

Ekko looked at the square. "Oh, all kinds of things."

"Like what?"

His eagerness was pathetic. "Well, like take the time I took the eleven o'clock out of New York for Boston. I got the window seat like now, and next thing you know this chick comes aboard and sits down beside me. Well, I was dead on my feet, hadn't slept for days. You know how it is in the big city."

"Sure do."

Ekko smiled to himself. "I look around and see there were plenty of other seats, so I figure she wants company. You could see she was a high-class chick and good-looking. She's wearing one of those coats that comes down to the ankles and when she takes it off, I see she's really built. So when she sits down, I say something like, 'It's a nice night for it.' You know, to get friendly and start the ball rolling. But she just says like 'M-hm,' and she opens this book of poetry and starts reading. So I says to myself, 'Okay, lady, if that's the way you want it,' and I close my eyes for a little shut-eye. Then in a couple of minutes the lights go off and we start rolling and I fall asleep. But you know how it is on a bus, you don't really sleep. You just like doze off and on."

"Sure. I never really can sleep on a bus."

"So once when I wake up, the broad is fast asleep with her head back on the cushion and her mouth open a little. And this little wisp of hair is across her face and every time she breathes out she like blows it away and then it falls back. So I twist around to kind of watch it and I fall asleep, watching. And then I feel something touching me and I kind of half wake up and it's the chick. She's curled up facing me and she's touching me in her sleep. Right where it counts."

The square was now excited. "So what did you do?"

"Well, I hitched up closer to her and I got this long coat she had on her lap to kind of cover us."

"And then?"

"What do you think? I put my hand on her boobs, and when she didn't wake up I hinched closer and put my other hand up her dress."

"And then what did you do?"

"What could I do? We were in a bus. I couldn't try to put it to her right then and there. We just held each other like that and I fell asleep that way."

"And in the morning?"

The guy was dying.

Ekko grinned. "Nothing. When I woke up, we were just pulling in to Boston and she was gone. She must've got off at Newton. Anyway, that's why I like to take a bus ride every now and then."

"So nothing happened?" the man said regretfully. "You never saw her again?"

"Naw."

"I think maybe you dreamt it."

Ekko grinned in the darkness. Let him suffer. "No, I didn't dream it."

The other sat silent and made no further comment. After a while Ekko dozed off. It seemed only minutes later that he was awakened by the bus driver announcing that they'd be arriving in Springfield in ten minutes. The man removed a small overnight bag from the rack overhead, and then sat down again holding it on his lap.

"Springfield," the man said. "That's where I get off."

"Oh, Springfield already?"

"Uh-huh. You know, you had me going for a minute," he said.

"What do you mean?"

"Oh, all that about taking a bus ride just because you felt like it and not knowing where you're planning to get off." He chuckled. "You young people are always trying to let on that you do whatever you like, just the way you feel, but it's only a lot of talk. You go someplace because that's the place you want to go, just like anybody else. You're on this bus right now because you were planning to get on this bus."

Ekko tensed up. "How do you know?"

The man laughed his deep gurgle. "Because I saw you. I saw you get on the train at Charles Street. I was right behind you, and I saw you. You were carrying a canvas duffle bag and it's up there on the rack. And I saw you get out at Boylston and head right for the bus station. No strolling along the street and suddenly deciding to take a bus ride on the chance that some girl might sit down beside you so that you could feel her up."

"Were you following me?"

"No, but I was right behind you. Then when we got to the bus station, I went into the cafeteria, and you went to the ticket booth."

"Must've been some other guy," Ekko muttered.

"Oh, no, it wasn't. It was you. I noticed you particularly, because I could see you was wearing a wig. And that moustache is phony, too. I could spot it in a minute on account I'm a barber and hair's my business. You bald or something?"

"Yeah, I'm pretty naked there," he said sheepishly.

The bus came to a halt and the man rose. "You get head colds all the time, do you?"

"Naw, it's just that the chicks don't go for baldies."

The man laughed. "Well, there's passengers always get on here. Maybe you'll have better luck the rest of the way." He waved genially and headed down the aisle.

17

Like all district attorneys, Matthew Rogers of Suffolk County, which included all of Boston, was first and foremost a politician and only secondly, and it was a poor second, a lawyer. Rogers was tall, strikingly handsome, and one of the youngest men ever to hold the office. The party bosses foresaw a bright future for him: certainly attorney general of the state, then, who knows? possibly even governor. Although of good Irish Catholic stock, he did not look it; and his name—neither name—was flagrantly Irish, so it was easier for the other ethnic groups to accept him.

Shortly after finishing law school—and he had gone to Harvard Law rather than to Catholic Boston College—Rogers' father-in-law, who was in politics, told him that he had sounded out "the boys" and they were willing to back him for political office. "With the boys backing you, Matt, you're practically a shoo-in for the state legislature."

"I was thinking of running for school committee," said Matthew Rogers.

"That's crazy, Matt. It don't pay nothing. You've got to think of Kathleen and the girls. And for school committee you got to run city-wide."

"But in the legislature I'd be only one of a couple of hundred, and on the school committee I'm one of five. And I'm not worried about the pay. With the millions the school committee dispenses every year, I ought to be able to pick up enough law business to more than equal what I'd be getting in the state legislature."

Matthew Rogers ran as a family man, as the concerned father of children who attended the public schools; all his campaign posters and cards showed him seated, with his lovely wife standing beside him, and their two pretty little daughters sitting at their feet. He won handily.

On the school committee he had espoused the cause of the teachers. His father-in-law remonstrated, "Why do you want to get tied in with a pay raise for teachers? It's going to mean a jump in the tax rate, Matt, and you won't get a damn thing out of it. The teachers ain't like the cops or the firemen. They're a bunch of rabbits, they got no clout. They won't go to bat for you come election time. They'll vote for you, but you won't get those snooty bastards going around ringing doorbells."

"But they've got better contacts with the media," said Matthew Rogers.

The pay raise was compromised, but he was now the one liberal on the committee, and when reporters and TV newscasters covered a meeting of the school committee, he was the one they usually interviewed.

After a couple of terms on the school committee, he had run for district attorney of the county, again projecting the family-man image in his campaign, with the slogan "Vote for Matt Rogers and make Suffolk County a decent place to bring up your family." This time his campaign pictures showed him seated beside his now somewhat more matronly wife, with the two older girls, quite the young ladies, standing on either side of their parents, a third sitting on the floor, and a fourth on her mother's lap. Again he won handily.

He had taken office just as the student riots were beginning. When trouble broke out in Hollings College, he had seized the opportunity to demonstrate his capacity for leadership—against the advice of his chief assistant, the senior assistant district attorney, Bradford Ames.

"Don't do it, Matt," Ames told him. "These aren't hoods, they're college kids from nice families, some of them with a lot of political influence. And you'll find when you go into court that the college authorities won't back you up. Keep out of the line of fire and let the cops handle it, or you'll get clobbered."

Rogers had stared at him, uncomprehending. "They've taken possession of one of the buildings, haven't they? They've destroyed buildings. Do you expect me to stand by idly while private property is seized? It is private property, isn't it?"

Bradford Ames was in his fifties, quite a bit older than his chief. He came from an old and wealthy Boston family and had no difficulty wangling an appointment as assistant district attorney immediately after passing the bar exam. A bachelor, he found his niche in the district attorney's office, where he was content to remain. Although of medium height, he looked short because he was well-fleshed. His suit, though tailor-made and expensive, looked rumpled and ill-fitting because, sitting or standing, he slouched. He wore old-fashioned stiff detached collars, which appeared too tight for him and tended to make his head look bigger than it was. He was a smiley, chuckling, Dutch uncle of a man, so that when on occasion his face became stern and grave, as it did sometimes when addressing a jury, everyone in the courtroom felt that a horrendous crime indeed had been committed. He knew intimately all the clerks, criminal lawyers, and judges, knew their special characteristics and idiosyncrasies, but he also had an instinctive feeling for political considerations and he had been invaluable to a succession of district attorneys, unobtrusively training them in their jobs.

He shifted uncomfortably from foot to foot under Rogers' stare and then emitted an embarrassed chuckle. "Well, it is and it isn't private property. A college is actually a community of scholars that developed into a corporation with trustees and officers who appoint the president. In the Middle Ages, on the other hand, a lot of colleges were set up by the students. They hired the faculty and fined them when they were late for their lectures. What I'm saying is that it could be argued that the college belongs to the students as much as it does to the administration."

But Rogers had persisted—and he had indeed got clobbered. For a few days he'd had a fine time, issuing statements to the press, getting photographed, conferring with the college president and the dean, planning strategy with the police. It had resulted finally in a heated confrontation between police and students with physical injuries sustained on both sides. And suddenly, he was the villain, target of dozens of denunciatory letters in the press and even an editorial or two. He discovered, to his surprise, that many of the faculty sided with the students and that even the administration was having second thoughts. To his great disgust, when the case of the ring leaders finally came to trial, the administration showed great reluctance to prosecute, and even the judge, who imposed a small fine, suggested in his summation that perhaps the authorities had over-reacted.

Rogers was a politician and he learned his lesson. From then on, whenever there was student unrest, he followed the advice of his chief assistant, Ames, and let the police take the lead. When it was absolutely necessary for his office to appear, he assigned the case to the most junior member, some youngster fresh out of law school, and Ames would brief him, "Keep a low profile, and don't push. Remember, you're just going along for the ride. The chief considers this basically intramural, something for the college to work out, and doesn't want to get involved."

So Bradford Ames was surprised when he found the folder for the Windemere College case on his desk with a note from his superior, "Brad, I want you to handle this one personally." He came in to Rogers' office to discuss it. "How come, Matt?"

"Because this time I want the book thrown at them."

"Why?"

It was not easy for Rogers to explain. A scion of the Massachusetts Ameses looked at things differently from the son of Timothy Rogers, a mail carrier. Take this matter of these college kids raising hell all the time; Brad didn't exactly side with them, but he didn't get too indignant either, as though he thought they might have a point. Then, too, the man was a bachelor. How could he understand the feelings of a man with four daughters? To a man with daughters, the direction the world was taking was frightening: a girl living openly with a man and no one, not even the college authorities, thinking anything of it; kids using dirty language to their dean—a lady dean at that—and expecting to get away with it.

Occasionally Matthew Rogers found himself feeling defensive before the aristocratic coolness of his subordinate, so he now said more emphatically than he normally would: "This one is different, Brad. I know you feel these student riots are none of our business, and I go along with you; but this involved arson, and arson by its very nature is not an intra-mural sport."

"There is that of course."

"And a man was killed."

"Well, that appears to have been an accident."

Then defiantly: "And I think it's good politics. I think we're at a turnaround, Brad. I think the public is goddam fed up with these goddam radical kids doing whatever they goddam please. So by taking control now, I think I can demonstrate leadership."

Ames smiled. "You planning to run for attorney general next time around, Matt?"

"I've thought of it," said Rogers evenly.

Ames saw he meant business.

"We don't have too much of a case, you know. The youngsters claim they had nothing to do with the bombing."

"Naturally."

"And there isn't much evidence that they did, not anything that would stand up in a court."

"How about the fact that one of them ran away?"

"We don't know that he did," said Ames. "He could have just taken off someplace the way kids do."

"How about the time?" Rogers persisted. "The dean says she left her office around quarter of three. The kids admit they remained until three. A few minutes later the bomb goes off. Who else could have done it?"

"The caretaker stated the doors of the building are left open. Anyone could have come in. It could be another student group. I understand there are at least half a dozen of various shades of radicalism."

"Look," said Rogers, "have we got enough to hold them?"

Ames temporized.

"Well, it would probably depend on who was acting for them and which judge they came up before. Somebody like Sullivan, he'd hold them just for the way they're dressed."

Rogers nodded. "So arrange to have them come up before Sullivan, or even Visconte. In the meantime I'll put enough investigators on it to make sure he'll hold them."

"All right."

"And I want them held, Brad. No bail."

"Oh cummon, Matt! Even Sullivan wouldn't go for that."

"Why not? It's murder, isn't it? A homicide resulting in the course of committing a felony is murder in the first, isn't it? Exploding a bomb is a felony, isn't it? So the professor getting killed is murder. Is that the law, or isn't it?"

Ames hedged. "It's not as simple as that, Matt. The rationale behind felony murder is that malice is presumed when a homicide takes place during the commission of a felony. But the homicide has to be so closely connected with the felony that it is within the *res gestae*. Coincidence is not enough. Now this was done late Friday afternoon when the building is usually empty, and the victim was in another room."

"That's something for a trial judge to decide, Brad."

"Yes," said Ames. "But these kids are in school. If we hold them without bail, they won't be able to attend their classes."

Matthew Rogers smacked his hand on the desk.

"As far as I'm concerned, kids that blow up their school with a bomb aren't too interested in attending classes. I want those bastards held, understand? We're in an adversary system. If their lawyers can get them out on bail, I got to go along, but I'll be damned if I'll help them. I'm pushing for no bail. And if the judge won't go along on that, then push for the highest bail you can get."

"If that's the way you want to play it."

"I do," said Matthew Rogers.

"Look here, Matt," Ames said earnestly, "the chances are that it was the missing one, the one they call Ekko, who did it and that the others didn't know anything about it."

"How do you figure?"

"Well, he's not like the others. He's quite a bit older and has already served in the Army. He was in Vietnam." He raised an admonishing forefinger. "In Ordnance. What's more, on what we were able to gather from preliminary questioning, he was the only one who was alone in the dean's office for any length of time; the others were searching for her all over the building. And he had a dispatch case with him. Finally, he was the only one who ran."

"Did any of them suggest that it might have been him?"

"No, but—"

"And if they don't know for sure, it's a cinch that they won't say a word. Those kids stick together."

"So?"

Matthew Rogers grinned. "So isn't it to our advantage to keep them in jail? When this Ekko hears of it, especially that we've got his girl, there's a good chance he'll give himself up."

"That's like holding them for ransom, Matt," Ames protested.

"Uh-huh."

"Matt, that's a dirty Irish trick."

Rogers grinned broadly. "Uh-huh."

18

The rabbi was dressing for the Friday evening service when the phone rang. The baby-sitter took the call, and as the rabbi came to the door of the living room, knotting his tie, he saw the girl's eyes widen.

"Who is it?" he asked.

She covered the receiver with her hand and whispered, "It's the police, Rabbi! From Boston."

"All right, I'll take it." She handed him the instrument quickly as if eager to relinquish it.

"Rabbi Small?" said a gruff voice. "This is Sergeant Schroeder of Boston Homicide."

"How do you do, Sergeant," said the rabbi pleasantly.

"What? Oh yes. Look, Rabbi, I'd like to ask you a few questions about Professor Hendryx."

"All right. Ask."

"No. Not on the phone. I want to talk to you, and I'd like to get a signed statement. I'd like you to come down to headquarters here in Boston."

"That's out of the question, Sergeant."

"I can send a car."

"I'm afraid not, Sergeant," said the rabbi. "I'm on my way to the temple right now. This is the Sabbath and we hold an evening service."

"What time does it end?"

"Around ten. Why?"

"Well, suppose I come out to Barnard's Crossing, say around ten-fifteen."

"There's nothing I can tell you."

"You were probably the last person to see him alive, Rabbi."

"That may be true, but I left him shortly after two o'clock and he was alive then."

"I'd still like to talk to you," the sergeant said.

"Then I'm afraid it will have to wait until tomorrow evening. I don't discuss business matters during the Sabbath."

"But this is a homicide, Rabbi."

"There's nothing I could tell you that would justify my breaking the Sabbath."

"What if I came out there?"

"I would not talk to you."

The receiver at the other end banged down. Rabbi Small listened for a moment and then gently hung up the instrument.

Baffled and angry, Sergeant Schroeder sat staring at the phone. Then he remembered Hugh Lanigan, Barnard's Crossing's police chief, whom he had met at numerous police conferences and who had once invited him to come out sailing some Sunday during the summer.

He called Lanigan. "I wonder if you'd do me a favor, Hugh. I'd like you to pick up somebody for me and bring him in for questioning. . . . Yeah, on this Windemere College thing. . . . No, there's no charge against him. I just want him for questioning. . . . Who? A Rabbi Small. You know him? . . . Yeah, well, I asked him to come in, even offered to send a car out for him, but he said he wouldn't talk to me because it's the Sabbath."

"That's in character."

"Oh? A tough guy?"

Lanigan laughed. "Far from it, but he does observe his Sabbath. They don't transact business or even talk about it from Friday to Saturday night."

"That's what he said, but—"

"Look, Bill, don't let your pee steam. I wouldn't intrude on the rabbi on his Sabbath any more than I'd interrupt Father Aherne during a mass. If I asked him to go, he wouldn't come. And if I tried anything stronger, I could get into trouble. This isn't the big city, Bill. We're a small town and everybody knows everybody. We do things differently here. Tell you what, why don't you drive down tomorrow afternoon and take Saturday night supper with us? It's ham and beans and brown bread, but Gladys has a way with it. Then afterward, we'll drop in to see the rabbi. I guarantee he'll cooperate with you then a hundred percent."

The next evening Lanigan and Schroeder appeared at the Smalls'. Lanigan introduced the sergeant and said, "Why don't you two start fresh?"

The rabbi grinned. "Gladly." And led them into the living room.

The sergeant said, "Sure. You understand, Rabbi, I didn't want to interfere with your religious holiday, but with us homicide takes precedence over everything."

"With us too," said the rabbi, "but I'm sure there is nothing I can tell you that will be of any help. Professor Hendryx was alive when I left him."

"And what time was that?"

"Shortly after two. Ten after at the latest."

"Was he usually there then?" asked the sergeant.

"I really couldn't say. I have a class that ends at two, and afterward I stop into the office to pick up my coat and to leave my books. Sometimes, not always, he'd be there; I understand his cleaning woman comes to his apartment on Fridays so he escapes to the office—it's only across the street, you know."

"Yes, Rabbi, we've got the setup."

"But yesterday," said the rabbi, "he did say something about the dean having phoned him, asking him to stand by. She was scheduled to see a student committee and wanted him there in case they got obstreperous."

"Aha!" exclaimed Schroeder. "So you *did* have something important to tell."

"I did?"

"Why sure. In her statement, the dean didn't say anything about phoning Hendryx and asking him to hang around."

"And how is that important?" asked Lanigan, interested.

"Well, say she was involved." He looked from one to the other. The rabbi's lips were pursed in doubt; Lanigan was smiling. "I mean—" Then Schroeder surrendered completely and laughed. "Sorry, Rabbi, but I guess I was still a little sore because you wouldn't see me last night," he said sheepishly. "So after you left on Friday, did you see anyone, anyone at all, on your way out?"

"Well, the door of the dean's office was closing as I came down the hall, so although I didn't exactly see her I assume she was in her office. And then downstairs I saw Professor Fine in the English office. He said he was waiting for a phone call."

"What time did you get home, Rabbi?" asked Schroeder.

"It was quite late," the rabbi admitted. "About half-past three."

Lanigan raised his eyebrows. "Have trouble on the road?"

"No, I stopped for a cup of coffee."

"That shouldn't have taken long," said Schroeder.

"Well, it was one of those places where you eat in your own car," the rabbi explained. "I began reading a book and must have lost track of the time."

When they left, Schroeder asked, "What do you think of your friend's story?"

"You don't know him," said Lanigan. "I assure you it's completely in character."

"Still . . ."

"Look, Sergeant, there never was an investigation without its little inconsistencies. And the quickest way to get bogged down is to concentrate on them instead of the main line. But I guess you know that better than I."

"Yeah," said Schroeder, "but sometimes you can't help being bothered by them. For example, why didn't the dean tell me she'd phoned Hendryx and asked him to stand by?"

"You find that hard to understand?" asked Lanigan. "She didn't tell you because she forgot, and she forgot because she wanted to forget, and she wanted to forget because otherwise it would mean that she was responsible for his death."

19

The Sunday morning *minyan* was usually well attended. For one thing, it was held an hour and a half later than on weekdays—nine instead of seven-thirty—for another, it was followed by a meeting of the board of directors at ten, so most of them came early and participated in the twenty-minute service.

Although Malcolm Selzer rarely attended the weekday *minyan*—he was already in the warehouse at seven-thirty—he never missed the one on Sunday. He was one of the handful with a traditional upbringing who knew the liturgy and often was asked to lead the prayers. But this Sunday he did not show up. His absence did not pass unnoticed.

Although the name was reported variously as Abner Seldar, Adam Sellers, and Aaron Selger, no one in Barnard's Crossing, certainly no one in the Jewish community, had any doubt that the person referred to in the newspaper accounts of the bombing was Malcolm Selzer's boy, Abner. And the somewhat larger attendance at the *minyan* that Sunday was no doubt due in part to the quite human desire for more information.

The late Saturday night broadcast and the Sunday papers had provided a somewhat fuller account: that the dean, Millicent Hanbury, had met with a student delegation to discuss student grievances; that she had left the meeting—reason not given; that shortly afterward the committee of five had left her office and the building; that less than five minutes later the bomb had gone off. The district attorney's office had issued a statement saying it was planning to question each of the students.

As the men were folding up their prayer shawls, Dr. Malitz, one of the older men, remarked, "He was too embarrassed to come, I suppose."

Dr. Greenwood, a dentist like Malitz, shook his head. "Why does it have to be a Jewish boy?"

"What do you mean a Jewish boy?" said Norman Phillips indignantly. "There were five of them and the Selzer kid was the only one who was Jewish. And what's being Jewish got to do with it? He's an American, isn't he? He got the same rights as anybody else, hasn't he?"

Dr. Malitz came to the defense of his fellow dentist. He was a peridontist and Greenwood sent him patients. "You see in the papers that someone with a Jewish name has made some scientific discovery—you know, has done something good—you feel kind of proud it was one of ours, don't you? We all do. So naturally when one of us sees something not so nice, we feel—"

"You feel guilty. Right? Well, I don't," said Phillips stoutly. "I feel that as an American citizen I got just as much rights as any other citizen, and that means I'm no more responsible for what someone named Cohen or Levy does than I am for someone named Cabot or Lodge. Naturally, I'm sorry for Mal Selzer, but, you know, in a way he was asking for it."

Greenwood stared. "What kind of crack is that? What father deserves to see his son in trouble?"

"Well look, my kid goes to college, Rensselaer Polytech. Doc Malitz here has a boy in college. I don't know about your boy, Doc, but I know my kid acts up a little now and then. He's a kid, see. Last year, for example, they had a riot at his school. The cops turn up, reporters, the works. My kid says he was just looking on, you know, watching the fun. Maybe he was; maybe he wasn't. I'm not one of those fathers that thinks their kid can't do no wrong. Anyway, he gets pinched and he spends the night in jail and he has to pay a fine. He? Me. I had to pay it."

"So?"

"So my point is, did I go around bragging how my kid was a big student leader?"

"So you brag about something else that your boy did, maybe that he got into Rensselaer."

"I just mentioned that because—"

"Makes no difference," said Greenwood. "Fathers brag about their children. I'm sure Malcolm Selzer would rather brag that his boy was getting high marks and scholarships."

Dr. Malitz had a sudden thought. "How do we even know the Selzer boy had anything to do with the bombing? All the paper said was he was one of those at the meeting and the D.A. was planning to question him."

"When the D.A. questions somebody, like as not he ends up in jail," said Phillips. "What I'd like to know," he went on, "is what the rabbi knows about it. He teaches there. I notice he didn't come today, either."

"He's the guest speaker at the men's bible study class at the Lynn Methodist church this morning," said Dr. Malitz. "There was a notice in the Lynn paper."

"Just our luck," said Phillips disgustedly. "So that means *they'll* get the inside dope, not us."

20

The rabbi arrived home shortly before noon to find an impatient Malcolm Selzer waiting for him. "Your wife said you'd be along any minute," he said. "Besides, my wife was so sure you'd be able to do something I didn't have the heart to tell her I'd missed you."

"Just calm down, Mr. Selzer, and tell me what's on your mind."

Selzer looked at him gratefully, then took the seat the rabbi offered. "Well, Friday I heard the news same as everybody did. And I'll admit I had this little funny feeling maybe my Abner might be mixed up in it." He held up a hand. "I don't mean that I thought he could do anything like a bombing, a thing like that. I know my boy; he wouldn't hurt a fly. But I thought maybe he knows about it, maybe some group he could be connected with— You know how you think, how all kinds of funny ideas can come into your head?"

"Of course. Take your time and tell me what happened."

Selzer nodded. "All day Saturday, I thought of calling Abner. You know, not asking him point-blank, but just how's tricks, what's new. That way, if he was involved he could say something. It wasn't so much me as my wife who kept nagging me. 'Call him up; you got a son; talk to him once in a while.' And to tell the truth, I would have, except I was afraid it was like asking for it. My mother, may she rest in peace, always used to say, 'Don't start anything.'"

"Like tempting fate," said the rabbi with the ghost of a smile.

"That's right," Selzer said, pleased that the rabbi understood. "So I suggested to my wife we go to the movies. You know, to give us something else to think about; besides, I know she's not going to ask me to go out in the middle of the picture to make a phone call."

He looked off into space as if marshalling his thoughts. Then he continued. "I thought maybe we'd go out for a cup of coffee afterwards, like we always do, but my wife insisted we go right home, like her heart told her. As soon as we drive up to the house, I know there's trouble because the light in the kitchen is on, which means Abner has come home, and why would he come home on a Saturday night if he weren't in some kind of trouble? Nevertheless, my wife tries to act as though nothing happened. 'Have you eaten, Abner? There's some chicken left. Let me make you a sandwich. He's so thin. Look how thin he is, Malcolm.' Of course, this doesn't fool anybody; not me, not Abner, not even herself. She's just stalling, putting off the time when we'll have to ask him why he came home. But me, I'm a businessman and I don't horse around. So I put it to him straight: 'Are you in trouble, Abner? Are you involved in this bombing?'" Selzer raised a forefinger to call for special attention. "'Involved,' I said, Rabbi. Not did he do it. I just asked him if he was involved. What's involved? Anybody can be involved. If it's my son, I'm involved. My wife is involved. The police are involved. It's no crime to be involved."

He shook his head sadly. "That started it. He starts yelling I don't trust him. He comes home and all I can think is he must have bombed the school or done some terrible crime. That I'm part of the Establishment and the Establishment is trying to suppress the non-Establishment and they're trying to make this a decent world and my generation is not letting them. And how we use the pigs to keep them in line. By pigs he means the police, you understand."

Selzer got up and began pacing the room. "He yells and I yell, I suppose, and my wife cries, and after an hour of it I know as much as I did before. Finally, we all quiet down, and I say to him nice, quiet, calm, 'Look Abner, I'm not accusing you. I'm just asking, not because I'm nosy but just because I want to help. Do you want me to get in touch with my lawyer?'" He rapped the coffee table with his knuckles. "This table answered me? That's how he answered me. Not a word, like suddenly he's deaf and dumb. He just sits there smiling a little to himself like it's all very funny, and then he finally speaks. What does he say? He says, 'I think I'll hit the sack. Tomorrow could be a long day.' And he gets up and goes to bed. And my wife? She opens up on me. Why did I talk to him that way? Why can't I believe in him? Why am I driving my son away from us? You know, my wife, God bless her; for her, Abner can do no wrong. Whatever he wants, give. Whatever he does, fine. When I try to get him to shape up, to study, to act like a responsible citizen, she accuses me of nagging him. He was an honor roll student in high school, so if I want him to get good grades in college, that's nagging him. Why was he on the honor roll? Because I kept after him. I'm in business and I know what it takes these days for a young man to make it. You don't go to a decent college, you're nothing these days. So he gets into Harvard. That was bad? That was nagging? And if he had lived at home, like I wanted, instead of in the dorm, like he wanted and his mother went along with, he'd still be in Harvard right now. That would be bad? I tell you, Rabbi, the trouble with kids these days is their parents *don't* nag."

The rabbi had not interrupted because he sensed Selzer wanted to talk, but now he brought him back sharply to the main issue. "So what happened, Mr. Selzer? Why did you come to see me?"

"So this morning," said Selzer in a flat monotone, "the pigs came and took him away. Who were the pigs? Lieutenant Tebbetts, who was his scoutmaster, who Abner would talk about so much I would get practically jealous. He was the pigs."

"In that case, I think you had better get in touch with your lawyer, Mr. Selzer."

"Two minutes!" cried Selzer. "Two minutes after my son was out the door, I contacted Paul Goodman. And half an hour later he came by—he wasn't even dressed when I called —and picked me up and we went down to the police station."

"And?"

"And nothing. My son wouldn't even talk to me, or to Goodman. Just, 'Oh, it's you.' This is the way a boy talks to a father, Rabbi?"

"So what did you say?"

"Nothing! I was embarrassed in front of Goodman. So I didn't show I was sore. I didn't holler at him. I didn't say anything, just told him this was Mr. Goodman who would be his lawyer. And I left them together. But later, when Goodman came upstairs—we saw him in his cell in the basement, you understand—he said the boy had refused to cooperate."

"But he agreed to defend him?"

"Oh sure. What's he got to lose? He won't be sitting in jail." He got up when Miriam entered the room. "Look, I'm keeping you from your dinner. I just came to ask you to go and see him. Talk some sense into him. I know he thinks a lot of you from when he was in your post-confirmation class. He'll listen to you."

"He must've been terribly hurt," said Miriam after Selzer had left.

"What do you mean?" asked her husband. "By whom?"

"By his father, of course. Suppose there was a rumor that you had done something terrible, something inherently abhorrent to you. And suppose if instead of knowing you could never do such a thing, I asked you if the rumor was true. You *might* sit down and patiently explain how unlikely it was. On the other hand, you might feel so terribly hurt, especially if you were a youngster of Abner's age, that you just wouldn't say anything."

"Yes, I see what you mean."

"Go and see the boy, David."

"And tell him what?"

She smiled. "You could tell him to try to forgive his father, I suppose."

21

"The Boston police asked us to pick up the Selzer boy, so we picked him up," said Chief Lanigan. He was sitting at his dining room table with the Sunday paper spread out before him.

"Do they have any real evidence against them?" asked the rabbi.

Lanigan shrugged. "You know how these things are. It's the D.A. who looks over what they've got and who issues the orders. He certainly wouldn't tell *me*. Even the D.A. of our own county wouldn't necessarily take me into his confidence on a matter that occurred right here in my own bailiwick. But from what Schroeder said, what they have on him is obvious. He was one of a committee that met with the dean. They talk for a while and then one of them gets vituperative and the dean walks out. They wait around for her to come back, and when she doesn't, they leave. A few minutes later a bomb goes off in her office. Now I put it to you, that's certainly grounds for suspicion. Add a couple of other little items: one, there was a bombing in the school during the spring semester; two, a member of the committee, somebody called Ekko—I don't know if that's his real name or just a nickname—skips. That suggests guilt certainly."

"On the other hand," the rabbi observed, "none of it is what you would call real evidence. The building is open and anyone can walk in. Dean Hanbury left her office unlocked, so anyone could get in after the committee left. From what little I myself know about conditions in the school, there are other student groups, more or less revolutionary, who are seemingly as opposed to each other as they are to the administration."

"Well, you don't have to convince me, Rabbi. It's the people in Suffolk County you've got to convince."

"Is it all right if I see the boy now?"

"Sure. Let me get my shoes on and I'll run you down to the station. You can talk to him in my office if you'd like."

The young man was visibly surprised when he saw the rabbi. "Oh, it's you," he said. "I thought it was the lawyer guy again." He walked the length of the room and looked out the window. Then he faced around. "Cops!" he exclaimed. "They're not human. Do you think he'd bother to tell me who's here? He just says somebody wants to see me in the chief's office, and when I tell him I don't care to go—thinking it was the lawyer or my old man—he says, 'On your feet, bigshot,' and practically hauls me up here."

"He probably didn't know who it was either," the rabbi said mildly.

"Rabbi, you don't know these guys. You just haven't had the experience."

"All right," he said good-naturedly. "Now what's your objection to cooperating with the lawyer?"

Abner Selzer spread his hands and let his shoulders droop in exasperation. "Goodman! He didn't ask me a thing. He just said if I was planning on making a speech, forget it. I'd be standing before Judge Visconte and he's hard as nails. He'd throw the book at me. If the judge asks a question, he says, I'm supposed to stand up and address him as Your Honor. Otherwise, keep quiet, don't whisper with the others. Just sit up straight, look straight ahead at the judge, and look interested. That's planning a defense? Then he takes a look at me and tells me he wants me clean-shaven and wearing a regular suit when I come to court tomorrow morning. Rabbi, how can I communicate with a man like that? So I asked him how would it be if I wore a kilt and crossed my legs and showed part of my behind to the jury."

The rabbi laughed and the young man grinned. "What did he say to that?"

"He got sore and just said he'd see me in the court in Boston."

"I don't suppose it makes much difference," said the rabbi. "The arraignment is largely a formality. As I understand it, the law requires you to be brought before a magistrate within twenty-four hours of your arrest."

"But what if a guy's innocent?"

"That's not the judge's concern at an arraignment, Abner. He's there just to determine whether the police have enough evidence to hold you for the grand jury. If they want you held, the judge will usually go along. All right, I can understand about your lawyer, but why don't you want to see your father?"

"So he can yell at me? We can't talk for five minutes before he starts yelling."

"What does he yell about?" asked the rabbi curiously.

"Oh, almost anything, but mostly—until now, at least—about marks. 'Shape up,' he's always saying. Why don't I shape up, or sometimes, 'Shape up or ship out.' He was in the naval reserve for a while. That's where he got it. When I was in high school here, it wasn't so bad. I was one of the smart kids, and besides the other kids' fathers did the same thing. But at Harvard, I was up against all the other smart kids, and I wasn't living at home where he could keep tabs on me every night—C or even B-minus wasn't good enough for him. It had to be A's. And for a while, I tried, but the competition was tough and I thought, the hell with it."

"So you slacked off completely."

"Sure, why not? I was working so hard and got a B-minus, but it wasn't good enough for him. So I thought it won't be any worse if I have a little fun and get a C or even a C-minus."

"But you felt guilty about it."

The young man considered. "All right. I suppose I did—at first. I don't now."

"Are you sure?"

"Yeah, I'm sure. I'll tell you something, Rabbi. My father didn't care if I learned anything or not. He was just interested in my getting good marks so I could get into a good law school and get good marks there, even if I never learned any law, so I could get into a big law firm."

"I suppose he's trying to fit you for the world as he sees it."

"So what's wrong with trying to change it?" demanded Selzer.

"Well, you might change it for the worse," the rabbi observed wryly. "But in any case, by your own admission, whatever your father is doing, whether he's going about it the right way or not, he's doing it for you."

"Rabbi," said Abner solemnly, "this is going to shock you, but the fact is I don't care very much for my father. I don't respect him and—"

But it was Abner who was shocked when the rabbi interrupted to say, "Oh, that's perfectly normal."

"It is?"

"I would say so. That's why it's one of the ten commandments. 'Honor thy father and mother.' If it were perfectly natural, it wouldn't require a specific commandment, would it?"

"All right, so why should I accept help from somebody I don't respect?"

"Because it's childish and peevish to refuse help when you are in need," said the rabbi. "You're going to have a lawyer whether you want one or not. If you don't use your own, the court will appoint one for you. He may be better than Mr. Goodman, but it's not likely, and he's certain to be less experienced. Common sense would suggest that you get the best you can."

22

Judge Visconte's head nodded slightly as he read the complaint. When he put the paper aside, his head continued to nod, for he was an old man, well over seventy, with snow-white hair surmounting a high, slanting forehead. His handsome Italian face with its long Roman nose looked benign and grandfatherly.

He turned to Bradford Ames. "The Commonwealth has a recommendation on bail?"

"The Commonwealth has a recommendation, Your Honor," said Ames. "It is the Commonwealth's opinion that since a man was killed as a direct result of the explosion of a bomb, this is a case of felony murder and hence that bail should be denied."

The judge nodded vigorously in apparent agreement. Then he inclined his head and nodded at a somewhat different angle, which the clerk interpreted as a sign that His Honor wanted to confer with him. He leaned over the judge's desk and they whispered together. It looked as though it was all over.

Paul Goodman rose beside the attorney's table. "May I be heard, Your Honor?"

The judge nodded graciously.

"To save the time of the Honorable Court, I am speaking not only for myself but for my three colleagues who are each representing one of these young defendants. It seems to me, Your Honor, that the recommendation of the Commonwealth is punitive rather than designed to insure the appearance of the defendants at their trial. These young people are not professional criminals; they have clean records. They are enrolled in college; if they are prevented from attending classes they will be unable to pass their courses. To hold them in jail pending their trial is to punish them before they have been proven guilty."

The judge nodded benevolently. "It's always punitive, isn't it?" he said gently. "A workman loses his wages; a businessman sometimes has to close down his business or office. And in every case, the family suffers."

"If I may, Your Honor," said Goodman. "Isn't that all the more reason not to hold these young people unnecessarily, since the danger of their not appearing for the trial is slight?"

"But the charge is murder, Counselor."

"I recognize that it has been the prevailing practice in the Commonwealth to deny bail to prisoners charged with murder. But my understanding is that the rationale—"

"Did you say rationale?"

"Yes, Your Honor. I was saying that the rationale behind denying bail in such cases is that money becomes secondary when a man's life is at stake. However, since the Supreme Court of the United States has held the death penalty to be cruel and unusual punishment, that fear no longer obtains."

"On the other hand," the judge interposed, "these young people—and I have had a lot of experience with them; oh yes—are apt to be rather cavalier about money. If I were to set bail, even very high bail, which their parents might arrange to meet, there is a strong possibility—and I speak from experience—that they may fail to appear, having no regard for the loss which their parents would thus incur. No, Counselor, I think I'll go along with the Commonwealth recommendation and order them held without bail."

23

When the rabbi arrived for class Monday morning, he found the flag on the administration building of Windemere College at half staff. All classes had been cancelled, and many of the students and faculty had already left. A memorial service was scheduled for Professor Hendryx in the chapel at noon, and those who remained behind were milling about on the Marble.

The rabbi was undecided whether to return home or attend the service when Professor Place, whom he knew slightly, invited him to have a cup of coffee.

It was the first time the rabbi had been in the faculty cafeteria and he looked about him with interest. It was a small room with two large tables, both of which were half occupied; the rabbi noticed that older members of the faculty sat at one and younger members at the other. Professor Place went over to a large coffee urn and poured a cup for the rabbi.

"Ten cents a cup." He dropped a quarter into a slotted carton. "The honor system. No, I've just paid for yours, and a little over," he said, as the rabbi reached for some change. "Sometimes you forget. Our coffee committee reports that pennies, buttons, even unsigned I.O.U.'s appear from time to time, just as I suppose they do in your collection plate after a service."

"We don't pass a collection plate. Our regulations forbid carrying money on the Sabbath," said the rabbi.

"Very commendable. Our method of collecting at each service smacks altogether too much of a business transaction, a *quid pro quo* of sorts with the Deity." He led him to a table. "Let me introduce you to some of your fellow faculty members. Professor Holmes, Professor Dillon, and Miss Barton. Or is it Professor Barton or Dr. Barton, Mary?"

"Dr. Barton at mid-years," she said happily, "and probably Professor Barton shortly after, Dean Millie says. But right now it's still officially Miss Barton." She had a good-natured, homely face.

"You shared Hendryx's office, didn't you?" asked Professor Holmes. His narrow face was accentuated by a long nose and pointed chin.

"Yes," said the rabbi, "although I didn't use it much."

"Your trouble was that you didn't come in at enough rank," said Mary Barton. "What are you listed as? Lecturer? Instructor? If you had played hard to get, they would have hired you as associate at least and given you decent office space. Of course, if you had held out long enough, and they wanted you badly enough the way they did Professor Malkowitz, you could have come in as a full professor and then you would have got a private office with a secretary. A professor, Rabbi, is just an instructor who can strike a better bargain."

"Mary, as you can see, is cynical about professorships," Professor Holmes said.

"Well, I'd say she has reason to be," commented Professor Dillon, a cheery, round-faced man with a walrus moustache. "She's been teaching here for how long, Mary? Fifteen years?"

"Sixteen."

"For sixteen years; and because she didn't have her doctorate, she's been kept an instructor. That, and because she's a woman—in what used to be a woman's school, mind you, and is still more than sixty percent women."

"Ah, the champion of Women's Liberation," murmured Professor Holmes.

"Well, it's true, isn't it?" demanded Dillon.

"Of course it's true," said Holmes, "but you know the reason as well as I do. Mary chose to invest her energies in teaching rather than research and publication, and these days it just doesn't pay off. You see, Mary, you made the natural mistake of assuming that college was a place where students come to learn and the faculty teaches. It's been years since that was true. As soon as the administration discovered there was more endowment money, even more student applications, when someone on the faculty made a discovery that hit the headlines, the old order was dead and you were one with *dinosaurus rex*."

"But she's getting her doctorate," Professor Place pointed out.

"Well, of course," said Holmes. "She finally surrendered. You can fight just so long. Right, Mary?"

The rabbi had no way of knowing if they were teasing Miss Barton, and if she minded. He turned to Holmes and asked, "What about the students?"

"How's that?"

"You said that before the order changed, the students came to study and the faculty taught. Now the faculty does research instead of teaching. What about the students who came to learn. Did they also change?"

"Of course," said Holmes. "They now come to get credits, to get degrees for better jobs. It's like green stamps. You save up a bookful and get a degree. And nowadays you don't even have to earn the credits. Bookstores, even the college bookstores, openly sell detailed outlines of all the major courses. On a quiz you get the same answers, even the same phrasing, from all your students."

"They had those outlines when I was in college," said Dillon.

"But using them was considered cheating," Holmes objected. "And they were sold furtively under the counter. Now you can even buy a term paper for two dollars a page."

"Three dollars," said Place.

"Three dollars for an original," Mary Barton corrected.

The rabbi looked from one to the other, wondering if they weren't pulling his leg. "I'm sure there must be some students who study."

Professor Place agreed. "Of course. Maybe as many as half. But even their credits are tainted. The last two years, Rabbi, we had student strikes—in memory of the Kent State shootings, I believe. They came just before finals, so the students don't take their exams. We permit them to make them up later, but none of them do. Instead they play it safe and take a pass mark in the course, which is one of the alternatives we offer. So a kind of Gresham's Law applies and bogus credits drive out real ones. Nobody questions them. Nobody cares."

"I care," said Mary Barton.

"That's right. Mary cares, because she's young and foolish," Place went on, looking fondly at her, "and we here care a little because we remember how it used to be. And word has come to me via the grapevine that you care, Rabbi."

"Indeed?"

"One of my better students is taking your course. According to him, you're taking a very hard-nose line." He looked at the rabbi quizzically.

"Just doing what I'm being paid for."

Professor Holmes shook his head. "Not good enough, Rabbi, not if you lose your health over it. I would have thought your erstwhile roommate, whose memory we'll be honoring at noon, would have set you straight. I didn't know him too well, but it seemed to me he had the right attitude about the contemporary college scene. He'd been here only two or three years and he was made department head—"

"Acting head," Mary Barton amended.

"All right, acting head. But he would have been given the full appointment before long."

"I wouldn't bank on it," she said. "The faculty rules call for the concurrence of the department."

"Oh, and there was opposition to him?" asked Holmes.

"The older members of the department didn't care one way or another," she said. "I had nothing against him. But the younger men didn't care for him at all. He was apt to be sarcastic with them. One of them, Roger Fine, almost came to blows with him."

"Roger Fine?" Dillon looked to her for enlightenment, and then remembered. "Oh yes, the fellow that wrote that article in *The Windrift*." He shrugged. "I shouldn't think he'd count for much. He was only appointed for the year."

"Don't you believe it," she said. "He had lots of friends among the younger men, not only in our department."

Professor Place asked about his fight with Hendryx.

She colored and shot a quick glance at the rabbi. "Roger considered him—well, an anti-semite. Once when they were alone in the English office they got to arguing pretty violently. I came in just then and I heard Roger say he'd ram his stick down his throat if he made another crack. My appearance cooled things off," she added almost regretfully.

"How about it, Rabbi?" asked Holmes. "Was he given to making anti-semitic remarks?"

"Not really, not to me," said David Small.

"What I don't understand," said Dillon, "is how he even got to be acting head with Hallett and Miller both in the department."

"I suspect Millie Hanbury liked him," Mary Barton said. "He came from Barnard's Crossing originally, you know, her hometown."

"They grew up together?"

"I shouldn't think so," she said. "He was a good five or six years older than she is, and his folks moved away when he was about fourteen, he told me."

"Still—"

"Sh," Mary Barton who was facing the door hissed a warning. "Here comes Dean Millie now. Hello, Millie."

24

That afternoon, when he returned home from the memorial service, he finally got around to telling Miriam about the sit-down strike in his class the previous Friday.

She listened without comment until he finished and then said, "Weren't you being a little stuffy, David?"

"Well, I—yes, I suppose I was," he said gloomily.

"It's not like you," she commented.

"It wasn't just that they sat on the floor, you understand. It's everything; I resent having only a third of my class show up on Fridays."

"But don't the same ones come every Friday?"

"What of it?"

"Then why resent them and not the others, the ones who stay away?"

"Well, of course, but—yes, I see what you mean. I shouldn't have let out my frustrations on those who show up faithfully. But . . ." his shoulders drooped disconsolately. "I'm disappointed in the whole business," he said quietly. "It's not what I expected. I can't help feeling that they're not getting anything out of the course. They come in, open their notebooks, and all I see of them during my lecture is the tops of their heads as they write down my precious words of wisdom."

"At least it shows they're interested."

"It shows they're interested in passing the examination in the course, that's what. If they were truly interested in the subject matter, they wouldn't write, they'd listen. And occasionally, a face would light up so I'd know I was getting through to them and they were learning."

"Don't any of them ever ask questions?"

"A few, but they're not so much questions as challenges."

He shook his head. "They're not looking for information, just for an argument—I suppose to make the time pass quicker. They don't know anything, but they're full of opinions. There's Henry Luftig, the representative of the Radical Left. He is deeply concerned for the oppressed—the blacks, the Arabs, everyone except the Jews. And his sidekick, Harvey Shacter, a nice-looking young man who doesn't seem concerned about anything but who always seconds Luftig, more out of loyalty than conviction, I suspect. And there's a girl, Lillian Dushkin, who appears to side with them, perhaps because she's interested in the Shacter boy. It wouldn't surprise me if she came from a traditional home and knew a lot more about the subject than she lets on, but she conceals it, as though she's ashamed of it."

"She's rather plain, I suppose."

"Why do you say that?"

"Because a pretty girl can develop naturally; a plain one has to look for a role to play, and until she finds one, she never feels quite sure of herself."

The rabbi nodded. "Yes, I guess she is on the plain side, although it's hard to tell because she's so heavily made-up with all that stuff on her eyes, like a raccoon. But if she's looking for a role to play, I guess I am, too."

She gave him a sharp look. "You never felt sorry for yourself before, David."

He laughed shortly. "I suppose it sounds that way, and maybe it's true. Whenever I had doubts of my ability as a rabbi of a congregation, I always thought of teaching as a possible alternative. I always thought I'd make a good teacher. Well, now it appears that I'm no better as a teacher than I am as a rabbi. That's rather disquieting."

"What makes you think you're not a good teacher?" she demanded. "Because so many stay away on Friday afternoons? Would it be any different for any other teacher of any other subject?"

"Perhaps not."

"You think you haven't succeeded in interesting them. Well, maybe you're not giving them what they expected to get."

117

"They expected to get three easy credits," he said scornfully. "That's what they expected. And when they found they weren't going to get them—" He stopped as she shook her head.

"No, David. That's not the reason students take a snap course, at least not the only reason. When I was in college, I occasionally elected a snap course, and I imagine you did, too. But it was because I was interested in the subject, and the easy credit was frosting on the cake. I remember there was a music appreciation course that almost everybody took. Maybe a few did so because the prof was an old softy who passed everyone, but most of us were there because it was interesting and something we felt we ought to know. There was also a course in something called research methodology where no one ever got less than a B, but the professor could never manage to get more than ten to sign up for it. That's because he was dull and the course was dull."

"Then maybe my students just aren't interested in the history and development of fundamental Jewish ideas," he said bitterly.

"Probably not," she said amiably. "But how can they be interested in how our concepts of charity and justice and all the rest developed if they don't know what they are? Don't you see, David, most of them probably never received any religious instruction at home or went to a religious school. It just wasn't fashionable when they were growing up. But there's been a change in recent years, especially since the Six Day War. They always knew they were Jews and somewhat different from their Gentile friends and neighbors, but they and their parents tended to minimize the difference. But now they're of an age when the differences are important: they're dating seriously and thinking of marriage. I'll bet most of them signed up for your course to find out just what those differences are and whether they were something to be ashamed of or proud of."

"But college students—"

"They're not college students, David, at least not just college students. They're Jews. You tell them what they want to know, and believe me, they'll be interested."

25

As he waited for Mrs. O'Rourke, the cleaning woman, to arrive, Schroeder wandered about Hendryx's apartment, trying to get the feel of the place and the man who had occupied it.

A rental agent would have listed it as a three-room apartment although a prospective tenant would have countered that the kitchen was tiny and that one of the rooms was little more than a closet. The smaller room evidently had been the professor's workroom, because it contained his desk, chair, and a bookcase. The other room was of decent size and served as both bedroom and living room, with a large studio couch, bureau, TV, rocker, and an oversize easy chair of simulated leather with a matching hassock. Beside the chair stood a large mahogany smoking stand. The large glass ashtray contained a pipe and the half-dozen burned kitchen matches used to light it. A book, open, rested face down on one of the broad arms of the chair. On a side table were several books between bronze bookends, a large brass bowl, and a pipe rack with five pipes lined up in the half-dozen slots.

Schroeder went into the kitchen and opened the refrigerator. It contained a carton of milk, a package of bacon, a box of eggs, and some processed cheese. Obviously the professor took breakfast at home and relied on restaurants or the faculty cafeteria for the rest of his meals.

He stepped out of the apartment and walked down a short, dimly lit corridor to the rear door leading to the alley outside. The door was not locked. The key found in Hendryx's coat pocket opened not only the apartment but the front door to the building as well. It never failed to amaze him how people could be so careful about security at one point and downright careless at another, like installing special locks on a door and then using a cheap latch that could be easily forced on street-level windows.

He returned to the apartment and began to go over it more systematically. Apparently Hendryx had been neat and methodical. His clothes hung neatly in his closet. The bureau containing his linen was tidy. In a shallow top drawer he kept handkerchiefs and a tray of the usual men's appurtenances—cuff links, tie clips, a couple of discarded cigarette lighters, a billfold evidently no longer used, a wristwatch and a pocket watch, and a little glass dish with less than a dollar's worth of change. The next drawer contained his shirts, the next his underwear, shirts, shorts, and socks, each separated from each other by thin wooden dividers. Then a drawer for his pajamas. The bottom drawer was empty. He decided that Hendryx was a man who didn't like to bend over unless he had to.

The desk was equally well organized with drawers full of notes and manuscripts, the latter in folders with the subject matter carefully inked on the tabs.

A police car delivered Mrs. O'Rourke, a thin, hard-working woman, close to sixty. Although the day was quite warm, she wore a heavy imitation fur coat and a shapeless hat of crocheted purple wool.

"Just a few questions," he said. "You were working here Friday?"

"Yes, sir."

"What time did you arrive?"

"Around ten I got here, a few minutes before or a few after, I'm not sure. I plan to come at ten, but it depends on the bus."

"And when did you depart?"

"A little before three, sir, maybe as early as a quarter of."

"Are you sure? Now I want you to think carefully. It's important," he said. With this type you had to be stern to insure exactness.

"Yes, sir. I plan to make the three o'clock bus at the corner, so I always try to leave a few minutes before, or else I have to wait sometimes as much as half an hour. Isn't it terrible the way the buses run."

"Yes, yes. And you made the three o'clock bus?"

"Yes, sir. I made it in time."

"All right. What did you do here in the apartment?"

She looked at him in mild surprise. "Why, I clean the place up. I dust and vacuum. I polish the furniture. I make the bed. I wash the tub. I clean the whole place up."

"You straighten out the things in the bureau?"

"I do not, sir," she said indignantly. "I don't open the drawers, and no one can say I did. Professor Hendryx told me not to touch anything in the bureau or his desk and I don't, just the things on top like his comb and brushes, so I can dust and polish."

"All right, Mrs. O'Rourke. I was just asking. So you left the place exactly as it is now."

"Oh no," she protested. "I wouldn't leave the ashes and burned matches in the ashtray. And if there's a book open like that, I'd put it back. But I didn't because there was no book there." She looked about. "And the hassock, I always put it in front of the TV there because the way it is now it would get in my way."

"Just a minute. Are you saying that someone was in here after you left?"

"Oh no, just Professor Hendryx. He was always dodging back and forth between here and the school." She sighed. "If he'd only stayed here, he would have been alive today, the poor gentleman. Isn't it terrible the way the students behave these days?"

26

They were unusually quiet and subdued when he entered the classroom Wednesday morning. The dozen who had been present last Friday must have told the rest what had occurred. Or was it their reaction to the bomb explosion?

All the way from Barnard's Crossing, Rabbi Small had wrestled with his conscience. He hadn't seen his class since he walked out on them. Should he proceed with his lecture as though nothing had happened, or should he apologize? True, their behavior had been intolerable, but on the other hand he now realized no personal disrespect had been intended. On the contrary, they evidently believed they were doing something fine and noble. But why hadn't they explained? But why hadn't he asked? But they were younger, and they owed their teacher respect. But he was older and should have had more understanding. But they should have realized . . . But he should have realized . . .

"For those who were not here last Friday," he began, "I would like to announce that there was no lecture. To those who were here, I wish to apologize for having walked out. I did not know at the time the reason for the strange conduct of some of the members of the class. Subsequently I did discover it and apologize for not having inquired at the time." He was about to go on, when Mazelman raised his hand. "Yes?"

"I want to know if you think it was right for us—I was one —to sit on the floor?"

He said he had just explained he now knew the reason.

"No, what I mean, isn't it part of Judaism, like aren't Jews supposed to protest injustice?"

"Everyone is supposed to," said the rabbi carefully. "It's not a monopoly of Judaism. But are you sure an injustice was done? As I understand it, the chairs were removed from the prison recreation room as a temporary precautionary measure because they had been used for rioting."

"Yeah, but all the kids didn't take part in the riot, but they all had to sit on the floor," one student observed.

"And President Macomber admitted he was wrong," another called out.

"I read his statement," said the rabbi firmly. "He said he had not intended to comment on the merits of this particular case, only to indicate his general confidence in the head of the institution."

"Yeah, but he backed off from what he said the first time.

And he wouldn't have if it hadn't been for the student demonstration."

"Did it convince him, or did it force him?" demanded the rabbi. "If his statement indeed represents backing off, was it caused by your sitting on the floor for a couple of days or because he felt that in the present atmosphere in the college it was wiser to defuse a minor situation before it got out of hand? And where is the justice in bullying somebody to agree with you?"

"Well, how do you know he wasn't convinced?"

And now from all over the room:

"What good is just sitting and talking?"

"How about civil rights? They talked for four centuries."

"How about Vietnam?"

"Yah, and Cambodia?"

"How about the Arab refugees?"

The rabbi pounded on the lectern and the yammering came to a gradual stop. In the moment of silence that followed Henry Luftig's voice could be heard, dripping with sarcasm: "Aren't we supposed to be the Chosen People?"

The sally was greeted with shouts of laughter which quieted down, however, when they saw that their teacher was obviously angry. But when he spoke, it was in quiet tones.

"Yes, we are," he said. "Some of you, I see, seem to regard that as amusing. I suppose that to your modern, rationalist, science-oriented minds, the thought of the Almighty making a compact with a portion of His creation is hilariously funny." He nodded judiciously. "Well, I can understand that. But how does it alter the situation? Your modern skepticism can be applied to only one side of the compact, God's side. You can doubt He offered such a compact; you can even doubt His existence. But you cannot doubt that Jews believed it and acted accordingly. That's fact. And how can one quarrel with the purpose and goal of Chosenness: to be holy, to be a nation of priests, to be a light unto the nation?"

"But you got to admit it's pretty arrogant."

"The idea of being chosen? Why? It's not confined to the Jews. The Greeks had it; the Romans, too. Nearer our own time, the English felt it their duty to assume the white man's burden; the Russians and the Chinese both feel obliged to convert the world to Marxism; while our own country feels it must prevent the spread of Marxism and indoctrinate all peoples in democracy. The difference is that in all these other cases, the doctrine calls for doing something to someone else, usually by force. The Jewish doctrine alone calls for Jews to live up to a high standard so that they might become an example to others. I don't see anything to laugh or sneer at about that. Basically, what it calls for is a high standard of personal behavior. It manifests itself in restraints which we impose on ourselves. Some of these, such as the restrictions of kosher food, may strike you as mere primitive taboos, but their intention is to maintain purity of mind and body. In any case, we don't try to foist it on others. Perhaps more to the point is the admonition that you have occasionally received from a parent or more likely, a grandparent, 'This is not proper behavior for a Jew.' Well, that's how the doctrine of Chosenness works in everyday life."

He looked around the room. "Which brings us to Mr. Mazelman's questions and its larger implication: is it our duty as Jews to be the leaders in all reform movements? I suppose we have a tendency in that direction as a result of our history. But there is nothing in our religion or basic tradition that imposes this duty on us. It does not call for us to devote our lives, like the Knights of the Round Table, to righting wrongs."

The class was attentive now. The rabbi felt he had the situation in hand, so he continued with less vehemence. "Ours is a practical religion calling for a practical way of life. There are so many injustices throughout the world that if we set out to right them all, even if we could, when could we live our own lives? And can we always be sure that we are right? And that our method of reform will improve things? Even in the small matter of sitting on the floor there was a difference of opinion. I, for one, was not convinced either that President Macomber was wrong or that the method taken to convince him was right. And remember what I said about the difference between our kind of Chosenness and that of other nations. Our religion calls on us to live our own lives in rectitude and justice, not to impose them on anyone else."

"How about Israel then," Henry Luftig called out. "Why aren't they treating the Arabs justly?"

"Compared to whom?" the rabbi shot back.

"I don't understand, Rabbi."

"It's quite simple, Mr. Luftig," he said. "We criticize Jews and Judaism by disparaging comparisons with some ideal. But to be fair, you must compare them with what's real, not imaginary. So I ask, what other nation has dealt with its foe better, or even as well, as has Israel with the Arabs?"

"What about the way the United States treated Germany and Japan?"

"But that was after they had signed a peace treaty; not while the other country still considered itself at war."

"Yeah, but everybody says they ought to be a lot less obstinate."

The rabbi smiled grimly. "There is also in our religion a doctrine against suicide."

"But the Palestinians were driven from their homes."

"They *left* their homes," Mark Leventhal called from across the room. Like Mazelman, he came from a traditional home and had had some religious schooling. "The Arabs promised they'd be able to return once they'd driven the Jews into the sea. They were promised the Jews' property as well."

"I don't believe it."

"Well, it's true."

Lillian Dushkin said in a high, shrill voice: "This boy I know told me there are lots of Jews in Israel who feel the Jews have no right to be there until the Messiah comes."

"Yah? So what are *they* doing there?"

And they were off again, but this time the rabbi made no effort to stop them. He sat on the edge of the desk and listened, vaguely annoyed, but occasionally interested in spite of himself. The bell rang at last and the class began to gather their books.

"Just a minute," he called out.

They halted.

"You seem to have a lot of questions more or less relating to the subject matter of this course. So I'm setting aside the next class, Friday, and perhaps succeeding Fridays, to deal with them. You can bring in any questions you like, and I'll do my best to answer them."

"You mean in writing?"

"In writing or orally, or write them on the blackboard for all I care."

As he came down the broad granite steps of the administration building, Luftig and Shacter, lounging against the iron railing, fell in step with him as he made for the parking lot.

"That was quite a class today, Rabbi," said Luftig, his thin face aglow.

The rabbi looked at him. "You think so? You feel you learned something?"

Luftig looked surprised—and hurt. "Why sure."

"What, for instance?"

"You mean specifically? Well, I didn't know there were Jews who thought they had to wait for the Messiah before they could live in Israel. And—and that business about the Arabs expecting to take over Jewish property. And—oh, lots of things."

"Well, that first, about the Messiah, that's wrong," the rabbi said. "The objection is not to living in Israel, but to establishing a state. As for the rest, if you want to hold a bull session why bother to come to college and pay tuition for it?"

"But this was fun, Rabbi," Shacter protested.

"It's not my function or the college's to amuse you," he said stiffly.

As the rabbi drove off, Shacter said, "Gee, what's he so uptight about?"

27

In the short time that had elapsed since the incident, the Windemere folder had assumed sizeable proportions. There were photographs of the offices of Professor Hendryx and Dean Hanbury, as well as floor plans to show their relation to each other. Most of the folder, however, consisted of typed statements made by the various people questioned by Sergeant Schroeder.

He read over the statements now in preparation for his conference with the assistant district attorney. He had worked with Bradford Ames before and had great respect for him. When Ames prepared a case, nothing was left to chance. Schroeder smiled as he came to Dean Hanbury's statement.

> . . . The girl then said something insulting and I decided to leave.
>
> QUERY: What did she say, Miss Hanbury?
>
> ANSWER: I'd rather not repeat it. It was a four-letter word.
>
> QUERY: Was it directed at you?
>
> ANSWER: It was addressed to me. I'm not used to—I cannot tolerate that kind of language spoken to me by a snip of a—by a student. In any case, I decided that it was pointless to continue the discussion, so I said, "I must go now" and I left. I left the building and went to my car and drove home.
>
> QUERY: And what time was that, Miss Hanbury?
>
> ANSWER: About half-past three. If the exact time is important, I'm sure you can get it from the Barnard's Crossing police, because I called them almost as

soon as I arrived home. I suppose they register all
calls. You see, there was a window open—

QUERY: No, no, I'm interested in what time you left the
meeting.

ANSWER: Well, it was scheduled for two-thirty. They were
prompt, I'll say that for them. We talked for about
ten or fifteen minutes when that girl—

QUERY: Yes, Miss Hanbury. Then would you say it was two
forty-five?

ANSWER: That's about right.

QUERY: Two forty-five to three-thirty. That's pretty fast time
to Barnard's Crossing isn't it?

ANSWER: Well, traffic was light, and it may have been that
I left as early as two-forty. Are you going to charge
me with speeding, Sergeant?

The four students in their statements d'ffered markedly
with the dean, and to some extent with each other, as to the
reason for her departure, insisting that she had not really
been offended but had used the remark as an excuse to break
off the discussion. Judy Ballantine, who had precipitated the
incident, naturally was most insistent that it was merely a
ruse. Abner Selzer, on the other hand, was inclined to feel
the dean may have been genuinely distressed. "You ought to
see my mother when someone talks like that, especially a girl."
He also confirmed the dean's time of departure.

ANSWER: It was a few minutes of three when we all got back
to the office after looking for her because I looked
at my watch and said we'd wait until three and
then split. It must have taken us five or ten minutes
to search the building, so that would mean she left
between two-forty and ten of.

QUERY: And you all left at three?

ANSWER: That's right.

QUERY: Then what did you do?

ANSWER: Oh, we wandered down to the corner diner for a

cup of coffee and to talk it over. And we just about got there when we heard this boom. So we ran out and saw smoke coming from the administration building. So naturally we ran back to take a look, and in a couple of minutes—Jeez, there's a whole mob and fire engines. We stood around for a while and then split.

QUERY: Where'd you get the bomb?

ANSWER: Where'd I—Look, get this. We had nothing to do with the bombing.

QUERY: Then who did?

ANSWER: How do I know? Maybe the guy that tossed the last one.

QUERY: And who was that?

ANSWER: How would I know?

QUERY: Look, Abner, if you cooperate with us—

ANSWER: I'm not saying another word, not another goddam word.

He had tried it on each of them, a series of innocuous questions followed by the sudden accusation, not in any real hope of getting them to confess but on the chance of upsetting them enough so he could bore in. He could have saved his breath. Yance Allworth said, "Man, I wouldn't know what a bomb *looks* like." O'Brien said, "You got the wrong picture, Sergeant. We're just a bunch of do-gooding liberals." Judy's response had been, "Why don't you get off the jerk, copper?" And when he asked who could have done it if not her group, she had said, "Maybe the dean laid an egg and it exploded."

The last sheet in his folder was a time chart based on the testimonies of those he had questioned:

1:00–1:15: Hendryx leaves apartment and goes to his office. (Mrs. O'Rourke's statement. No corroboration.)

2:01–2:03: Rabbi enters his office. (Class runs from 1:00– 2:00.)

2:10: Rabbi leaves building. (His statement.)

2:30: Committee arrives at dean's office. (Statements of all members of committee and dean.)

2:40–2:50: Dean leaves meeting and starts for home. (Statements of committee and dean. Earlier time probable on basis of time of her arrival home.)

2:45–2:55: Mrs. O'Rourke leaves to catch 3:00 bus. (Her statement, not corroborated.)

3:00: Committee leaves building. (Their statements. N.B.: Selzer looked at his watch.)

3:05: Bomb explodes. (Statement of Lt. Hawkins, Station 15.)

He remembered he did not as yet have the report of the medical examiner. It was not particularly important in this situation with the cause and time of death known. On the other hand, not having it would mean sloppy preparation, something Ames would never permit.

He called the receptionist and asked whether the medical examiner's report had come in yet.

"About half an hour ago. I put it in your box."

"Jennie, be a good kid and get it for me."

He slit the envelope and ran an expert eye over the report. Cause of death was given as a blow from an object weighing approximately sixty pounds. ". . . skull crushed . . . fragments of cranial bones embedded in brain . . ." Death was practically instantaneous. "Time of death: between 2:10 P.M. and 2:40 P.M., November 13."

He spotted the mistake immediately. The good doctor had no doubt meant between 2:40 and 3:10. Probably his secretary had transcribed her notes incorrectly.

He called the receptionist and asked her to get him Dr. Lagrange.

He waited impatiently, gnawing on his lower lip in vexation. Then the phone rang, but it was Jennie. "He's not in. He's gone away for a few days and won't be back until Monday."

"Where'd he go? Did they say?"

"On a camping trip."

"Well, doesn't he call in or keep in touch?"

"I asked, but his girl said he hasn't so far. I told her to have him contact us when he does."

"Call her again and let me talk to her."

When he was put through, he said, "Oh look, miss, I've got Dr. Lagrange's report in front of me. Did he dictate his notes to you?"

"Yes sir."

"Well, I think you must have transcribed them wrong. It says here that time of death was between two-ten and two-forty. I'm sure he reversed the figures and meant between two-forty and three-ten."

"Just a minute, Sergeant. I'll check my notes." There was a pause while she got her notes. "Here it is, Sergeant, 'Time of death: between 2:10 P.M. and 2:40 P.M. . . .' I remember his remarking that he was able to pinpoint it so closely because the examination was made so close to the time of death. I'm sorry, Sergeant, the report is correct."

28

"Schroeder is a good man," Matthew Rogers said as he glanced through the bulging folder. "You can always depend on him to do a thorough job."

Bradford Ames chuckled and told him to take another look at the medical examiner's report.

"Why?" But he picked up the sheet again and this time saw the time of death. "Obviously a clerical error. Call Dr. Lagrange."

"I did, Matt. He says it's correct as he gave it in his report."

"Then he made a mistake. He's new at this. This was his first time, wasn't it?"

"Yes, but Dr. Slocumbe says that if Lagrange pinpointed it that close, then that's when it occurred."

"But, Brad," Rogers was exasperated, "it just doesn't make any sense. I don't know what buggered up his analysis, but something did. It may have been something ridiculous, like his watch stopped, but this is one case where the medical examiner's analysis of the time isn't important because we have other and better evidence of when death occurred."

"It's no good, Matt. The other side would raise the question the minute they saw we didn't introduce it. Then you'd have to offer it and we'd catch hell from the judge, and the papers too, for having suppressed evidence. No, you'll just have to let the kids go."

"What do you mean, let them go?" the district attorney asked belligerently.

"Because according to the evidence of our own expert, the medical examiner, Hendryx was killed *before* the bomb went off. We can't hold them responsible for his death."

"And he can't make a mistake? How about the time the corpse was locked in the freezer and it threw off all of Doc Slocumbe's calculations?"

"Put it this way, Matt, if I had presented the medical examiner's report when they were arraigned before Judge Visconte, would he have withheld bail?"

"Maybe not, but—"

"They're college kids. If the grand jury should refuse to bring in a true bill against them and charges are dismissed, they still will have served time and their lives will be messed up."

"Something you're forgetting, Brad. There's no doubt in my mind, and I guess there was none in Judge Visconte's, that they planted the bomb."

"They deny it."

"Of course."

"Maybe it was the missing one, Ekko, who did it," said Ames doggedly. "The others might not know anything about it."

"That's hard to believe."

132

"Why is it? He was the only one who skipped."

"Oh, I'm willing to admit that he may have been the actual perpetrator, but what grounds do you have for thinking the others didn't know about it?"

"Because he's different from the others. He's a lot older, for one thing. If the defense had taken this line, I think the judge might very well have gone along and set bail and they'd be out and back at school right now."

"School!" the district attorney echoed scornfully. "What the hell does that bunch of hippies care about school, except to cause trouble? Check it out and you'll find they never go to class. They just hang around and smoke pot and start riots and sit-ins, and when they're not doing that they're busy screwing. That Ekko guy was living with that girl, Ballantine, just as open and free as you please. The hell with them!"

"You're judging their life-styles, Matt, not their guilt."

"Sure, I'm taking their life-styles into account in making up my mind about their guilt, just as every jury does in deciding on the credibility of every witness they see on the stand. And every judge does the same. What's wrong with that?" demanded Rogers. "If we couldn't judge on things like that, then the only people we'd ever find guilty would be those who confessed. What are you getting at, Brad? Do you want me to appoint somebody else, maybe Hogan, to this case?"

"I don't know," said Ames soberly. He shifted unhappily in his seat, then decided to make one last try. "Let's just say, as a kind of exercise in logic, that Dr. Lagrange is absolutely on target."

"All right, then I'll tell you what follows," said Rogers. "Lagrange says death occurred sometime between two-ten and two-forty? Let's call it half-past two. Now that means that Hendryx didn't go back to his apartment, but stayed there in his office. And that means that he was dead even before the committee came in to see the dean. And *that* means that someone had to come into his office, go around behind his desk, reach up somehow to where that statue is resting on the top shelf, and pull it down. Who can reach that top shelf? That's an old building there with eleven- or twelve-foot ceilings. Our mysterious assailant would have to hop up on one of the lower shelves, maybe hang on with one hand while he grabbed at the statue with the other. And all the while Hendryx just sits there? He doesn't ask what the guy is doing?"

"What if he were asleep? What if he dozed off?"

"Then how did the person get into the office?" challenged Rogers. "It's locked."

"The door could have been open. I mean, the latch might not have caught when the rabbi left."

"Possible, but just barely."

"And if the murderer had a long stick with a curved handle, like a cane, for example," said Ames, "then he could just hook the statue and pull it down."

"Sure, Brad. And then?"

"And then what?"

"And then how do you figure the pipe and the hassock and the open book in Hendryx's apartment?"

"Well, it's possible that the cleaning woman fibbed about that," said Ames. "Naturally, she'd want to get out as early as she could. And if she thought Hendryx wasn't likely to come back and check on her, she might have skimped and not done a thorough job."

"Then why didn't she say so?"

"Well, all I know is that if it was my cleaning woman she wouldn't want to say. They have a kind of professional pride."

"So question her again," said Rogers good-naturedly. "If you can make her change her story, I'll reconsider Lagrange's finding on the time of death."

29

At class reunions and other nostalgic get-togethers, the name of Bradford Ames always was good for intensive discussion.

"You saw Brad Ames? What's he doing now? Still assistant district attorney? It just goes to show how money can mess up a man's career." Karl Fisher, like the three friends he was lunching with at his club, was in his early fifties. They were all prosperous.

"How do you mean?"

"Well, the rest of us, when we got out of law school we were all running around looking for a job," said Fisher. "And you know how many law firms were hiring and what they were paying in those days! So you opened an office of your own with the loan of a couple of hundred bucks from your father or your wife's father for some secondhand furniture and a Corpus Juris Cyc."

"When I got out," said Gordon Atwell, "I shared an office with six other guys, and let me tell you, we had to scratch between the seven of us to pay the one secretary her wages every week. And believe me, there was no chance of her getting rich on what we paid her."

"Right," said Fisher. "But we persisted, and gradually things got a little better, and after a while, lo and behold! we were making a living. And then it got to be a good living. And by the time we were in our forties, some of us had big practices, and some of us had become judges, and some had gone into politics and were in the legislature, and some got to be chief counsels for large corporations. I mean, most of us made good. Some of us awfully good.

"But that's because we all had to scratch. But when you're an Ames, and money doesn't mean anything, you don't think the same way. And your family doesn't think the same way, so you're not subject to the same kind of pressure we were. We had to go where the dough was. And we had to get cracking right away. Now *I* was interested in criminal law, but luckily I decided that I couldn't afford to practice it, or else I might've found myself working for the mob like Bob Schenk or more likely defending two-bit criminals whose widowed mothers had to mortgage the old homestead to pay my retainer. So I've been practicing real estate law, and as you guys know we've got a pretty sizeable outfit and I'm doing all right.

"Now Brad Ames was interested in criminal law, too. But for him it was no problem. His family got him a job as assistant district attorney for the county, and he's been there ever since. He not only practices criminal law, but he doesn't have to worry about bleeding some poor bastard's life savings for his fee, or worry that maybe the money he's paying him with is the money he stole, which is why he needs a lawyer in the first place.

"Of course, the salary of assistant district attorney isn't anything much. None of us could live on it, at least not the way we're accustomed to live. But to Brad Ames, it's just cigarette money anyway. He has no wife and there's no pressure from his family to keep scratching."

"Maybe," said Gordon Atwell, who looked younger than the others, "and then again, maybe there's a more personal reason."

"What do you mean by that?" asked Fisher.

"Well, you know the way Ames looks—that round head on the fat torso and the way he grins and chuckles all the time like some idiot—"

"Some idiot!" Andrew Howard laughed. He had a general practice and was the only one who engaged in criminal law. "You forgotten he made *Law Review?*"

"I didn't say he *was* an idiot; I said he *looked* like an idiot. What I mean is he doesn't make the sort of impression that's apt to inspire confidence in a client." Atwell looked to Fisher for support.

"Don't let any of that fool you," said Howard. "Maybe it's a kind of nervousness, but let me tell you, he can turn it off when he wants to. And when he does, watch out! I appeared against him once on a rape case. My client was a clean-cut young fellow, very cool and very much at ease. I had to put him on the stand, but I figured it would be all right, that he'd be able to handle himself. He told his story well, and I could see he was making a good impression on the jury. Then Brad Ames started to cross-examine. He asked his questions, and they were good-natured. You know what I mean? No pressure. And that manner of his. He looked like a grinning buddha.

And always with that little giggle as though it was some kind of joke. Pretty soon my client was relaxed and grinning, too. It was a regular tea party between them. Every once in a while Ames would slip in a question that wasn't according to Hoyle and my client would answer before I could object. The judge, Judge Lukens it was, would order it stricken, but the jury had already heard it. It went on like that for almost an hour, all nice and friendly. And then suddenly, Brad's face tightens up and suddenly—goodbye, buddha. He holds up the girl's dress so the jury could see how it was ripped. 'And is this the way she took off her dress?' he asks. My client began to stutter and stammer, and right then and there I knew he was a goner."

"Oh, I don't deny he's good," said Fisher. "But it's still no sort of career—assistant district attorney. If he really had any drive, he would have got out of the D.A.'s office after a few years and used it as a stepping stone to private practice in criminal law, like Clyde Bell, or Amos Mahew."

"I don't agree," said Sam Curley, who had been silent until now. "I've had dealings with Brad off and on over the years. Our firm doesn't handle criminal business as such, but every now and then one of our clients, or some relative of a client, gets into trouble and they expect us to act for them. If it's anything serious, of course we'd farm it out to a Clyde Bell or somebody like that. But a lot of times, we'll handle it ourselves. About two or three years ago, I had a case and Brad was acting for the Commonwealth. It was during the summer and when I called Brad about it, he invited me to come down to their family place in Barnard's Crossing for the weekend. They got quite a place on the Point and the weather was nice and we did a bit of sailing. Well, Sunday his older brother Stuart came down for dinner—"

"The judge?"

"That's right. Well, after dinner, we were sitting on this great big verandah they have, overlooking the water, with this telescope mounted near the railing so you can look at any boat in the harbor and see who's aboard, and a pitcher of Tom Collins right there on the table. It was nice. And we were just talking the way you do after a good dinner, and the judge says, half-joking, something to the effect when was Brad going to realize his potential and perform the duties that were expected of him. And do you know what he meant? He meant that it was Brad's *duty* as an Ames to serve society and the country, to his fullest capacity.

"Now, ordinary people don't talk that way because—well, because they don't think that way. I mean, normal people might say when are you going to realize your potential and be a big shot? If you're so smart, why aren't you rich? That kind of thing. But Stuart Ames wasn't thinking of that. He was thinking that his brother had a duty to society that he wasn't fulfilling. He actually thought that way. And the funny thing was that Brad felt the same way, too. So he started to tell about his job, half-kidding at first, like his brother, but really in dead earnest just the way his brother was. I'll never forget it to this day. He said, 'District attorneys come and go. The better they are, the quicker they go, too, because it's just a stepping stone for them to the next office. But assistant D.A.'s, they stay on. Now somebody's got to train those D.A.'s, and I guess a lot of it falls to me, mostly because I've been around so long.'"

"I hadn't thought of that, but I can see how it could be true," said Andrew Howard.

"Then he went on to point out that it was the assistants in the D.A.'s office that run the whole shebang. They decide who is going to stand trial and who is going to get a second chance. Not the judge, mind you, not the defense counsel, and not even the D.A., but the assistant D.A. He's the one who decides to prosecute or not. He's the one who makes the deals. Well, you know, he made out a good case. I know I was convinced and I'm pretty sure his brother was. And it gave me a new slant on him. I'd been thinking all along, like you, that he was doing it as a kind of hobby: that he liked criminal law and since he could afford to practice it at this level, he was indulging himself. But by the end of that afternoon, I saw him as a kind of top sergeant who does all the work and makes all the decisions, but lets the lieutenant or the captain give the actual order and get the credit. What keeps the whole legal apparatus of the city running is not the judges and the defense counsel or even the cops, but the lowly assistant D.A."

Bradford Ames unhappily stared after the departing district attorney and tried to decide what to do. In his own mind, Rogers had already tried the four students and found them guilty—of what? Of being radicals, of using bad language, of following a life-style he did not approve of, and for all those reasons he was determined to keep them in jail as long as he could, all the weeks and months to the day of the trial. It was those four daughters of his that were warping his judgment, Ames decided, and thanked God that he was a bachelor.

Of course, once the case reached trial, the medical examiner's report would have to come out and there would be a directed acquittal on the murder charge, however it would go with them on the arson charge. But in the meantime, the students would have remained in jail all that time. There was also the danger of a judicial backlash; if the case came up before a prima donna like Judge Harris, for example, he would have plenty to say about the suppression of evidence by the district attorney. He wondered at his chief's blindness to the political implications and then reflected wryly that he probably *was* aware of them and assumed his constituency would not mind in the least if he stretched the law a bit to keep these young radicals out of circulation.

Normally, a hint to the defense attorney would take care of the matter, but each of the four defendants was being represented by a different attorney, all of whom were strangers to Ames. The O'Brien boy had retained a young lawyer who had just passed the bar exam; Allworth had someone furnished by one of the radical black organizations; and the girl, Judy Ballantine, whose father was well off, was being represented by a firm of New York lawyers. Only Paul Goodman, the attorney for the Selzer boy, seemed a possibility, but even he was an unknown quantity since he practiced largely in Essex County, not Suffolk. Still, Ames thought he might get a line on him, and if he measured up, risk it.

From his years of summering in Barnard's Crossing, Ames had got to know its chief of police. He called him at home that evening. "Hugh Lanigan? This is Bradford Ames."

"Oh yes, Mr. Ames. How are you?"

"Look, do you know a lawyer in your town, name of Paul Goodman?"

"Yes, I know Mr. Goodman."

"He's acting for Abner Selzer. That's the boy who—"

"Yes, I know, sir."

Ames sensed the caution at the other end of the line and hastened to reassure Lanigan. "I'm not planning any skull-duggery. At least not against him or his client. In fact, I'm trying to help him out a little, but it's pretty confidential and I'd like to know the sort of man Goodman is."

"Well," Lanigan began doubtfully, "I don't know that I can tell you much. He's the lawyer for the temple here, and he's appeared before the board of selectmen a couple of times on zoning matters, usually. I guess he's well enough thought of."

"What kind of man is he?" Ames began to suspect he may have made a mistake in approaching Hugh Lanigan. "Is he accessible? A reasonable man? You know what I mean?"

"Look," said Lanigan, "I got an idea. Why don't you call the rabbi of the temple here, Rabbi Small. Now he's a good man, and bright. Ask him about Mr. Goodman. This Goodman is a sort of vestryman of the temple, one of their board of directors, so the rabbi would know all about him."

The rabbi? Of course! He could tell the rabbi and thus transmit the information to Goodman at one remove. And if the rabbi was adroit, Ames' name need never come into the picture.

He thanked the police chief, hung up, and immediately called Rabbi Small. He identified himself and explained that he wanted to discuss the case with him.

"Certainly," said the rabbi. "I have a class tomorrow from nine to ten. I could come to your office any time after that."

Ames hesitated. He felt a certain reluctance in having the rabbi seek him out when it was he who was going to ask a favor. So he said, "Why don't I meet you outside your class-room at ten, Rabbi?"

30

The bell rang, and the rabbi dismissed his class. He gathered up his books and papers and left the room. In the corridor, just outside the door, a plump middle-aged man was standing.

"Bradford Ames, Rabbi. I hope I'm not putting you to any inconvenience."

"Not at all. My office is just down the hall."

As the rabbi inserted his key, Ames asked, "The office is kept locked all the time?"

"All offices. This one has a door-closer which shuts it auto-matically."

Ames looked about him curiously. "And that's the desk where Hendryx was sitting?"

"That's right."

"And the bust?"

"Was on the top shelf just above."

They sat down, the rabbi in the swivel chair, Ames across the desk, silent as his eyes roamed around the room. As he continued to maintain his silence, David Small asked politely, "Do you have any other questions?"

Ames chuckled. "I didn't really come here to question you, Rabbi. I suppose that's what I implied over the phone, but it's more that I want to tell you something."

"All right."

"I'm sure you know the nature of the charges against the four students?"

The rabbi nodded. "I think so. Arson and felony murder?"

141

"That's right. Setting off a bomb is arson, which is a felony. It's our assumption that the explosion caused the statue to fall on Professor Hendryx and kill him. That makes it a felony murder which is first degree murder."

"I understand."

"And since in this state there's no bail for first degree murder, we've got the students sitting in jail waiting for arraignment before the grand jury. If they find a true bill, they'll remain in jail until they go to trial."

"Yes, I know that."

"What do you think of it?" Ames asked unexpectedly.

It caught the rabbi by surprise. "I don't understand. Does it make any difference what I think?"

"No, I suppose not, but I'd like to know anyway."

The rabbi smiled. "It's not really much of a coincidence, but only yesterday I was doing some research in the Talmud for a sermon and I came across a passage which bore on a somewhat similar problem."

"Talmud? Oh, that's one of your religious books, I believe."

"It's actually our book of law. And the passage was not concerned with murder, but with the law of bailment and the responsibility of the bailee."

"You mean this Talmud deals with civil law?"

"Oh yes," said the rabbi. "And criminal law, and religious law—all the laws by which we were governed. We don't separate them in our religion. Well, this case involved a loss by accidental damage and there was evidence of negligence on the part of the bailee. The question concerned his liability. One rabbi held, as a general governing principle, that if negligence in the beginning results in damage in the end, even by accident, then the bailee is liable."

"Well, that's the point of view we take."

"But another rabbi held that the basic principle should be different. Even though the beginning may be negligence, if the damage results by accident he is not liable."

"And how was the case finally decided?" asked Ames, interested in spite of himself.

The rabbi smiled. "It wasn't. As in a number of such cases,

the final decision was held in abeyance until the coming of the prophet Elijah."

Ames laughed. "Very good. I wish we had a device like that."

The rabbi laughed too. "You can't," he said, "unless you believe that Elijah is actually coming."

"That *would* make a difference, of course." Ames found himself liking the rabbi and decided to go ahead with his plan to confide in him. "To get back to the matter in hand, Rabbi, I don't mind admitting that I am not too happy with the situation as it stands. These young people can be kept in jail for some little time even though they have not as yet been tried and found guilty. Of course, that's one of the hazards of citizenship. It could happen to anyone. It's unfair to the individual, of course, but on the other hand the state must protect its citizens. We take all sorts of precautions to insure that the innocent are not harassed in this way. The police cannot hold people for more than twenty-four hours without the consent of a magistrate, just as we don't subject people to the annoyances and vicissitudes of a trial until a grand jury has decided that there is a good case to be made out against them."

"Surely, Mr. Ames, you didn't come here to lecture me on the virtues of our legal system."

Ames giggled. "True enough, Rabbi. Well, the medical examiner has just filed his report, and according to his analysis the death of your colleague occurred some time before the explosion. Now, the M.E.'s findings are not conclusive, you understand. He can make a mistake, and probably did, but I'm sure that if the judge had had the medical examiner's report he would not have refused bail."

"I see," said the rabbi. "So what do you do in these cases? I'm sure it must have happened before—not exactly like this perhaps, but where some new piece of evidence has been introduced."

"Oh, it occurs often enough. And what I'd be apt to do is call the defense counsel and tell him, so that he could file a motion to quash or to reduce bail. But in this case, the district attorney has rather strong views, which makes it a little

143

difficult. You understand?" He peered up at the rabbi expectantly.

"I think so," said the rabbi doubtfully. Then, "In the other cases, did you get the district attorney's permission first?"

"Oh no. I handle my own cases as I see fit. Normally, there's no interference."

The rabbi looked at him. "So why couldn't you do the same here?"

Ames tried to find a more comfortable position in the visitor's chair. "Because we've *already* discussed it, and he's against it."

"Suppose you didn't bother to tell him and just did it, wouldn't he assume the defense attorney had thought of filing the motion on his own?"

"Well, if it were a lawyer I knew, one I'd had dealings with, I could manage it that way without any trouble. I'd let them know I was going out on a limb and to keep it quiet. You understand, there are only so many lawyers practicing criminal law in the county and over the years I've established good working relations with most of them. But here I don't know any of the people who are acting for these students. Besides, there are four of them, and it would be bound to get out."

"Ah, I see the problem." The rabbi was silent for some little time. Finally he said, "In talking to me about the case, did you feel that because I'm a rabbi, that is, a clergyman, that what you said was privileged and that I was thereby bound to respect your confidence?"

Ames chuckled. "You catch on fast, Rabbi. To answer your question, let's put it this way: if you were on the witness stand and refused to answer on those grounds, the examining attorney would be sure to point out that since one party to the conversation was a Jewish rabbi and the other a Unitarian, the principle of privilege of the clergy certainly would not apply."

"All right, I'll proceed on that basis. Tell me, Mr. Ames, how did you happen to come to me?"

"Well, of the four lawyers, I thought only Paul Goodman seemed at all possible. He's mature and he's local, but I thought

I'd better get a line on him first. So I called Chief Lanigan, and he suggested I talk to you. I gather you two know each other."

The rabbi smiled. "Yes, we've had dealings."

31

Bradford Ames slowly circled the apartment, stopping to glance at the titles of the books on the shelf, staring at a picture on the wall.

"What are you looking for?" asked Sergeant Schroeder.

"I don't know." Ames shook his head. "I don't have any idea. That hassock, the cleaning woman says it wasn't there when she left?"

"That's what she said."

"And the pipe and the ashtray, she's positive they weren't there?"

"Just the pipe," said Schroeder. "She said she cleaned the ashtray and doesn't remember whether there was a pipe in it, but if so she'd have returned it to the rack."

"It's true, Sergeant. As a bachelor of long standing, I can testify to the fact that cleaning women always clean ashtrays whether they need it or not."

"Wives, too."

"Is that so?" he said abstractedly. "Well, Sergeant, I'm inclined to believe her."

"And you didn't before?" asked Schroeder in surprise. "Why?"

"Because if her story is true, then the whole thing just doesn't add up."

"Why not?"

Ames raised a pudgy finger. "She says she left here a little before three, maybe ten to. We know the bomb went off just after three. That means Hendryx had to go to his apartment, pull over the hassock, select a book from the shelf, light his pipe, sit down to read and then hightail it back to his office in time to get killed by the statue—all in fifteen minutes."

"He could have been smoking the pipe when he came in."

"Good point. And yet not so good, because there are half a dozen matches in that ashtray."

"They do it all the time," said Schroeder. "They smoke more matches than they do tobacco. Are you saying it couldn't be done in fifteen minutes?"

"Well, it's possible," said Ames. "But that's all it is—possible, in the sense of racing against a stopwatch. Does it satisfy you?"

"No, it doesn't, sir," admitted the sergeant. "But you know what they say: when you've ruled out everything else, what's left has to be the answer. Then again, Mrs. O'Rourke could have been fudging a little on the time and actually left quite a bit earlier. But why would she lie about it?"

Ames shrugged. "They always fib. If they answer the phone in your absence, they always pretend they can't hear, or the connection is bad, rather than go to the trouble of getting a pencil and taking down the message properly. And when they break things, they hide them instead of telling you. I had one who would put something she'd broken where I'd be sure to trip over it and think I did it myself."

"We could question her again," Schroeder suggested.

Ames agreed that was in order.

"What about the medical examiner?" asked the sergeant. "Did you get him to admit he'd made a mistake?"

Ames shook his head. "No. He insists the time is correct as he gave it."

"Then it doesn't make sense, none of it," said Schroeder, shaking his head.

Ames chuckled. "Sergeant, let me tell you something about doctors' testimony as to the time of death. There never was one I couldn't have tied into knots on cross-examination on the witness stand. I never do, of course, because usually they're on my side; but you have only to check the literature to find there is enormous variation in the process of departing this world. The doctor says that death occurred, say, between two-ten and two-forty, as here. So you ask if it couldn't have been just a little earlier and a little later, say from two-five to two forty-five, and of course he has to admit that it's possible. So you keep extending it five minutes at a time until he calls a halt and says, no, it couldn't have been as early as that or as late as that. But by that time the jury is a little suspicious of him. And then you ask why he said between two-ten and two-forty when he now admits it could have been between a quarter of two and a quarter past three. Even if he manages to keep cool —and there's a good chance that he won't—the jury may think he's not such an objective, scientific witness after all, but he's only trying to help the side that's paying him."

"Well then!"

"Now, Sergeant," Ames cautioned, "that's only legal pyrotechnics. If he were a good man and knew his business, I'd know he was telling the truth even while I was making hash out of him."

Schroeder was thoroughly confused. "Then is he mistaken or isn't he?"

Ames began to stride about the room as he tried to organize his thoughts. "That's a problem, Sergeant. Because if the medical examiner is right, we've got to find another reason besides the explosion for that statue falling. I suppose there could be reverberations from a passing truck or sonic boom of a passing jet—but surely those have happened before and the statue hasn't fallen. No, the only possibility that seems to make sense to me is that someone pulled it down. Deliberately. And that would be murder, not felony murder, not an accident occurring during the commission of a felony, but out-and-out murder."

"We could backtrack Hendryx on the chance that someone might have wanted him dead," suggested the sergeant.

Ames nodded vigorously. "Yes, do that. By all means. I'd question everyone who was in the building that afternoon. I'd also question the people in his department. I'd especially want to know why he didn't have a desk in the English office along with the rest of the department."

"All right, sir, I'll get on with it."

32

Dean Hanbury sat placidly knitting as she answered the sergeant's questions. "Let's see . . . between two and three I was here of course, awaiting the student committee. President Macomber might have been in his office, but my own secretary leaves at noon on Friday. And then there was Rabbi Small and his class."

"He saw you close your door."

She laughed. "Oh, did he see me? I *am* sorry. I'm afraid it was not very nice of me. He's a dear man, but so serious about his course. Every Friday he stops by to tell me how few students have shown up for class. That afternoon, what with the student committee and a rather hectic morning, I just didn't want to see anyone."

"Can you tell me anything about Professor Hendryx?"

"Like what, Sergeant?"

"Well, his personal life, his friends, his close associates—"

She shook her head regretfully. "He came from my hometown originally, from Barnard's Crossing. I actually knew him when I was a little girl. He was much older than I, of course, but in a small town everyone knows everyone else. When we hired him, we went into his academic qualifications quite thoroughly, but that's all. He has family out West somewhere. As a bachelor, he had no ties here."

In response to a cheery "Come in," Sergeant Schroeder entered President Macomber's office to find him stroking a golf ball across the carpet toward a drinking glass lying on its side at the far end of the room. The president looked up. "Oh, it's you," he said. "I thought it was my daughter. What can I do for you?"

"We're just tying up some loose ends, checking on everyone who was in the building, say, between two and three."

"Well, I was here, all right. Must have left around half-past two, a few minutes before or after."

He picked up the glass and emptied the golf ball into his hand. He was about to return the glass to the carpet but thought better of it and set it on his desk. Sliding the ball into his pocket, he sat down, still holding the putter. "A most unfortunate business, Sergeant. You know, Dean Hanbury had been after me for quite a while to appoint Hendryx permanent head of the English Department. He was only acting head. Well, that very morning I notified her I was going to make the appointment. It goes to show you—man proposes, and all that sort of thing."

Sergeant Schroeder remarked that Dean Hanbury hadn't mentioned it to him.

"Well, of course. Under the circumstances, where no public announcement had been made, she wouldn't be likely to. Besides, she'd feel it ought to come from me."

"I suppose so," said the sergeant. "Now, is there anything you can tell me about Professor Hendryx's personal life, his relations with other members of the faculty, with the students, women students particularly. After all, he was a bachelor and living alone—"

"I can answer that, Sergeant." It was Betty Macomber. She had entered the office and overheard his question. "Professor Hendryx had no relations, not the kind you hinted at, with any of his women students. I knew him very well and saw a great deal of him. You see, we were going to be married."

Mary Barton, soon to be Dr. Barton, was plain as an old shoe. She prattled on without guile and without restraint. "Oh, I liked him, but he wasn't everybody's cup of tea. He was inclined to be sharp and sarcastic, given to making snide little remarks that annoyed people. It didn't bother me any. In fact, I rather enjoyed them. College professors tend to be pompous and our English Department is no exception, so I didn't mind hearing him prick their little vanities. . . . No, I can't say that anyone actually hated him, but when he announced that he was moving out of the office, I don't remember anyone urging him to stay. . . . Like what? Oh, like when Professor Hallett remarked that he'd like a vacation and Hendryx said, 'I'm sure your students would profit from it.' That kind of thing. And he'd make little sly digs about Jews, like once when he was going to lecture on *The Merchant of Venice*, he said, 'I'm sure I'll get some interesting reactions from The Chosen on this lecture.' We have two or three Jews among the younger members of the department." She laughed. "You know, when I came here in the fifties, it was the policy not to hire Jews for the English Department. Math, the sciences, economics, that sort of thing, O.K., but not for English. I remember they turned down Albert Brodsky. . . . Oh, he's the one who did that marvelous book on linguistics. . . . Professor Brodsky of Princeton? You never heard of him? Well, believe me, he's tops, absolute tops, and they could have had him here, but then he probably wouldn't have stayed anyway. . . . Oh, yes! Well, what I was going to say is that they'd naturally be a little embarrassed, but they'd just pretend they hadn't heard. All except Roger Fine. He'd stand up to him. And more. I once heard him say he'd ram his stick down his throat if he didn't shut up. He's a little lame and walks with a cane. . . . I'm sure it was about some remark that Fine considered anti-semitic. I suspect he was over-sensitive, but then I suppose I shouldn't say since I'm not one, a Jew, I mean, or maybe I should say, Jewess. I mean, I might feel differently if I were. I remember asking Rabbi Small if he considered Hendryx anti-semitic, and he said no. Of course, it was after Hendryx's death and the rabbi might have felt *De mortuis*. . . . It was just be-fore the memorial service they were having for Hendryx. . . . Oh, I thought you'd know it; it's a common expression. It's

Latin, *De Mortuis nil nisi bonum*. It means you say nothing but good concerning the dead."

"Hey, did the cops come to see any of you guys?" Mazelman called out to the class. "This guy, a sergeant yet, turns up to the house and starts to grill me—"

"What do you mean?"

"Like who was in class Friday, you know, the Friday Hendryx got his? Did I see anybody in the building? Well, then it turns out he's especially interested in the time from two to three o'clock. So I tell him how by two o'clock I'm already at the airport because the rabbi walked out of class. Boy, was he surprised."

"Asshole!"

Mazelman colored. "What's with you, Luftig?"

"What did you have to tell him that for?"

"Why not? It's a secret?"

"I don't see why we should wash our dirty linen in public," maintained Luftig.

"Well, it just came out. Besides, since when are you so buddy-buddy with the rabbi? You're always fighting with him."

"So what? That doesn't mean I got to throw him to the wolves."

"Who's throwing him to the wolves? Anyway," said Mazelman, "don't worry about the rabbi. A smart cookie like that can take care of himself."

"You start digging and you find things," said Sergeant Schroeder with grim satisfaction as Bradford Ames finished reading his progress report. "For instance, why didn't the dean tell us about Hendryx getting appointed head of the department?"

"Because when you first questioned her she didn't think it germane, I suppose. And the reason President Macomber gave is probably correct."

"I don't get it. A man's been killed."

"They'll have to appoint somebody to the job, won't they?" said Ames. "Why tell him he was just second choice?"

"Well . . ." The sergeant was not convinced. "Of course, I've still got more to question."

"Yes, you said you'd speak to the cleaning woman again."

"You wanted to be in on that one, sir."

"That's right. I certainly do. Anything on the missing student, this Ekko?"

Schroeder smiled complacently. "I think we've got a lead on him. Late Friday afternoon a young fellow hops the bus to Albany. He sits down next to a man who turns out to have a barber shop in Springfield. Well, it seems the barber was telling one of his customers about this young fellow, how he was bulling him and how he puts him in his place by spotting that he was wearing a wig and phony moustache. Just our good luck, this customer happened to be a plainclothesman with the Springfield police and he'd seen our flyer on this Ekko, who's bald as an egg. So the plainclothesman had their artist add some hair and a moustache to the picture on the flyer and got a positive ident from the barber. I expect we'll be picking him up in a couple of days."

"That's good work," said Ames. "Are you about through at the college?"

"All except this Professor Fine and the remainder of the rabbi's class and the rabbi, of course. I figure I'm going to have to bear down on him a little."

"Bear down? On the rabbi?" Ames looked up in surprise.

"You bet. That man has a lot of explaining to do. I told you about the first time I called him and he wouldn't talk to me on his Sabbath. Well then, when I finally did get to talk to him, not a word about walking out on his class right after it started."

"And what significance do you attach to that?" asked Ames.

"Well, think about it, sir. If he left his class a few minutes after one and didn't leave the school until after two, then he was with Hendryx for an hour or more. Now what were they doing there together?"

"What anyone would do, I suppose—talking."

"Right!" said Schroeder, as if this was conclusive. "But remember what this Barton woman said about Hendryx being anti-semitic."

"What are you suggesting, Sergeant?"

"Well, if the rabbi admits he left around ten past two, and the M.E. puts the time of death at between two-ten and two-forty, and the rabbi was alone with Hendryx right up to that time, and with Hendryx a known anti-semite and the rabbi a rabbi and all. Suppose they argue. Suppose the M.E.'s a little off—the ten, fifteen minutes you yourself mentioned, sir—only it's *earlier* not later. The point is, sir, if it's easy, if it involves no planning, just a spur-of-the-moment thing . . ."

Bradford Ames stared at the officer as though he were seeing him for the first time. The man obviously was still aggrieved at the rabbi's refusal to talk to him when he first called.

"And how does he go about pulling the statue down, Sergeant?" Ames asked gently. "Have you thought of that?"

"Yup, I have," Schroeder said smugly. "There's old books and papers on those shelves. Suppose the rabbi spots a book he wants to read or just look at. Now if it was on the top shelf the only way is to climb up and get it. So he climbs up right next to the statue. Then all he's got to do is give a little shove. Or maybe it was really an accident." A sudden thought occurred to him. "That may be what he wanted to see the dean about, to tell her there was an accident and to call a doctor, but the door shuts. He'd be all in a stew, not thinking clearly. Now I put it to you, would a man who'd just been through an experience like that go right home?" He shook his head. "No, sir. He'd ride around for a while, trying to make up his mind what to do. That's why he got home late. And then when I call up, he'd heard about the bombing. Naturally he wouldn't want to talk to me until he'd figured out what line to take."

"But—"

The sergeant leaned forward for emphasis. "Here's the clincher," he said. "You remember how we wondered how the killer could enter the office without Hendryx getting up to open the door for him? Well, there's one person who could, and that's the rabbi. *Because he had his own key!* Oh, I've got a lot of questions to ask that rabbi—"

"No."

"No?"

"No, Sergeant, I'll talk to him myself."

33

It wasn't a party; a few of the Selzers' closest friends just decided to drop in to congratulate them on the release of their son. Now they listened to him with rapt attention.

"So the rabbi comes in and I offer him a cup of coffee. Not that I was particularly interested in entertaining visitors at that time, you understand, but if I told the Boss Lady the rabbi was here and I didn't give him something, well, I'd sure hear about it." He glanced affectionately at his wife beside him on the sofa and she patted his hand.

"But he says he's in a hurry, he can't stay. And then he says: 'I think it would be a good idea if you speak to Mr. Goodman. Tell him to file a motion for your son's release on his own recognizance or on reasonable bail.' Just like that!

"Well, you know, ever since it happened I've been getting advice from people—not only from friends and acquaintances but from people I hardly know, even perfect strangers. One calls me to tell me I should get this lawyer that's been in the newspapers, how he always gets his clients off. Another one calls to suggest I ought to write a letter to all the papers and start a publicity campaign. Then there are some real crackpot calls to say how if I surrender to Jesus, he'll handle it. Believe me. And one guy actually came to see me and he said I could get Abner home tomorrow if I just concentrated certain vibrations in my own head, which would link up with the same type vibrations in the head of the judge or the D.A. and

154

tell them they had to release Abner and send him home. Honest to God, he was dead serious and he spoke like a college professor. Listening to him, you'd swear it was legit, like making a telephone call."

"My kid brother is a reporter," said Ronald Berkowitz, "and he tells me they get these crackpots calling up the paper all the time."

Selzer nodded. "I guess you're right, but you know something? It was kind of nice—I mean, that he was concerned and wanted to help me. Because there were others—letters and even phone calls—that were just the opposite. Like one night a lady calls up and asks if I'm the father of the boy who is in jail. And when I ask who I'm talking to, she lets out a string of dirty words. I didn't hear such language even when I was in the Navy."

"You got to remember, Malcolm, crackpots come in all shapes and sizes."

"I know," said Selzer. "And there were plenty of my friends who didn't call me or come near me—"

"We were out of the country, Mal—"

"Oh, I'm not blaming you, or them," Selzer assured Berkowitz. "These friends of mine weren't avoiding me because they were ashamed of me, or anything like that. It was just that it was embarrassing for them and they thought it would be embarrassing for me."

"So get on with the story," his wife urged.

"Right, hon. So here was the rabbi telling me what I should tell my lawyer. He didn't say I should discuss it with Goodman, mind you, or that I should ask him if maybe it wouldn't be a good idea. No, he says, 'Tell him.' But you know, I'm a guy like this: if I get sick, or some member of my family, God forbid, I'm not going to call a doctor and then tell him what pills he should give me. He's the expert. That's why I called him. Right? And that's why I pay him. It's the same way with a lawyer. If I'm going to tell him what to do, what do I need him for?"

Selzer looked around the room. "On the other hand, I'm not going to tell this to the rabbi's face because—well, because

155

he's a rabbi. I mean, maybe I'm funny that way, or maybe it's the way I was brought up, but I don't talk to a rabbi the way I would to a regular-type person. If a rabbi told me to do something, I might do it and I might not, but I wouldn't argue with him. Now it so happens that I think Rabbi Small is a good man and we're lucky to have him," said Selzer. "But that's as a rabbi, you understand. This is a practical matter, and I just don't think of Rabbi Small or any rabbi as a practical man. So I thanked him very polite for his interest, and I would've forgot all about it but I happened to walk down to the drugstore for a copy of the *Times* and who do I run into but old Jake Wasserman taking a walk with Al Becker."

"Oh yeah?" said Berkowitz. "How is the old boy? I haven't seen him in months."

"He looked fine," said Selzer, "just fine. Of course he's terribly thin and his skin it's so pale it's almost transparent. And he shuffles when he walks, and he holds onto Becker's arm like he'd fall down if he let go, but otherwise he looked pretty good to me. So naturally, we stop to *shmoos* for a few minutes, and he asks me what's new with my boy's situation and I tell him that there's nothing new, everything is status quo. And while we're talking, I happen to mention that the rabbi was down to see me and what he said.

"So Wasserman says, 'So did you tell Goodman?' So I explain to him how I couldn't see any sense in my telling a lawyer how he should practice law. But old Jake shakes his head like he don't agree with me and then he says, 'The rabbi came to see you? You didn't happen to bump into him like to us just now?' 'That's right,' I says, 'he came to see me.'

"So then Al Becker asks, 'Was it just about this, or did he come to see you about something else?' 'No, just about this,' I says.

"So then Wasserman, he puts his hand on my arm and he looks me right in the eye and he says very serious, 'Believe me, Mr. Selzer, if the rabbi went out of his way to tell you, then that's what you should do.' "

Selzer looked around at the others. "Well, to tell the truth, I was going to kind of laugh it off, because Wasserman, after all, he's an old man."

"And everybody knows he thinks the sun rises and sets on the rabbi."

"That's right," Selzer agreed. "That's why I was going to pass it off, but then Al Becker who is a practical and successful businessman says, 'That's good advice, Selzer, and if you don't follow it, you're apt to spend a long time wishing you had.'

"Well, sir, I don't mind saying I began to worry a little. I mean, a man like Becker, a big businessman, he's had all kinds of dealings with lawyers. I mean he knows what's what. And I began to think, maybe I'm passing up a chance. And what am I afraid of Paul Goodman for? I mean, I'm paying him, ain't I? I'm not a charity case. So when I got back home, I called him, and to make a long story short, he files the motion. And what's the result? Thanks to our rabbi, Abner is upstairs, catching up on his sleep right this minute."

34

"Just one question, Rabbi," said Bradford Ames, smiling genially as if to assure him it was not very important. They were once again in the rabbi's tiny college office. "Why didn't you tell Sergeant Schroeder that you left your class early on Friday?"

Rabbi Small blushed. "Sheer embarrassment, I suppose," he said. "Of course he didn't *ask* me what time I had left my classroom, only what time I had left the building. I suppose I should've mentioned it, but Lanigan was there and my wife, and I just didn't like to admit I'd had trouble with my class."

"Well, I'm asking now, Rabbi. What time *did* you leave the classroom?"

"It couldn't have been more than ten minutes or a quarter past one," said the rabbi promptly. "And I came straight here."

"Hendryx was in the office?"

"Sitting, or rather lying back, in this very chair."

"And you stayed here until a little after two?"

"M-hm."

"The two of you sitting here for an hour or so just engaged in friendly conversation."

"That's about it, Mr. Ames."

"And were you friendly, Rabbi? Did you consider him a friend?"

"Not particularly," said the rabbi. "We shared the same office, that's about it."

"But this time you talked for a whole hour," mused Ames. "Why? What were you talking about?"

"Oh, largely about educational theory." Once again the rabbi blushed. "At first, I was just marking time on the chance that someone from my class might come along to apologize for their behavior earlier. And then I stayed because—well, I was being paid for the time."

Ames looked at the rabbi curiously. "A refreshing notion, if you don't mind my saying so. And then on your way home you stopped for a cup of coffee, got immersed in a book and didn't get home until quite late."

"That's perfectly true," the rabbi insisted.

Ames chuckled and then laughed out loud. "I believe you, Rabbi," he said. "You know why? Because it's the damndest unlikely explanation I've ever heard, so I can't imagine you making it up."

The rabbi grinned.

"Have you told it all now?" he said, teasing him slightly. "Nothing you're keeping back because it might be embarrassing or because you consider it unimportant?"

"How would I know?" said the rabbi. "How can I tell what is and isn't significant when I don't know what you're after or what stage your investigation is at?"

Ames nodded. Should he tell him? Normally he would never reveal to an outsider the results of an investigation still in progress, but on the other hand, the rabbi might be of some help. He was intelligent and sensitive and had talked with Hendryx for almost an hour shortly before his death. If he knew what they were looking for, he might remember a remark, a phrase, something that could be linked to the evidence they already had. No doubt Sergeant Schroeder would disapprove, and probably the district attorney, too. And this as much as anything decided him. Delighted at the idea, he proceeded to relate in detail what they had discovered to date. "So you see," he said in conclusion, "it all boils down to one of two possibilities: either Mrs. O'Rourke is lying, or the medical examiner made a mistake."

The rabbi sat silent. Then he got up and circling the desk, he began to walk up and down the room. "The two do not balance," the rabbi said at last. "They are not of the same weight. For i–if you believe the medical examiner"—and unconsciously he lapsed into Talmudic argumentative sing-song —"the–en you have to assume not only that Mrs. O'Rourke was lying but that the explosion of the bomb did not cause the statue to topple. But if you believe that the medical examiner was mistaken and that Mrs. O'Rourke was telling the truth, then it is possible Hendryx was killed by the bomb. But it is not probable. So you have an impossibility on the one hand and an improbability on the other."

"Ah, I see what you mean by the two not balancing." Ames chuckled and shifted in his seat. "This chanting of yours—"

"Oh, was I doing it? I didn't realize. It's the normal accompaniment to Talmudic argument. I do it without thinking, I suppose."

"I see." Ames returned to the matter at hand. "Of course you're quite right about our being left with an improbability at best. The open book and the hassock could be a matter of a minute or two. You could sit down to read and then remember something you've got to do and put the book down without having read a line. But the pipe and all those matches . . ."

The rabbi had resumed his striding, but now he stopped. "Do you smoke?" he asked.

"No, thanks."

"Oh, I wasn't offering," said the rabbi. "I just wanted to know if you did."

"No," said Ames. "I never did, as a matter of fact. I had a

touch of asthma when I was a kid so I never got around to it."

"Well, I used to smoke," said the rabbi, "but I gave it up when I found it was too hard to smoke during the week and then stop for the Sabbath. When I was in college I tried a pipe for a while. It's almost irresistible to the young student, at least it was when I was in school."

"In my time, too."

"I never really acquired the habit," the rabbi went on. "Most young men don't. There's a trick to it, you know, and long before they've learned it, they've burned their tongues raw and given it up. Now, if I had sat down in that easy chair and smoked a pipe, the half-dozen burned matches you found would make sense. Because I never learned how, and until you've learned how, your pipe keeps going out and you have to keep relighting it. You make a regular bellows of your mouth and puff and puff, and still it keeps going out. But not Professor Hendryx. He knew how to smoke, and he really enjoyed his pipe. I used to watch and even envy him a little. He'd light it —he never needed more than one match—tamp it down carefully, and then keep it lit, effortlessly, a little puff of smoke coming out of his mouth every now and then."

"What are you trying to say, Rabbi?"

"That if it took half a dozen matches to light that pipe, or to keep it lit, then it wasn't Professor Hendryx who was smoking it!" said the rabbi.

"You're suggesting that someone came into the apartment and smoked one of his pipes to make it *appear* that Hendryx had returned after the cleaning woman had left."

The rabbi nodded.

"But that can only mean Hendryx was already dead and this person wanted to make it appear he was still alive."

Again the rabbi nodded.

"And that means the pipe smoker was establishing an alibi for himself because he had murdered Hendryx."

"At least it offers a third possibility," said the rabbi with the ghost of a smile.

"A third?"

160

"You said there were only two: that either the medical examiner was wrong or the cleaning woman was. This suggests that they both may have been right, that the medical examiner gave an accurate estimate of the time and that the cleaning woman was telling the truth."

Ames nodded slowly in agreement. A thought occurred to him. "Suppose the fingerprints on the pipe turn out to be Hendryx's?"

"It's only what you'd expect," the rabbi replied. "His prints would be on all his pipes. The murderer only had to be careful not to obliterate them. The cleaning woman wouldn't wipe them; a pipe is personal like a toothbrush."

Bradford Ames sat back. "You know, Rabbi," he said, "you're quite a guy. All right, tell me, how did the murderer get into the apartment?"

The rabbi shook his head. "I don't know."

35

Ames could see that Sergeant Schroeder was highly pleased. "We picked up that student, Ekko," he said, the minute he entered Hendryx's apartment.

"Good work," said Ames. "Has he talked?"

"No, but he will," said Schroeder confidently. "We'll let him stew for a while and then pull the cork and it'll all gush out. You'll see—" He broke off as a police cruising car drew up. "Here's Mrs. O'Rourke now."

The cleaning woman looked quite confused, and not a little apprehensive. Schroeder began brusquely. "We're going to ask you some questions, Mrs. O'Rourke, and this time we want the truth."

"Let me handle this, Sergeant," said Ames.

The cleaning woman visibly relaxed. "Now, Mrs. O'Rourke,"

he said in a mild voice, "here's what I want you to do. Would you please clean this apartment, just the way you did it the last time. You understand?"

"Yes, sir. Now?"

"Now will be fine, Mrs. O'Rourke," said Ames.

"Well, I start here usually." They followed her into Hendryx's small kitchen, and she made motions of removing dishes from the table and placing them in the sink. "Like this?"

"Just a minute, Mrs. O'Rourke," said Ames. "Do you do all this in your coat?"

"Oh, I take that off first, of course, and hang it up in the closet."

"Then please do so now," said Ames. "And how do you get in?"

"Well, I ring the bell and Professor Hendryx lets me in."

"All right. Then please go outside and we'll start from the beginning."

"This is like a—a play, isn't it, sir?" said the delighted Mrs. O'Rourke.

"Yes, Mrs. O'Rourke," said Ames seriously. He and Schroeder watched in silence as she simulated cleaning the apartment.

"When I finish this room," she said, warming to the scenario, "I usually empty the wastebasket."

"Go ahead."

"But it's empty."

"Well, for God's sakes, woman, make believe it's full," snapped Schroeder.

Dutifully, she picked up the wastebasket and opened the door.

"You leave the door open?" asked Ames.

"No. There's a draft sometimes and it slams shut."

"So you close it and Professor Hendryx would open it for you when you knocked?" Ames persisted.

"Oh no, sir, I wouldn't want to disturb him. I put it on the latch."

Ames directed her to do so. They watched her walk down the corridor to the back hall and make motions of emptying the wastebasket in a large trash barrel. She returned with the presumably now-empty basket and set it back in place.

"Don't you release the catch on the door now that you're back?" asked Ames.

"Oh, no, sir, on account I got to keep going out to empty the other wastebaskets and the newspapers and shake out the mops."

"I see," said Ames. "And when Professor Hendryx is not here? Say, he's gone across the street to the school?"

"Same thing. Nobody's going to come in, and I'm just down the hall."

"And when you finished and left for the day," said Ames, "did you remember to set the catch again?"

Her hand flew to her mouth in guilty embarrassment and she stared from one grim-faced man to the other.

"Well?" Ames' voice was suddenly hard.

"I don't remember, sir," she wailed. And then in automatic defense, "But it don't make any difference. The professor would be in and out all day, and he was just across the street. Besides, it didn't happen here; it happened over there." And suddenly she buried her face in her hands and began to weep.

36

The story of the rabbi's part in releasing young Abner Selzer gained wide currency; the Selzers made no attempt to conceal it—quite the contrary. Reactions were mixed.

"I'm not so sure the rabbi did such a good thing. After all, the kids did bomb the place, didn't they? And for my money, jail is exactly the right place for them."

Others were pleased. "Our rabbi, you got to hand it to him. I don't know how he does it, and I'm not sure he does either; it's like he's got a kind of sixth sense about these things. Re-

163

member that time with Hirsh, where everybody thought the guy was a suicide and made all this fuss about burying him in our cemetery, and then the rabbi found out the guy had been murdered so it was okay after all."

Some were inclined to minimize the rabbi's role. "You want to know what I think? I think the rabbi talked to Selzer, all right, and suggested he get him out on bail, like anyone might. Then when it worked out, Selzer made a whole spiel because to the Selzers, especially Mrs. Selzer, the rabbi is God's gift to Barnard's Crossing. Mind you, I'm not saying anything against our rabbi, because personally, I'm strong for him—a little. Let's put it this way, if you were to split the congregation into pro-rabbi and anti-rabbi, I guess I'd line up with the pro-rabbi side. But there's no sense losing your sense of proportion. What's such a big deal?"

Paul Goodman, when asked directly by a friend, smiled and said enigmatically, "That's why they don't allow hearsay evidence in court."

"You mean he had nothing to do with it? But Selzer says—"

"I'm not suggesting that," said Goodman. "Mr. Selzer did come to me and ask me to file a motion. But we were planning to do so anyway, as soon as the other boy was apprehended by the police. It all reminds me of something Doc Simons, the pediatrician, was telling me. Most of the time he finds it's the mother he has to treat, not the infant. It's the same way in criminal practice when your client is a minor. It's the parents you have to worry about. And when it's a Jewish parent. . . ."

Not surprisingly, those who were not his supporters downplayed the rabbi's contribution. While conceding he had brought it off, they thought the rabbi probably had got a hint from his friend Lanigan, the police chief, who had got it from the Boston police "because all these cops hang together."

Lanigan met the rabbi a short time later. "Bradford Ames played that one pretty close to the chest," he said. "Even my friend Schroeder was surprised. He thinks the D.A. let the kids off because he figures he can make out a better case against this Ekko than against all five of them."

"They've found him then?" asked the rabbi.

"I thought you knew. Yes, it was a bit of luck, according to Schroeder. You need luck, because nowadays you've got a regular underground with these young kids. Any city you name, there's places they can go. In the old days, a hood on the run had it rough. The more heat there was, the rougher it was to find sanctuary. But with these kids, it works the other way. And if it's the police he's running from, instead of just his parents, then they're all the more eager to help him. It's become a little easier the last year or so because the Feds have infiltrated a lot of these groups, but still we don't find too many that don't want to be found. They all look alike—with the clothes and the beards and the hair. And the girls wear their hair down covering half their faces. Usually when we catch them it's because they got tired running."

"Did Schroeder say what the young man was charged with?" asked the rabbi.

"My guess is that they won't press the felony murder charge; they'll just stick to arson because it's easier to get a conviction. And I wouldn't be surprised if nothing came of that, either. These college cases are tough. There's no push behind them because the public doesn't exert any pressure."

Lanigan shook his head. "You ought to hear the way some of the men on the force complain. To John Q. Public these kids may be mistaken or misguided, but criminals? Never! When a college kid steals, it's so he can give the money to the peace campaign or to promote ecology. They're a bunch of regular little Robin Hoods."

Lanigan ran a hand over his face in exasperation and his tone was bitter. "In the old days a hood stole to buy himself a new car, some flashy clothes. But these kids drive old jalopies and wear beat-up clothes. So that proves they're a bunch of idealists. Right? Wrong! The law enforcement people know that they're also apt to have a couple thousand dollars worth of hi-fi stereophonic equipment and that they're supporting a dope habit that may run to a hundred bucks a day."

Lanigan had talked himself into a state of gloomy cynicism. "You mark my words, Rabbi, nothing will come of this case at your college. It wouldn't surprise me if the Commonwealth were to drop the charges because they know they won't get a conviction. And the police are left in the middle, unable to do a thing."

But the next day, Roger Fine was arrested and charged with the murder of his acting department head, Professor John Hendryx.

37

"Do you think she'll turn up?" asked Selma Rosencranz as she riffled a deck of cards. Of the four women in her Wednesday afternoon bridge group, she was the only serious card player; the others played to be sociable and it showed in their game. Selma also belonged to another foursome on Mondays and still another group that played Mah Jong Tuesday nights when her husband had his regular poker game.

"I could certainly understand if she didn't," said Annabelle Fisher, this week's hostess. She passed into the kitchen to check the tiny toasted sandwiches she was planning to serve. She was the least skillful player, with frequent lapses in concentration, but whenever the girls met at her house they were sure to get something different to eat—and delicious. She reappeared from the kitchen. "If my husband had just been arrested, believe me, I wouldn't have the heart to play cards."

"But she ought to call," insisted Flossie Bloom, a thin, sallow girl with a small hard mouth who prided herself on being candid and outspoken—"It's the way I am." Her husband was a salesman and not as successful as the husbands of the others. "If Edie doesn't come—"

"Then we won't play," said Selma. She set out the cards for solitaire.

"Do you believe he did it?" asked Flossie.

"Absolutely impossible," said Annabelle Fisher.

"Harvey says he has it on ve—ry good authority that Roger is tied in with all these radical students," said Flossie. "You know, the ones who have been staging all these riots and seizing college buildings and breaking up the furniture."

"Oh, I don't think that's so," said Annabelle Fisher, who found it impossible to think badly of anyone she knew.

"The eight can go on the nine," said Flossie. "Have you girls heard the talk that's going around about the rabbi—and Roger, I mean?"

"I've heard Roger make some cracks about the rabbi," said Selma, deftly shifting a line of cards from one column to another. "And it's certainly understandable after all the grief he gave him and Edie about the wedding."

"Oh, that was something else," said Flossie. "No, the story I heard is that the rabbi got that Selzer boy off by accusing Roger instead."

"That's absolutely ridiculous," said Annabelle.

"I don't find it so ridiculous," said Selma imperturbably, her eyes scanning the cards in front of her. "Everybody is saying the rabbi was the one who got the Selzer kid off. Well, how could he know, in advance, that they were going to let the kid off if he didn't know they were going to arrest Roger? And how could he know that unless he had something to do with it? I for one certainly don't think our rabbi has wings. Remember how nasty he was to Edie before the wedding and how at the ceremony butter wouldn't melt in his mouth? You think he wouldn't hold a grudge like anybody else? And if the chance came along—no, I wouldn't be surprised in the least if the story were true. Where'd you hear it, Flossie?"

"Oh, I've heard it several places," said Mrs. Bloom vaguely. "It's going around."

Selma saw that she was stymied and scooped up all the cards. "Well, let me tell you girls," she said, "if that story should turn out to be true, I for one wouldn't take it lying down."

"Why, what would you do?" asked Annabelle.

"I'd think of something, I know that," declared Selma. "And I'd make sure that the rabbi and the whole congregation knew exactly how I felt about it, too."

The doorbell rang.

"That must be Edie now," said Annabelle. She ran to the door and they could hear her say, "We thought you weren't coming."

"Sorry I'm late, girls," said Edie Fine. "I got held up. I went to see Roger."

"How is he?" "Are they treating him all right?" "It must've been terrible for you."

She sat down at the table with them. "Such a place," she said. "You get such a funny feeling when you go in. And the people, the types you see hanging around." She shook her head in disbelief.

"What happened?" asked Flossie.

"Well, first," said Edie, "you make out this form and hand it in. And then they not only search your handbag, but they make you walk through this place with this metal detector—"

"Like going on a plane."

"Yes, only more so. They're terribly careful. I asked Mr. Winston, that's Roger's lawyer, how they can sneak in all these guns and things that you hear about, and he just smiled and said, 'They don't search the guards.' How do you like that?

"So then I went into this little room, which Mr. Winston got special permission for us to use. Otherwise we would have had to meet in this big room with a barrier between us like you see in the movies. Well, I came in and Roger was already there waiting. He looked at me as though he weren't sure just how I was going to take it, so of course I smiled. And then he smiled back and I felt everything was all right.

"We sat down at this little table and he asked me if I thought he had done it, and of course I told him it never entered my mind. And that made him very happy. Really, he was quite cheerful after that, almost as though he was enjoying himself. He assured me that I was not to worry. Of course, he may have been putting on an act the same way I was at first, but I really didn't think so."

"But how did he—" Flossie started over again. "I mean how did the police decide to arrest— Did he talk about it?"

"Oh yes," said Edie. "You see he was in the administration building at the time. You know, he's involved in all this social justice business, and he was waiting for this important call. The whole point is that the building is practically empty on Friday afternoons, and the rabbi—"

"The rabbi?"

"Yes, the rabbi has a class on Friday afternoon. And after he finished as he was leaving, he passed by Roger's office and happened to see him there."

Selma looked significantly at Flossie Bloom and then they both looked at Annabelle Fisher.

As she had on similar occasions, Aggie Nolan walked slowly along Commonwealth Avenue, alert for the three short blasts of an automobile horn. She had called the FBI earlier and told the agent she worked with: "Commonwealth at Fairfield. Eleven o'clock."

At a quarter past eleven she finally heard the signal. She stepped into the roadway and stuck out her thumb. Almost at once a car slowed down and came to a stop beside her.

"You're late," she said, sliding in beside the driver.

"I passed you twice," he said. "The first time there was a guy standing on the corner. I thought he was looking at you."

"Well, guys do, you know," said Aggie.

"I sure as hell do know," he said appreciatively. "The second time you hadn't thumbed. I told you before, you've got to thumb."

"Yeah, well, all that cloak and dagger jazz is a drag."

"Maybe so," he said, "but while you work with me, you'll do it my way. It's for your protection as much as mine. All right, what's up?"

"They've picked up Ekko and they're holding him."

"What do you care—he a boy friend of yours?"

"He was once. That's all over, but he's a decent guy," she said.

"Well, you don't have to worry about him. They let the others go and they'll let him go, I'm sure, especially now that they've charged this professor with the murder."

"There's still the arson charge. The others are out on bail. Ekko couldn't raise the bail."

"I still don't think there's anything to worry about. Believe me, I don't think the case will go to trial. The D.A. just doesn't have the evidence. And if it does go to trial, they'll be acquitted for sure."

She turned on the seat to face him. "Not good enough," she said. "You told me to get in solid with the Weathervanes, and I did. I even went along with this crazy bombing scheme of yours to show I meant business."

"It worked, didn't it?"

"I didn't expect anybody to get killed!"

"But nobody did. This Hendryx guy, the bomb had nothing to do with his death."

"And I didn't expect anybody else to get blamed. I got nothing against any of them, especially Ekko. Well, I want him out."

He sighed. "All right, I'll talk to my boss and have him tip off the D.A. Okay?" He patted her on the knee.

She slid away from him. "You can drop me right along here."

"What's your hurry? How about a little ride?"

"No. At the corner there. It's right near school."

He shrugged. "Whatever you say, baby."

39

District Attorney Matthew Rogers felt he ought to grumble a little. "I don't see why they can't tip us off when they set up something in our bailiwick."

Bradford Ames chuckled. "Because even where the local people are completely trustworthy, there's a chance they may slip up and blow the cover of the federal operative."

"I suppose. But at least they could give us some advance warning. Not let us arrest these decent young people and keep them in jail for days on end and cause their families all kinds of grief, when by passing the word we could have just let things simmer."

"Maybe they felt that would look suspicious," suggested Ames.

Rogers gnawed at the thought in silence for a moment. "I don't mind cooperating with the FBI. I'm anxious to, especially when they have secret information that people we've charged are actually innocent. We can always file a motion to quash for lack of evidence, although if you do that too much, you're suspected of being too eager to jail people. Remember that, Brad."

Ames nodded dutifully.

"But I like to be kept informed of developments."

"You were busy with the budget business," Ames said. "I didn't think you'd want to be bothered with the routine."

Rogers looked at him sharply. "Well, that's exactly right, Brad, but still—"

"And I don't mind admitting," Ames added, "that it occurred to me it might be better for you to have no official knowledge of this business, since it was slightly irregular."

"You're absolutely right, Brad. But you know if you got into a jam, I'd stand by you and back you up."

"I was thinking politically."

"Yes, that's true," said the district attorney. "In politics you sometimes have to disclaim knowledge of some of the things that are done in your name. But even then, you could rely on me to accept full responsibility." He scanned his assistant's face.

"Precisely. So I thought I'd go ahead. If my judgment was wrong—"

"Not at all, Brad. I have every confidence in you. You know that. Now what are your plans for proceeding against the real culprit?"

"We were asked to do nothing, Matt."

"Nothing? But Brad, a serious crime has been committed in my jurisdiction. A bombing. I can't just wash my hands of it and make believe it never happened."

"Not such a serious crime, Matt."

Rogers was indignant. "You don't call blowing up a school a serious crime?"

"Oh, there was some damage to the wall in the dean's office," said Ames, "some scorching, and a pane of glass in the door of an adjoining office was broken. Probably not a hundred dollars damage altogether. A smart lawyer could get a sympathetic judge to call it a misdemeanor. Besides, it was the government agent who did it."

"Good Lord!"

Ames squirmed in his seat, his round head wagging as he adjusted the various portions of his body to the chair. "It's a wicked world we live in, Matt. You see, when you plant an agent in a radical organization like the Weathervanes, he—although in this case it's a she—can't just sit back and observe. It's a small, close-knit organization, and everybody is expected to pull his own weight. And if they initiate action, so much the better. You can see that."

Rogers nodded seriously.

"But in this case, they weren't planning to do much damage,

just discredit the group that sent the committee to see the dean. Originally, they were only going to organize some sort of counter-demonstration. But when the government agent learned from a source on the committee that they were seeing the dean late Friday afternoon when the school is practically deserted, she seized the opportunity. She waited inside the building and when they left, set off a small charge. It wasn't expected to cause much damage but would do the job on the committee, since they'd be surely blamed for it."

"And you say this operative is a woman?"

"A mere slip of a girl, but with a heart full of patriotism."

Rogers looked doubtfully at his assistant, not sure he was entirely serious. "But dammit, Brad, it did do damage, and somebody got killed."

"Oh no, we know now that the explosion had nothing to do with that."

"Oh yes, this man Fine. I hope he's not going to turn out to be a government agent or anything like that, is he?"

"Don't worry." Ames chuckled. "We've got a good case against *him*."

"Well, that's good." Rogers rubbed his hands in satisfaction. "And the girl—after this, she must be in solid with the Weathervanes, I mean, after bringing off this caper, she'd be above suspicion?"

"Like Caesar's wife."

"What? Oh yes, yes, I see." He laughed.

"And she's above suspicion with us, too."

"Well, naturally . . ."

"Has it ever occurred to you, Matt, that we've come to a rotten state of affairs when we have to use double agents to maintain some semblance of law and order? That we have to wink at one breach of the law to prevent another? And we set ourselves up as the sole arbiters of which is more important. Now isn't that characteristic of a police state?"

Rogers looked at him doubtfully. He sounded perfectly serious, as though he actually meant this radical sort of talk. But then Ames chuckled, and he knew it was all right.

40

WHY DON'T JEWS EAT HAM?
WHY DO JEWS WEAR BLACK BEANIES WHEN THEY PRAY?
GOD IS DEAD. TRUE OR FALSE?
WHY . . . ?
WHY . . . ?

The rabbi stood in the doorway of the classroom, bemused, as he looked over the blackboard with its long list of questions, each written in a different hand.

"You said we could ask questions today," said Harvey Shacter.

"So I did, Mr. Shacter." He came into the room, his eye still on the board. "And with a list that long, we'd better get started. We'll take them in order. Now the first question, about ham: that involves our dietary laws. Briefly, we may eat only the flesh of an animal which has cloven hooves and chews its cud. It must satisfy both conditions to qualify as kosher, that is, ritually fit to eat. Fish must have both scales and fins, which rules out shellfish; and fowl with curved beaks and talons —that is, birds of prey—are taboo. Some try to justify these laws on scientific grounds—healthy and nourishing animals are permitted, those liable to disease and hence less fit for human consumption are taboo—but that's a modern rationalization. Traditionally, we observe the dietary laws because we have been so commanded in the Bible. Now since the pig does not chew its cud, it is considered unclean, and so ham is forbidden."

"But don't we have a special thing about the pig that we don't have about other non-kosher animals?" asked Leventhal.

"Yes, that's true, Mr. Leventhal. We have a special aversion for the pig, possibly because it was an object of worship among many pagan peoples. But I am inclined to think it is for a more fundamental reason. All the other domestic animals have some utility for man while they are alive: the cow gives milk, the sheep produces wool, the horse performs work and transportation, the dog guards the house, the cat controls mice. Only the pig, of all domestic animals, kosher and non-kosher, serves no purpose except to be slaughtered and eaten. Now our religion forbids cruelty to animals. In fact, there are dozens of regulations in the Bible and in the interpretations of the rabbis that require us to treat the lower animals with kindness: one must not muzzle the ox that treads corn; a donkey and an ox may not be yoked together; beasts of burden must be rested on the Sabbath; hunting for sport is forbidden. With that as our tradition, you can readily understand how raising an animal solely for slaughter would be repugnant to us."

The rabbi made a checkmark against the question on the board. "All right, let's go on to the next, the black beanie. Whose is that, by the way?"

Harvey Shacter raised his hand.

"I've never heard the *kipoh* referred to that way," said the rabbi smiling, "but it's a good enough description. Why do we wear it? It's just a matter of custom, Mr. Shacter. There's no biblical regulation, although I might point out that with us custom takes on the force of law. It doesn't have to be black and it doesn't have to be a beanie. Any head covering will do. At times it was the custom to go bareheaded, at other times to be covered, and the latter custom seems to have won out except in Reform temples where they usually pray bareheaded."

He checked off the question, and then after a moment's hesitation, checked off the next one, remarking, "'God is dead' concerns Protestant theologians rather than Jewish rabbis."

"Why is that?" called out Henry Luftig.

"Yours, Mr. Luftig?"

"Yes sir."

"Well, it's a theological question, and we have no theology, at least not in the generally accepted sense."

"Why not?"

"Because we don't need one," said the rabbi simply. "Our religion is based on the idea of a single God, a God of Justice. If you think about it, the concept of justice demands a single God because it implies a single standard. And because He is infinite, He is unknowable to finite minds. We don't forbid the study of Him, you understand, but we consider it pointless. Much as an engineer would who sees a young colleague trying to construct a perpetual motion machine. He might say: 'You can work on it if you like, but you're wasting your time because it's theoretically impossible.' So because we believe it's pointless to try to know the unknowable, we have no theology."

"Then why do the Christians have one?" demanded Luftig.

"I had intended this session to deal with your questions on Judaism, not Christianity," the rabbi said reprovingly.

"How can we know about Judaism if we don't have something to compare it to?" asked Shacter.

The rabbi pursed his lips and considered. "You're quite right, Mr. Shacter. All right, I'll try to explain. Like us, the Christians also believe in a single God. But in addition they have another divine being in the form of Jesus as a son of God. And since a son implies a mother, they also have Mary, who is at least semi-divine. Now these familial relationships, between God and Jesus, Mary and Jesus, Mary and God, and all the other possible permutations, to say nothing of the human-divine nature of Jesus—these are not easy to explain."

"Is that what they call the Holy Trinity?"

"No," said the rabbi, "that's the Holy Family. The trinity consists of the Father, the Son, and the Holy Ghost, and their relationship to each other is the concern of Christian theology. There are very fine distinctions on these matters between the various Christian sects."

"Yeah, but aren't those just word games played by priests and ministers?"

"Tens of thousands have been killed in religious wars, from the time of Constantine in the fourth century down to modern times, all because of these so-called word games," said the rabbi. "No, Mr. Luftig, the arguments of theologians are not to be dismissed lightly."

Lillian Dushkin waved her hand. "This boy I know, he's into this Jews for Jesus thing, and he says that Jesus is the Messiah Jews believe in and that he came to save mankind."

"Save them from what?" It was a young man who took copious notes, and it flicked across the rabbi's mind that for once, like most of the others, he had been listening rather than writing.

"Saved from hell, of course," said Mazelman scornfully. "Isn't that right, Rabbi?"

"Yes, that's the idea," he said. "Hell was an attempt to answer the age-old question: why do good men suffer while evil men frequently triumph and prosper? All religions have wrestled with that problem. The Hindus solve it by the doctrine of reincarnation. You get your just deserts in the next life for what you have done in this life. Christian doctrine holds that the wicked burn everlastingly in hell while the virtuous are rewarded by everlasting life in heaven."

"Pie in the sky," said Luftig sarcastically.

"That's a rather irreverent way of putting it, Mr. Luft'g."

"What's the Jewish answer?" asked Lillian Dushkin. "Don't we believe in heaven and hell?"

"Not really, Miss Dushkin. Oh, the concept has crept in from time to time, but it's never really taken hold. Our 'answer,' as you put it, is best expressed in the Book of Job, and I'm afraid it is not very comforting. We say it's just the nature of the world—the sun shines as brightly on the wicked as it does on the good and just—but that goodness is its own reward, while evil carries its own punishment. At least it has the virtue of being realistic and of focusing our attention on this world, and trying to improve it, whereas the Christian view can be said to focus on the next world, regarding this one as a mere stopping-off place. Of course, it developed at a time when the world was troubled, and traditional ideas and institutions were crumbling, much like the present."

"Like the present?"

"Yes, Mr. Luftig. Just look at the world-wide revolt of young people against what they call the Establishment."

"Well, maybe that does prove God is dead!" challenged Luftig. "I don't notice any movement to religion or any new cults—"

"No?" said the rabbi. "Then how would you describe your generation's sudden fascination with astrology and yoga and Zen and I Ching and Tarot cards and the macrobiotic diet and drugs and communes—Shall I go on?—all of them offering escape or instant knowledge or instant mystical ecstasy."

He realized from the tense silence that he had spoken with some feeling. To reestablish the easy informality, he went on in his normal voice: "Basically, Christianity is a mystical religion and offers the psychological satisfactions mysticism affords. It is other-worldly, heaven-oriented, while our religion is this-world oriented. We oppose what is evil in the world and enjoy the good things, spiritual and material, it has to offer. We do not shun the world by asceticism or try to rise above it by mysticism, which has no following among the main body of Jews."

"What about Hassidim?" ventured Mark Leventhal.

The rabbi nodded. "Yes, they lean in that direction, but I would not say the Hassidic movement is central to our tradition. It's significant that Martin Buber, the chief modern apologist for Hassidism, was a lot more influential with Christian theologians than he was with Jews. We do not believe that the single ecstatic moment of near union with God ensures virtue forever after. With us, it has to be a day-by-day conscious practice of justice and virtue. But it is human virtue we require, not the superhuman virtue of the saint. Our religion calls for us to make a practical adjustment to the world as it is. It is a religion of work and rest, of life and death, of marriage and children and their training and education, of the joys of living and the necessity to make a living."

"Well, their religion must work," said Shacter. "They're doing a lot more business than we are."

The class laughed and the rabbi joined in, relieving the tension. "Yes, Mr. Shacter, Christianity is a very pleasant religion. It offers a number of highly desirable responses to questions that have beset man down through the ages. He fears death and finds life too short, and the church offers him a world after death with a life everlasting. All we can offer in that respect is the hope that he will live on in his children and in the memory of his friends. He sees the good man suffering and the wicked prospering, and the church assures him that in the next world all will be redressed. And all we can say is that this is the nature of the world. For the everyday trials and tribulations of life, the church offers him the peace that comes with surrender to the mercy of Christ and the good offices of countless saints to whom he can pray for assistance, even for miracles. And periodically he can renew his faith through communion with his Lord by a magical act. And for us there is no magic, no short-cut, only a lifetime of effort. I suppose that gives another shade of meaning to the saying that it is hard to be a Jew."

Lillian Dushkin was bewildered. "But if theirs is so much better, why don't we go in for it?"

The rabbi smiled. "There's just one little hitch, Miss Dushkin. You have to believe. And we cannot believe."

"So then what's in it for us?"

"What's in it, as you put it so bluntly, is the satisfaction of facing reality." He saw the class were all attentive now. "It doesn't permit us to dodge problems, but it does help us to solve them, if only by recognizing they exist. And, after all, isn't that what the modern world is beginning to do? So after thousands of years it appears our way is at last coming into style. As for who's doing more business, Mr. Shacter, look about you and you will find that the great changes in thought and attitude that produced modern Western civilization are paralleled in Jewish religious thought—the equality of people, the rights of women, the right of all men to the good things of this life, the improvement of conditions on earth, respect for life in the treatment of the lower animals, the importance of learning."

"You mean they got them all from us?"

"Whether they did or whether they finally developed them

179

on their own is not particularly important. What is important is that these were inherent in our religion from the beginning, which suggests it accords with reality."

The bell rang, and with a start the rabbi realized that the hour was over. He realized, too, that he had not made his usual head count, and as he glanced about he saw there were twenty-one present, more than ever before on a Friday. He smiled and nodded to them in dismissal.

Annabelle Fisher was delighted when Selma Rosencranz called to invite her over Friday afternoon. It was so like Selma, to call up and have some friends on the spur of the moment, without planning, without preparation.

"I'll bake some brownies," said Annabelle Fisher.

Selma's home was modern, inside and out. Built of concrete with panels of black plate-glass set in chrome, it had been designed by an architect and even had been written up in a magazine—a fact Selma would casually mention to first-time visitors. "His idea is functional design for living," she would say, searching for the article. "But here, read it for yourself. He says it a lot better than I can explain it."

Annabelle pushed the button and the chimes responded with the first four notes of "How Dry I am." She giggled as always when she heard it; Selma went in for the craziest things. Selma herself, elegant in lounging pajamas and silver slippers, opened the door for her, and then called back inside: "It's Annabelle Fisher, and she's brought brownies. Any of you gals who haven't tasted Annabelle's brownies have a treat coming."

Annabelle gave Selma her coat and the box of brownies and went into the vast sunken living room. Flossie Bloom was there along with several others, all of whom Annabelle knew or had at least met.

When Selma reappeared, Annabelle asked whether she was planning on two tables.

"If we get around to playing," said Selma. "We've just been gabbing, waiting for you, and we thought it might be fun if we all went to the service tonight. You've been, haven't you? What's it like?"

"To the Friday evening service? Oh sure I've been—once or twice—with Joe. Why, it's like, you know, like a Friday evening service. The cantor sings and you pray, and then the rabbi gives a sermon."

"He gives a sermon?" asked Selma. "You're sure? Every Friday night?"

"Well, every time I've been. I'm sure he gives a sermon every Friday. Why?"

"Oh, we wouldn't want to go if the rabbi weren't going to give a sermon," said Selma.

Flossie Bloom giggled. "No point in going."

"How long does it last, the sermon, I mean?" asked Natalie Wolf.

"Why, I never actually timed him," said Annabelle, pleased to be the center of attention, "but I'd say anywhere from twenty minutes to maybe as much as a half-hour."

"Then say we figure on ten minutes," said Flossie Bloom, her eyes glittering at the others, "or even fifteen minutes. What happens next, Annabelle?"

"Next, I guess the cantor sings again and there's another prayer or two and then everybody goes down to the vestry for tea and cake."

"I think it would be better at the very beginning," said Selma.

"You're right," said Natalie Wolf, "then it wouldn't look as though it had anything to do with what he was saying at the time."

Annabelle looked from one to the other uncertainly, her friendly little smile frozen on her face. "Were you all planning to go together? It's really quite interesting, and it doesn't last

181

too long. I mean, I don't think you'll be bored." She saw their smiles and wondered if she had said something silly. Of course she knew all these girls, but some of them she didn't know awfully well. Natalie she knew was divorced and there were rumors that she was kind of fast. Of course, if she was a friend of Selma's she must be all right. And Genevieve Fox and Clara Nieman, well, she'd met them, any number of times, but they were really in a different circle altogether. Genevieve drove a white Jaguar, and Clara was single and had a studio apartment downtown right on the water.

"Yes, that was the general idea," said Selma. "We all thought we'd go together in a body. Would you like to come?"

"Oh wonderful! I'd like to. Of course, I'll have to ask Joe. He may have been planning to go tonight, and then of course, I'd really have to go with him."

42

The Friday evening service began at half-past eight, and it started right on time. The congregants began arriving at eight o'clock, but they remained in the foyer, greeting friends, talking, until a quarter past when they made their way gradually into the sanctuary. Once inside, they took seats and automatically lowered their voices to whispers in keeping with the sanctity of the place.

They usually found the rabbi's wife already in her seat in the twelfth row, which was far enough back for her to judge if the rabbi's voice was carrying and on the aisle so she could signal him if it were not. They always nodded to her if they caught her eye and she would smile back and form her lips in *"Gut Shabbes."* On the *bema*, next to the ark, the rabbi and the cantor sat together, the latter stately in his black robe, long silken prayer shawl, and high-crowned and betasseled velvet *yarmelkeh.* He sat straight and tall, inclining his head on occasion when the rabbi whispered a comment to him, nodding gravely afterward.

The rabbi, shorter, and seeming even shorter because he tended to slouch in the thronelike chair, cut a sorry figure beside him. In spite of numerous hints from the ritual committee, he refused to wear a black robe, and his prayer shawl, while clean, was of wool and looked yellowish beside the gleaming white silk of the cantor's. His *yarmelkeh,* too, was the ordinary close-fitting skullcap worn by members of the congregation. And since he walked to the temple, his black shoes, plainly visible to the congregation, were invariably dusty. There was a shoe brush in the enrobing room, but in spite of Miriam's adjurations he always forgot to use it.

The attendance varied from week to week, depending largely on the weather. On pleasant nights, about a hundred. They tended to congregate in the middle seats, that is, in the center section, third or fourth row back. After a few minutes of whispered conversation, they would begin leafing through their prayer books as if to get into the proper mood for the service. Those who came in late, or even just before the service began, would take seats in the rear as unobtrusively as possible.

But tonight, just as the rabbi was about to come forward to announce that the cantor would begin the service by chanting the *Ma Tovu,* How goodly are your tenets, O Jacob, half a dozen youngish women appeared at the back of the sanctuary. They glanced about them for a moment and then marched resolutely down the aisle to take up seats in the second row. The rabbi waited for them to get settled, then came forward to make his announcement.

Mrs. Nathanson, like most of the congregation, was annoyed at the interruption and whispered to her husband, "Selma Rosencranz and her crowd. I suppose they're slumming." But before Mr. Nathanson could answer, the cantor, his head thrown back, his prayer book held at arms' length, had launched into the chant.

He followed with *L'choh Dodi,* greeting the Sabbath bride,

and the congregation joined in the choruses. Then came the responsive reading of a psalm in English, conducted by the rabbi, and then the chanting of the *Hineni Heohni Me Maas*, the cantor's special prayer and a favorite of his, since his rendition of the chant displayed his vocal range to good advantage. Then the congregation pronounced the *Shema* aloud and then rose to recite the *Amidah* in silence. During all this, the women in the second row behaved with great propriety, standing when they were supposed to stand, reciting the responses when the occasion required.

The rabbi waited until all had finished the silent prayer and were seated, and then, adjusting his prayer shawl and fingering his skullcap to make sure it was securely in place, he came forward to the lectern in front of the *bema* to deliver his sermon. The congregation closed their prayer books and settled back. "In the portion which we shall read tomorrow," he began, and then stopped.

The women in the second row had risen in a group, shuffled out of their seats, and as boldly as they had entered marched up the aisle and out of the sanctuary.

For a moment there was a shocked silence and then muffled voices as people turned to their neighbors.

The rabbi waited until the sanctuary door had closed behind the women and then murmured, so that only those in the first few rows could catch the words, "They must have heard it before." Then he began again, "In the portion which we shall read tomorrow . . ."

They walked in silence until they turned the corner and the temple was out of sight; then Miriam said, "You handled that rather well, David. You didn't appear to be the least bit angry or disturbed."

"I wasn't. That's rather disturbing, isn't it?"

"What do you mean?" said Miriam. "I don't understand."

"I'm not sure I do, either," said the rabbi. "I should have been angry. The occasion certainly warranted it, but I wasn't. I just didn't care. I don't know why." He paused in his stride and looked at her as though expecting to be challenged. When she remained silent, he went on, "It may be that I've always resented this late service, its artificiality, the chanting of the *L'choh Dodi*, greeting the Sabbath hours after it's arrived, giving a sermon that's nothing more than a change of pace from prayers, carefully crafted so that it's not too tedious. I resent the fact that we get over a hundred people every week and have difficulty rounding up a *minyan* for the regular *maariv* service."

"But that's the way it's always been," she said at last.

"Perhaps so, but I've never had a basis of comparison."

She looked at him. "You mean because now you've been teaching?"

"That may have something to do with it," he admitted. "I'm far from satisfied with my class at the college, but at least I feel I'm doing something worthwhile there. Here, I'm not so sure. These women," he turned to her, "do you know them all? I thought I knew some of them, but there were some I'm quite sure I've never seen before."

"It was Selma Rosencranz and her bridge-playing friends," said Miriam tightly.

"Oh. I didn't realize they were so interested in religion. They chose a rather dramatic way of expressing their opinion of the Friday evening service, or perhaps of me, since they left the moment I began my sermon."

"Oh David," Miriam cried, "they don't care a fig about the service, or about your sermons."

"But they—" he stopped. "Is there something you know that I don't, Miriam?"

"Well," she said, "Selma is very friendly with Edie Fine, and there's been some talk—I can't imagine anyone taking it seriously—that you got the Selzer boy off by convincing the police that Roger Fine was a more likely suspect."

"Oh no!"

She nodded dumbly.

And now he *was* angry. She could tell by the way he strode along so that she almost had to run to keep up with him.

43

"What the hell kind of dumb play was that?" demanded Sumner Rosencranz. "What are you, some kind of hippie? Why don't you carry a sign and picket the place? How do you suppose it makes me look when my wife gets up in the middle of a service and walks out on the rabbi?"

"I thought you didn't care for him," said Selma coldly.

"What's that got to do with it? There are lots of people I don't care for, so do I go around insulting them to their faces in front of a whole bunch of people? I'm not so keen on your old lady—"

"And you show it. You show it every single solitary time she comes."

"I've never said a single goddam word to her that any reasonable person could call an insult."

"Oh, is that so? How about the time she gave you that shirt for your birthday? How about the time she asked you to stop off at the drug store and get that beauty lotion?"

"Now wait a minute. Just wait one goddam minute, will you? I've explained that dozens of times. All I said was that it wouldn't do her any good. Those expensive lotions are just a big fake and they wouldn't do anybody any good and she could put her money to better use. That's all I meant. And as for that shirt. I just said—well, all I did was criticize the shirt. That's no insult to your mother. And how about the way you treat my mother when she comes?"

"Look," said Selma, "I treat your mother the same way she treats me. If she wants to come here as a guest she's perfectly welcome, but a guest doesn't go snooping in the refrigerator and she doesn't make personal comments on my friends. My friends are strictly my business and I'm going to stand up for them. And Edie Fine has been my best friend for years. We went to school together and if someone says she's married to a murderer and what's more actually goes to the police and tells *them* he's a murderer, when she's pregnant and is supposed to stay calm and not get upset, well, I don't care if he's the rabbi of the temple or if he's the Chief Rabbi of Israel, I'm going to show him what I think no matter who's around."

"How do you know, Clare? How can you know that the rabbi fingered this guy Fine?"

"Oh Mike, it's known. Everybody knows."

"But how do they know?" he persisted. "Who told you, for instance?"

"No one actually told me. I mean no one person I can think of. We were just sitting around talking. How do you know that Columbus discovered America? Somebody told somebody who told somebody. How did everybody know that it was the rabbi who got that Selzer kid off? Everybody knew it and nobody denied it. All right, the same way people know that he was the one that accused Fine."

"Well, if Fine is guilty and the rabbi happened to know about it, isn't he supposed to tell? Isn't that what a good citizen is supposed to do?"

"Mike, how can you talk like that? A rabbi isn't supposed to do things like an ordinary citizen. Rabbis and priests, people like that, don't even have to go to court. I mean you can't even make them go on the witness stand. That's religious freedom. Besides, if the rabbi didn't do it, why doesn't he come right out and say so?"

"You got a point there."

"Well, that's what I mean. Now, Selma Rosencranz is one of my best friends. She put it before the girls and we all agreed. And I'm not sorry."

He shook his head in reluctant admiration. "I got to admit

that broad Selma's got guts. Still, it was kind of raw, getting up and walking out like that."

"Look, as far as I'm concerned, this Fine is a snooty sonofabitch. I like Edie all right. She's a nice girl, but as for that husband of hers . . ."

"You hardly know him."

"I know him well enough. The big professor! Remember that political argument we had over at Al Kaufman's house and how he jumped down my throat? He struck me as a downright radical, maybe even a Commie. And when you made some objection to something he said, he acted like you were some kind of idiot. Oh, very polite, and with high class, ten-dollar words, but anyone who disagreed with him got jumped on. Well, after hearing his Commie talk, I can believe he could do it. You know, to them it's not murder; they liquidate somebody."

"Believe me, you got him all wrong."

"Yeah? Well, if you want my opinion, if the rabbi fingered him he knew what he was doing, and this sonofabitch Fine is guilty as hell."

"This is a way for Jewish women to act? For a minute I didn't know what was happening. I thought maybe one of them got sick or something. I guess like me the rabbi didn't know what was happening either, at first. Then he couldn't help knowing. So if he got angry, who would blame him? Let me tell you, in the same position I would've been mighty sore. Anybody would. And I would've said some mighty nasty things, believe me. But not the rabbi. He stayed cool. He even smiled and made a little joke. He says everybody walks out after a sermon, but what kind of people walk out before?"

"So what was the joke he made?"

"That was it; I just told you."

"Some joke!"

"Well, it sounded funny at the time, and everybody laughed. Look, it's not whether the joke was funny or not. It's that he could make any kind of a joke at a time like that."

Gladys Lanigan handed her husband his gin and tonic and then poured one for herself. "I dropped in to the Shipshape for coffee this morning," she said. "A couple of women in the next booth were talking and I couldn't help overhearing."

"Didn't lean back and strain a little, did you?" asked Chief Lanigan affectionately.

"I did not!" She laughed. "They were talking loud enough so I didn't have to. Seems that there was some trouble at the service at the temple last night. A group of women got up and walked out just as Rabbi Small was about to give his sermon."

"They did? What for?"

"Well now, that's something I couldn't quite lean back far enough to make out. I gathered that these women were friends of the Fines, the one who was arrested for that Windemere business. They had some idea that it was the rabbi's fault. Do you know anything about it, Hugh?"

He shook his head, mystified.

"Why do people do things like that?" she exclaimed. "And the rabbi is such a nice young man."

"Just general cussedness, I suppose." He shook his head again, but this time philosophically. "They want to get rid of him. And do you know why? Because he's there. With them it's not like with us. There are plenty of people who don't like Father Aherne, but no one would think of trying to get rid of him. They wouldn't even know how to go about it. That's because he's sent here by the archbishop and we don't have any say in it. With them, they hire the rabbi and so they can fire him. But I'll tell you one thing, Gladys, for all he's so mild-mannered, David Small's as tough as nails. And he's going to stay here just as long as he wants to. There ain't no one going to push him out." He put down his glass. "I might drop by and see him tomorrow."

"Oh, I wouldn't do that," she said quickly.

"Why not?"

"Well, I gathered one reason they thought the rabbi had been able to bring it off was because he was friendly with you."

He stared at her in angry disbelief.

44

Although it was the Sabbath, a time of rest and relaxation, of quiet rejoicing, when mundane thoughts and worries are supposed to be banished from the mind of the observant Jew, the rabbi had been abstracted all day, speaking scarcely a word to Miriam. And now, in the early evening, the Sabbath over, he went into the living room and was soon lost in a book.

"Do you think he did it?" Miriam asked in annoyance. "Roger Fine. Do you think he did it?"

He shrugged. "How do I know?" And he returned to his book.

"Well, aren't you going to do anything about it?"

With a sigh of impatience, he closed his book. "What can I do?"

"At least you can go see him," she retorted.

"I'm not sure it's advisable," he said. "Fine hasn't asked to see me, and neither have his family here. What's more, considering the unpleasantness before the wedding they're not likely to, especially after this business at the temple last night. If they can spread rumors that I accused him or denounced him to the police, Lord knows what they'd make of my going to visit him at the jail."

"You never used to care what people thought," she remarked quietly. "You did what you felt you had to do, regardless of what people thought."

"So maybe I'm a little wiser now," he said cynically.

She looked up quickly. It was so unlike him. He caught her

look and felt he had to explain. "I've never been exactly a howling success here in Barnard's Crossing," he said quietly. "At first I thought it was the fault of the congregation and that once they came around, everything would be all right. Each time there was a crisis of some sort—and there's been one practically every year I've been here—when it was finally resolved, I've thought, now everything is settled and I can begin to be really effective. But then another crisis would arise. It was like that first car we had, remember? We had trouble with the ignition, and when we had it rewired we thought everything would be all right. And then the radiator went. So we got a new radiator and in less than a week the muffler let go. And then the transmission, and they wanted—what was it—two hundred dollars? Three hundred?"

"Three hundred is what we paid for the car," she murmured.

"Each time something went wrong, we thought it was a fluke, and once it was fixed everything would be all right. But when you have a series of flukes, then it's no fluke. Then Murphy's Law governs."

"Murphy's Law?"

"That's right. I first became acquainted with it when I was a chaplain in the Army. Murphy's Law states that if an accident or a foul-up can happen, it will happen. So after a while I began to think maybe it was I rather than the congregation." He smiled ruefully. "You know the old Talmudic proverb: when three people tell you you're drunk, go home and lie down."

"So you're going to lie down?"

"Miriam, if *you* don't understand—"

"I'm trying, David," she said passionately. "I'm really trying."

"Look, all the other times when I've had a row I've felt I had the respect of the congregation. While we differed on principles, at the very least they were respectful. But this—it was like a, well, a demonstration. Directed at me *personally* by my own congregation."

"Some of those women weren't even members of the congregation."

"But some of them were."

191

She was troubled. "Are you trying to say that you are tired of the rabbinate, David?"

He laughed bitterly. "No, I'd like to try that sometime, too."

"What do you mean?"

He got up and began to stride the room. "My grandfather was the rabbi of a small Orthodox congregation. He didn't make little speeches to bar mitzvah youngsters. He didn't get up to announce the page in the prayer book during holiday services. He spent his time largely in study. When anyone in his community had a question that involved their religion, they came to him and he researched it in the Talmud and answered it. When there was a dispute between two or more members of the community, they came to him and he heard all sides and passed judgment. And they abided by his verdict. He was doing the traditional work of a rabbi."

"But your father—"

"My father was a Conservative rabbi. His congregation is old and established. They have a feeling and understanding of the function of the rabbi, and they trusted him implicitly. They didn't go to him for judgment and they had no great concern for the kind of questions that my grandfather passed on. But they cared about their Judaism and they relied on my father to guide them in it."

"Well, isn't that what you do?"

"It's what I've tried to do. It's what I would do if the congregation let me. But they buck me at every turn. At first I thought I'd gradually win them over and that I'd be able to serve them as my father served his congregation."

"But—"

"But now I see that the rabbinate is not what I thought it was."

She looked at him. He seemed so dejected.

"Everything changes from generation to generation, David," she began softly. "You went into the rabbinate because you were inspired by the sight of your grandfather sitting in judgment. How about the doctor's son who was inspired to go into medicine by the drama of his father sitting through the night with a desperately sick patient? He has to be a specialist now with office hours five days a week and Wednesday afternoons off. Instead of treating the whole man, he deals with a series of hearts and stomachs. It's the same in the trades. When Mr. Macfarlane came down to fix the windows he told me his father had built the house they lived in single-handed. And during the winter, he made a lot of their furniture, too. And our Mr. Macfarlane, except for little odds and ends on the side, does nothing but lay floors. The methods change, but the profession doesn't. Doctors are still concerned with healing the sick and carpenters with building houses and rabbis with directing the Jewish community and keeping it Jewish. And how about teachers?"

"I don't feel that I've been any great success at that, either," he said glumly.

"You're talking nonsense!" She exploded. "You're an excellent rabbi and an excellent teacher, too. You have trouble with your congregation *because* you're a good rabbi."

"What do you mean by that?"

"If you want to get along well with your congregation, if you want to be popular, David, you go along with them, instead of directing them and leading them. You don't ever make them face hard truths. And if a teacher wants to be popular with his class he doesn't try to make them learn anything."

"Well, of course—"

But she could see that his mood had changed. So with a fine high scorn for logic, she said, "And you don't have to go to see Fine in jail, at least not right away. I should think you'd want to see this Bradford Ames first and find out the situation. After all, he owes you something for helping him with the Selzers."

The rabbi considered. "I might try to see him."

"Why don't you call him right now, at home? There can't be too many people named Bradford Ames, even in Boston."

Ames seemed glad to hear from him. "I'd be happy to meet with you, Rabbi. As a matter of fact, I'm coming down your way tomorrow to close up our place for the winter. Do you know where it is? . . . Then I'll expect you there sometime before noon."

45

The Ames house was on the Point, a rocky finger of land jutting out into the entrance to the harbor. It was a large, white frame structure completely encircled by a wide verandah; on the harbor side it thrust over the sea wall, and at high tide over the water itself, giving the feeling that you were aboard ship. It was a warm, Indian summer day, and Bradford Ames was enjoying it from a large wicker chair on the porch when the rabbi arrived. "Come right up, Rabbi," he said. "I thought we might sit out here in the sun while we've still got it."

David Small went over to the railing and peered into the water below. "Nice. Very nice," he said and inhaled deeply of the salt-laden air.

"I'm always a little sad when it's time to close the old place up for the winter," said Ames. "I make a point of choosing a nice day, and after I'm done I like to sit out here and take a last look at the ocean and have a drink or two before returning to the city." He motioned to the bottle on a glass-topped wicker table. "Can I offer you something, Rabbi? You people do drink, don't you?"

"Oh yes, we're not abstainers."

He filled the glasses, and seated in the large wicker armchairs they toasted each other silently. "I imagine you're interested in Roger Fine," Ames said at last. "He's a member of your congregation?"

"No, but he's a member of the Jewish community of Barnard's Crossing, and as the only rabbi in town—"

"You feel some responsibility." Ames chuckled. "And as the only rabbi on the Windemere faculty, you can claim similar responsibility for any Jewish faculty member, eh?"

"That hadn't occurred to me," the rabbi admitted, "but now that you mention it . . ."

Ames squirmed in his seat as though trying to scratch his back against the chair. "Well, I'm happy to discuss Fine with you, Rabbi. I guess you earned it when you pulled my chestnuts out of the fire by getting those students to file for bail." He had squirmed so far down into the chair that his round head was just above the level of the table top. "I mention that, Rabbi, to suggest that I'm not interested in convictions for the sake of mere convictions."

"All right."

"I'm going to tell you what we've got on Fine. I'll give you our whole case. I'll put our cards on the table, face up, all of them." He twisted his head around and peered up at the rabbi. "Now ask me why I'd want to do that?"

The rabbi grinned. "All right, why would you want to do that?"

"Because I want to help the young man. Oh, I've got a good case against him and I'm going to get a conviction. But the sentence, that's something else again. That can be anything from here to there." He held his forefingers an inch apart and then spread his arms wide.

"You mean you'd like me to influence Professor Fine, to convince him to plead guilty?"

"That might be a good thing—for him—" said Ames, "if you could bring it off. Oh, there's nothing underhanded in my suggesting it to you. I've discussed it with his lawyer, Jerry Winston."

"And?"

Ames shifted again so that he was back at full height. "It's a kind of game we play, Rabbi. In the courtroom we are distantly polite to each other, the assistant D.A.'s and the criminal lawyers. We're not above playing any courtroom tricks we can think of and lambasting each other. But outside the courtroom, we're all pretty friendly. That doesn't mean that Winston doesn't fight for his client for all he's worth, just as I do for the Commonwealth. We're professionals, you see. But there's one big difference. Winston will fight tooth and nail for an acquittal, but I'll fight for a conviction only if I'm convinced the man is guilty. That's because while we are in an adversary system, the district attorney is also concerned with the protection of the innocent."

"I understand."

Ames took another swallow of his drink. "All right, let me tell you what we've got, and then I'll explain how you can help. You understand Professor Fine was under suspicion from the beginning simply because he was in the building at the time. But we really got interested in him when we started checking *you* out." He chortled at the look of surprise on his visitor's face. "Oh yes, Rabbi, for a while you were Sergeant Schroeder's prime suspect. He was able to make quite a convincing case against you, too. There was your failure to mention you had left your class early."

"How would—"

"That meant that instead of just passing the time of day with Hendryx on your way home, you were closeted with him for about an hour. There you are, the two of you, in a dinky little office with only one desk and a somewhat rickety and uncomfortable visitor's chair, as I can personally testify." He wriggled against the fan shaped back of the wicker chair. "No chance of you two sitting there, each absorbed in his own work, correcting papers. If you were there for an hour, you were talking—a rabbi and someone who was generally considered an anti-semite. And in an hour there was plenty of time to argue and get angry, and if you got angry enough . . ."

"I see. I get so angry that I decide to kill him. And how do I go about it? I can't just reach up and pull the statue down. It's way above my reach. Did the good sergeant have an explanation for that?"

"Don't scoff, Rabbi. The sergeant made out a pretty good case. There are all kinds of discarded library books on those shelves, and in climbing up for one you happen to pull down the statue instead, thus winning the argument conclusively, you might say. The sergeant even conceded that it could even have been an accident."

"Very generous of him."

Ames chuckled. "So you are naturally flushed. Your first impulse is perhaps to tell someone, the dean naturally, but just as you round the corner you see her door close. Perhaps you take that as an omen; or perhaps it merely suggests to you that she had heard nothing untoward. In any case, you leave the building. But naturally your mind is in a turmoil, so you drive around for a while in order to decide what to do. And that is why you were late getting home. Then when you do get home, you hear about the bombing and you realize that this could give the incident another dimension. So when the sergeant calls up you make an excuse not to see him to give yourself time to find out just what happened and to prepare a story."

"It does add up to a good case," the rabbi admitted.

"And I might point out that since you had a key to the office, you could get in without making Hendryx get out of his seat. Anyone else would have to knock. It really is a good case," said Ames almost regretfully.

"But you didn't buy it."

Ames shook his head, his mouth set in a wide grin. "I don't know that Schroeder did either, really. I suspect it was merely justification for him to give you a hard time."

"A hard time? But why should he want to?"

"Well, he probably considered your treatment of him when he phoned pretty cavalier. It rankled. You've got to understand a man like Schroeder. He is pretty near the top of his ambitions. As a sergeant of detectives, he operates largely on his own. He takes orders from his superiors, of course, but with the general public, especially when he's on an important case, he's his own boss and not used to having his authority flouted."

"But he didn't give me a hard time."

"Because I vetoed it. I told him I'd question you myself. Your excuses for the long delay in getting home that Friday and for neglecting to tell the sergeant about walking out of your class were so ingenuous I could only believe they were the truth."

The rabbi grinned.

197

"But of course that was simply my gut reaction. In all conscience I couldn't dismiss the sergeant's interpretation out of hand. A stupid man will offer what seems to him a plausible explanation of his suspicious actions, but there'll be obvious holes in it and we'll be able to break it down just from its internal contradictions. A more intelligent man will offer a plausible explanation with no apparent holes or contradictions. It will not necessarily allay our suspicions but we'll probably have to find additional evidence to disprove it." He paused. "An extremely intelligent man, Rabbi, might present a completely implausible explanation."

"Are you saying I'm still under suspicion?" asked the rabbi.

Ames shook his head. "No, you cleared yourself when you pointed out the contradiction between the medical examiner's report and the cleaning woman's testimony. If you were guilty, there'd be no point in your demonstrating that the book and the pipe in Hendryx's apartment was an alibi, and then going on to disprove it."

"Well, it's a relief to know that I'm not a suspect," said the rabbi, "even though it never occurred to me that I ever was. But you said you began to suspect Roger Fine in the course of checking me out."

"That's right. You got us to thinking about how that statue could have fallen, now that we were quite certain it had not been jarred loose by the bomb. It could be knocked down by somebody climbing up there, like you, but it's not too likely. It's pretty heavy, for one thing. Sixty-two pounds, seven ounces, not easily toppled by a sideswipe of the hand. And Hendryx wouldn't just sit there watching."

"It's what occurred to me when you first suggested it," said the rabbi, "my preparation for the defense, you might say."

Ames nodded. "So what would knock it down? We cemented the shards together and experimented with it. You couldn't do it with a stick—no leverage. If you had a long pole, like a window pole, you could insinuate it behind the statue and then pull. That would do it, but it would fall to one side. But if you had a stick with a hook on the end—"

"A stick with a hook?"

"Like a cane. Then it's child's play. You just reach around with the handle of the cane and pull. So there you have opportunity: he was in the building at the time. And weapon—"

"But the statue was the weapon and anyone could have used it," the rabbi objected.

Ames shook his head. "It was there all right, but only a man with a cane could have used it. Professor Fine is the only man in the school who has a cane with him all the time."

The rabbi was silent for a moment and then asked quietly, "And motive? What was his motive?"

Ames waved a hand in airy dismissal. "Who knows what really motivates a man? Frequently he doesn't know himself. We can only surmise or guess—until he confesses. We know they had quarrelled, that Fine considered him an antisemite—"

"He made sly little digs, an occasional joke, nothing that would justify anything more than a sharp rejoinder," said the rabbi.

"From you. But Professor Fine is a much younger man. Still, I'll go along with you, not enough motive for murder. But then we picked up this Ekko, the fifth member of that student committee, and after a while he talked. And it turned out that Professor Fine had opposed that meeting with the dean and even had opposed the student campaign to make the school change its mind about dropping him."

"But why?" asked the rabbi.

"Exactly," said Ames. "That's what we couldn't understand. Until Ekko revealed something Fine had told him in confidence. You see, at the end of the summer session, Professor Fine leaked the final exam to one of the students. Hendryx found out about it and reported it."

"Fine admits this?"

"In writing, Rabbi, in writing," said Ames. "His written confession was in the safe in the dean's office. It was an earnest that he would not make trouble if they let him continue to the end of his contract."

"And Ekko tried to blow up the safe to destroy it?"

"No, no," Ames said hastily. "That's what we thought at first.

But it turns out he had nothing to do with the bombing, nothing at all."

The rabbi waited to hear who in fact was responsible for the bombing, but when he saw Ames was not about to amplify his remark, he said: "Surely you're not suggesting that Fine killed Hendryx because he reported him to the dean?"

"It gives him a motive," Ames pointed out.

"You say that all happened last summer. He certainly seems to have taken his time about it," remarked the rabbi dryly.

"Sometimes these things smoulder," Ames said.

"And they usually continue to smoulder until the resentment dies out and is forgotten," said the rabbi.

"But suppose something happened the day of the murder that was quite capable of puffing it into flame?" suggested Ames. "What if something happened that made it look as though Fine might never get another teaching job? How do you think Fine would feel about that?"

"What was that?" asked the rabbi.

"Well, I'll admit I don't know too much about college hiring practices," Ames said lazily, "but I'd guess that while references from an acting head might not be necessary, since his function is purely administrative, one from the permanent head of the department is. And the very day of the murder, Rabbi, Hendryx was made head of the English department!"

The rabbi pursed his lips. "Hendryx didn't mention it to me."

"He wouldn't be likely to since it had not been officially announced. President Macomber told the dean not to say anything until the board met and made it official."

"Then how could Fine know of it?"

"Ah, my guess is that Hendryx told him." He looked at the rabbi, obviously enjoying his puzzlement. "You see, Hendryx and Betty, the president's daughter, were going to be married and she got her father to make the appointment." He chuckled. "Dean Hanbury had been campaigning for the appointment right along without success, but then a daughter, an only daughter, carries more clout, I imagine. I can see how Macomber would find it hard to refuse her."

The rabbi still didn't see how that involved Fine.

"Oh come, Rabbi, use a little imagination. Remember, this Ekko has told us Fine was against the student campaign on his behalf because he has promised the dean, and presumably Hendryx, he will not make trouble. And here's a committee coming to present a petition in his behalf that very afternoon. So with the dean tied up, Fine goes up to Hendryx's office to assure him the committee was not his idea. I can imagine Hendryx, who'd heard of his appointment the night before from Betty Macomber, leaning back in that way you've described and relishing the situation to the hilt. I can imagine him taking a certain sadistic pleasure in informing the young man that now he was the regular head of the department, and that Fine was not to expect any letter of recommendation from him, perhaps he'd even better begin thinking of going into another line of work."

"Perhaps," said the rabbi. "It seems that the motive is mostly your imagination."

"You're not speaking objectively there, Rabbi," Ames said reproachfully. "You're speaking like the attorney for the defense. It's not time for that yet."

"All right, go on. Or is that all of it? How about the alibi? Have you worked out how Fine could have got into Hendryx's apartment?"

Ames beamed. "I'm rather pleased with myself on that score. I questioned the cleaning woman again, and it seems it was her custom to leave the door unlatched while she went in and out, emptying wastebaskets and things. She simply forgot to reset the latch when she left. Quite characteristic of cleaning women, I assure you."

"But how would Fine know that? Or is it your theory that he just took pot luck?"

"Ah, we have evidence from other people in the department that Hendryx was always complaining about his cleaning woman, about the way she always left the door unlocked, among other things."

The rabbi was silent and Ames waited a few seconds before going on. "So there we have it: opportunity, motive, weapon

—the last peculiar to the accused. So we picked Fine up and questioned him. He denied everything, of course, and refused to give an account of his actions for that afternoon."

"He's within his rights, isn't he?" asked the rabbi.

"Of course. But why should he refuse? If he has an alibi, he has only to tell us. We'd check it out, and if it stands up we'd release him. But if it's not a very good alibi, a rigged alibi, say, that he intends to spring on us at the trial so that we couldn't check it out in advance—and that sort of thing might occur to a smart young man like Fine—well, Rabbi, you'd be doing him a favor to convince him of his folly. Because we'd break that alibi, believe me. But the fact that he tried it could have a very serious effect on the judge and on the sentence. I've talked to Winston about it."

"And what does he say?"

Ames smiled. "Oh, defense lawyers never admit anything. It's part of the game. Even when they're plea bargaining, they don't admit that their client is guilty. I don't think Jerry would go for an alibi if he knew it was rigged, but he might if he didn't know for certain."

"Can I see him?"

"Fine? I think so. I'd like to clear it with Jerry Winston first, though. I'll call him tomorrow, and you can see him Tuesday."

She was small and thin. She was wearing a long cotton maxi-dress that all but trailed the ground. It was gathered under the breasts and served to emphasize them, especially since she was obviously not wearing a bra. Dangling against her cleavage was a large silver crucifix on a black velvet ribbon.

Her brown hair was combed straight down and held away from her face by the bows of her granny spectacles. She had large dark eyes and was attractive in a sad, subdued way.

"Rabbi Small?" She was waiting for him outside his classroom.

"Yes?"

"I'm—my name is Kathy Dunlop, and I wonder if I could speak to you for a few minutes."

"Certainly, Miss Dunlop." He looked at her inquiringly. "What do you want to talk to me about?"

"Well, it might take a little more than a few minutes. I thought if you had some time . . ."

"By all means. Why don't you come to my office?"

She nodded gratefully and followed him down the corridor. He offered her the visitor's chair and then sat down in the swivel chair behind the desk and waited.

She fingered the cross at her bosom and then took courage to begin. "Well, this friend of mine, this girl friend, Rabbi, she's Christian like me. She doesn't go to school here, but I told her about you, I mean about you being a rabbi and giving a course here, and she asked me to ask you."

"I see."

"Well, like I say, she's Christian and she's in love with this Jewish boy."

"And they want to marry?" prompted the rabbi.

"Well, not right away, you understand. I mean, she loves him and he loves her. She's sure of it. I mean, I know them both and there's no question about it."

"All right," he said softly, "I'll take your word for it."

"Well, what I want to know, that is, what she wants to know, what she wanted me to ask you, is if she should want to change over—"

"To convert to Judaism?"

"That's right," said Kathy. "What would she have to do?"

He smiled. "Well, she'd have to see a rabbi."

The girl dropped the cross. "Of course, I know a rabbi would have to do it, but what would *she* have to do?"

David Small leaned back in his chair. "I suppose it would

depend on which rabbi she went to see. Most rabbis would tell her that she should give up the boy and look for someone of her own faith."

"You mean the rabbi wouldn't do it?" she said with surprise. "But that's not fair. I mean if you believe yours is the true religion, I should think you'd owe it to anyone who was interested to—well—to show them the way, to convince them, to offer them salvation."

"But we don't deal in salvation, Miss Dunlop," he said.

"You don't? But you do convert people, because I know someone who was."

"Yes, we do, but we don't encourage it," he said. "It is not easy to be a Jew, so the rabbi usually discourages them, for their own sake. In theory we're not supposed to convert for any reason other than conviction, not just because someone wants to marry a Jew, for example."

"Well, if someone is in love with a Jew, and wants to—you know, share with him and think the way he thinks—I don't think it's fair!" she repeated. "I mean, if you know something that I don't know, and you think it's the truth, shouldn't you want to tell me? Couldn't this girl being in love with this boy, couldn't that be what gets her started in being convicted, I mean convinced?"

"Yes," he said. "In fact, I suppose that's the rationale used by most rabbis in these cases." He sighed. How to deal with this girl, so intense, so serious. He wondered if she was pregnant and if what he would say was necessary to help her decide what to do about her immediate problem. "Why do you wear that cross?" he asked.

"Oh, does that bother you?"

"No. I just wondered. Do you wear it all the time, or did you just happen to put it on today?" He wondered whether she regarded it as a kind of talisman to protect her when talking to a rabbi.

"I wear it because I'm a Christian," she said. "I told you that."

"Yes, but most Christians don't wear large silver crosses."

"Well, it's a gift, a special gift from my father. He's a minister," she said. "He converts people all the time. I mean, that's really part of his ministry, to bring people to Jesus."

"And how does he convert them?" the rabbi asked.

"He preaches to them, of course. He convinces them that the way of Jesus will make them into better people, that they'll be like born again, and they'll be rid of their sins."

"And what do they have to do?"

"They've got to just accept Jesus. That's all it takes—they've got to be willing to accept Jesus, to open their hearts and let Him come in, because if someone has faith in Him, that's pretty much all that's required."

"Well, it's a little different with us," he said. "You see, ours is not a religion in that sense. The things we believe in, I suppose many people who are not Jews also believe. That doesn't make them Jews, though. And there are many Jews who don't hold these beliefs and are still Jews. The rule of thumb is that anyone born of a Jewish mother who did not convert is a Jew. It's more a matter of belonging to the Jewish people, the family, than of accepting certain specific beliefs."

"But I don't understand. If it's a religion—"

"Did you ever study Roman history?"

She seemed surprised. "Yes, in high school, but what's that got to do with it?"

"Do you know what the *lares* and *penates* were?"

"Oh, let me see," she said, as if called on to recite in class. "Weren't they like idols or statues that the Latins or the Romans had in their houses?"

"Something like that," said the rabbi. "They were the household gods, the family gods. The gods that particular family took with them wherever they went. Well, Miss Dunlop, it's a little that way with us. Judaism is a family religion. It's a set of beliefs, practices, rituals, a way of life, that is peculiar to our people, to our family, to the descendants of Abraham. Conversion is like being adopted into the family. The convert even takes a new name, a Jewish name, usually Abraham for a male and Sarah for a female."

"So what do you have to do?" she asked, impatient now. "To be adopted that way, I mean?"

"First of all," he said, "you have to learn the practices and the rituals."

"Do all Jews know them?"

"No," he conceded, "but converts must."

"Does it take a long time?"

"Months, sometimes years."

"Years? But that doesn't seem fair. I mean where some Jews don't know them."

"I suppose the idea is primarily to discourage conversion," he said. "But there is also the theory that anyone who was born a Jew acquired the knowledge and the way of life subconsciously, imbibed it with his mother's milk, so to speak. Someone else would have to work at it."

"But years!"

The rabbi nodded sympathetically. "It hardly seems worthwhile, does it? Why don't you suggest to your friend that she try to forget this boy, give him up? At first it may seem impossible, that she can't live without him, but she'll find that she can. You know, people are always falling in love with people they can't marry. They may already be married, for instance." He smiled. "Well, they usually live through it."

She remained silent, making no move to leave.

"Does this, what I've told you, does it come as a shock to you?" he asked kindly.

"No, it's what *he* said." She drew a deep breath, and her face took on a new determination. "Rabbi, you know Professor Fine, don't you? The one who was arrested?"

"Yes," he said, "I know him. Why?"

"Well, he didn't do it. He couldn't have because he was with me. When it happened, I mean."

Slowly the rabbi brought the chair to an upright position. "Yes? And where was that?"

"It was at a motel, the Excelsior, on Route 128. I got us a room and then I phoned him here at the school to tell him the number and he came right out."

"And what time did he leave?"

"A quarter past two."

He looked at her. "How do you happen to be so sure of the time?"

"Because after I took the room I—I wasn't sure," she said. "I mean I was kind of scared. I'd never done anything like this before. And the way the motel woman looked at me when I told her my husband had stopped off to pick up some things and would join me later . . . See, it's right next to like a shopping center. So I thought maybe I'd go back to the office and tell her I changed my mind and ask for my money back. Then I thought I'd just get into my car and drive off without saying anything and just forget about the money. Then I thought I'd wait until a quarter past two."

"Why a quarter past?"

"Because it was a few minutes after at the time and a quarter past seemed a good time to decide definitely. My watch just shows the quarter hours. It doesn't show the minutes in between. See?" She held her wrist out to him.

"And that's when you called him?"

She nodded.

"Is there a switchboard at the motel, or can you call outside directly?"

"Oh, I didn't use the phone in the room. There's a pay station just outside in the parking lot. I used that. I thought the motel woman might listen in."

"I see. How did you happen to pick that motel in the first place?" he asked.

She dropped her eyes. "One of the girls in the dorm said it was a good place."

"I see. And what time did Professor Fine get there?"

"I—I don't know exactly. But he said he was starting right out, and he wouldn't—I mean, if he were coming out to me, he wouldn't—"

"No, I don't think he would, either," said the rabbi kindly. Then, "Did you have any occasion to notice the time when he arrived?"

She shook her head slowly. "Not until later when I thought it might be late for him, but he said he had plenty of time. His wife was going to some party and he'd told her he'd be staying in town."

"Do the police know any of this?"

"Of course not, or he'd be free now, wouldn't he?"

"If they believed him," he said. "Did anyone see you together at the motel?"

She shook her head vigorously. "I'm sure they didn't. We were very careful. That's why we arranged that I should take the room. He didn't want to be seen. He was afraid, with his cane and his red hair and all, that the manager would remember him and someday it might come out."

"I see."

"He wouldn't tell them," she insisted, "because he wouldn't want to involve me."

"Even though it means staying in jail?"

"Oh yes," she said positively.

David Small filled out his permit form and slid it into the shallow tray under the thick glass bullet-proof shield.

"Just like a bank," he said.

The guard laughed automatically. The remark was made dozens of times a day. "Yeah, it's a bank all right. Now if you'll empty your pockets and walk through the scanner."

The rabbi deposited his wallet, loose change, and wristwatch in a little pile and stepped under an archway.

"Now back."

The needle on the dial moved.

"You still got metal on you."

The rabbi patted his pockets. He inserted his hand in the side pocket of his jacket and felt the tear in the lining he was always forgetting to ask Miriam to mend. He came up with a stub of pencil. "It fell down inside the lining," he explained. "I forgot I had it."

"All right. Now walk through again. Okay now."

"You mean the pencil registered?"

"The metal eraser holder," said the guard.

Rabbi Small collected his belongings and was directed down a short corridor and through a heavy door of steel bars which clicked closed behind him. "First door on your left," the guard called after him. "You wait there."

It was a small room with only a few chairs and a table as furniture. As he waited, the rabbi wondered what he would say. Did Fine know what had happened at the temple Friday night? Should he ask him about it? Should he mention that he was here at Ames' suggestion? The door opened and Roger Fine entered. Behind him was a middle-aged black prison guard.

"I have to wait out here, Professor Fine," said the guard, "but you can close the door."

"Okay, John, thanks. By the way, this is Rabbi Small. He also teaches at Windemere. John Jackson, Rabbi. His boy is a student at Windemere."

"Hello, Rabbi," said the guard, and drew the door of the room closed behind him.

"His boy was one of those I tutored in the summer and managed to get in," said Fine. "Nice kid."

"I heard of your program," said the rabbi. "That took considerable courage, I imagine."

"Not courage, Rabbi; concern." He flung himself into the seat and hooked his cane on the edge of the nearby table. He seemed thinner than when the rabbi had last seen him, and his face was drawn.

"And how has it worked out?" asked the rabbi. "The ones you tutored, have they done well?"

Fine shrugged. "Some worked out all right; some not so good. You've been hobnobbing with the Establishment. What do they say about it?"

The rabbi laughed shortly. "I certainly wouldn't call it hobnobbing—an occasional coffee in the cafeteria. And I didn't realize they were the Establishment, just some of the older members of the faculty. But I gathered from them that the group you were tutoring hadn't had college preparatory training, that they were from Roxbury, and most of them had been out of school for several years."

"What of it?" demanded Fine. "The experience of making it in the ghetto was ten times more valuable than a course in Latin or algebra in high school."

"Perhaps so," said the rabbi, "but that's not the point, is it? A course in algebra might not be very useful in the ghetto, but it's probably necessary preparation for college physics or chemistry."

"Well that's why we were tutoring them during the summer," said Fine heatedly.

"But how much could you hope to accomplish? If you could cover several years of college prep work in a couple of months, then our secondary school system is a fraud. If not, your tutoring project would be a fraud intended only to gain them admittance to a course of study they couldn't possibly pursue."

"What of it?"

"What of it?" the rabbi echoed.

"Sure, what of it?" Fine laughed scornfully. "What sort of place do you think Windemere is? Or any college? It's a fossilized institution like—like the electoral college, or the British monarchy, or the House of Lords. The college today is simply an institution for maintaining a plutocratic class structure. It's intended for . . ." his voice trailed off as he saw his visitor's gaze fixed beside him. He turned and, following the rabbi's gaze, saw a cockroach scuttling along. He knocked it down with his cane and then calmly stepped on it. "It's not the Ritz, but it's free." He laughed. "That's one of the things they say here. Not very funny, but it keeps their spirits up, I suppose."

The rabbi nodded and then, after a suitable pause, continued. "It's curious. Professor Hendryx also thought the college was no longer for the purpose of educating young people. But he thought its present function was to subsidize college professors."

"He would," said Fine. "But if you examine its effect on society, you see all college does is to divide the sheep from the goats, the white collars from the blue."

"I'm surprised you're willing to be a party to it then," said the rabbi pleasantly.

"Ah, but there's a little side-effect maybe the Establishment hadn't figured on, and that's why we were in it and were willing to do this summer tutoring thing."

"And that is?"

"Anyone from the wrong side of the fence who does manage to make it is automatically socially upgraded. There's no denying college is the main road to social advancement. That's a fact recognized by all sociologists and most educators."

"I'm afraid I don't have the same faith in the wisdom of sociologists and educators that you have."

"But dammit, Rabbi—"

"My view is naturally the traditional Jewish one," he went on imperturbably, "that learning is to be pursued for itself. A college, that is a liberal arts college like Windemere, is a place for those who want to know more than they have acquired in high school. If you change it into a vehicle for social upgrading, as you call it, or into anything too practical, for that matter, it no longer performs its function."

"You mean you'd limit liberal arts schools just to the smartest kids?"

"Not at all, although I don't know what you mean by the smartest kids, or how you'd go about selecting them. Marks usually reward the most docile students, those who conform to their teachers' opinions. There's nothing competitive about learning, it's something everyone does for himself alone. A fat man who joins a gym to reduce is not competing with someone who is there to improve his muscle tone, or even with someone else who is there also to reduce. Each is there to satisfy his own needs."

"So according to you, the only ones who should go to the liberal arts college—"

"Are not the smartest, but those who really want to be there, who want to know more than they do," said the rabbi.

Fine could barely conceal a slight triumphant smile as he said: "Then why object to our program of bringing blacks into college?"

"I don't," said the rabbi, not in the least disconcerted. "For those who want to learn, no objection at all, provided they have the necessary preparation. Because without that, they won't be able to do the work, just as the fat man in the gym wouldn't be able to take advantage of the physical regimen if he had a serious heart condition. And you won't be doing them a kindness. Quite the contrary."

The red-haired young man sat back in his chair and shook his head slowly in wonderment. Then he grinned. Then he laughed aloud.

"Have I said something funny?" asked the rabbi.

"No, you're all right, Rabbi. You know, when my lawyer told me you were coming I wondered what for. Were you coming to see the condemned man to urge him to confess? To tell the truth, I wasn't too keen on it, but Winston, that's my lawyer, seemed to think it was worthwhile. And here we sit in a little room in the city jail and we're talking—of all things—about educational theory and philosophy. You've got to admit, Rabbi, that's funny."

The rabbi grinned. "You're right, it is funny."

Fine leaned forward. "I'd love to go along with your theory, Rabbi, but the system itself militates against your precious love of learning. Taking courses in a dozen different fields with no continuity, no association, the subject matter forgotten within days after taking the exam—all it does is prevent anyone from getting a decent education. Why, the average graduate can't write a decent paragraph—"

"And whose fault is that?" the rabbi countered. "You've relaxed your standards because you no longer think it's your function to teach, just to upgrade socially, and you don't care how it's done. Any way the student gets his pass mark will do, just so long as he gets by."

Fine eyed the rabbi narrowly. "Is that a general comment,

Rabbi, or are you perhaps referring to a little difficulty I had with Hendryx and the dean?"

"I know about it."

"Oh yes, you shared an office with Hendryx."

"But he didn't tell me," said the rabbi quickly.

"Then who—" Fine shook his head. "It doesn't matter now."

"Tell me," said the rabbi, "do you happen to know a Kathy Dunlop?"

The atmosphere chilled perceptibly and immediately. "Yes, I know Kathy," Fine admitted cautiously. "What about her?"

"She came to see me yesterday."

"And she told you?"

"No, she said nothing about the exam. She wanted to know how a girl would go about getting converted to Judaism. It seems that some friend of hers is in love with a Jewish boy."

Fine moved in his chair uneasily. "Is that so?"

"Of course," the rabbi went on, "it was quite obvious she was talking about herself. Preliminary inquiries are quite frequently made that way. Was it you she was thinking of marrying?"

The man remained silent. The rabbi waited, and when it looked as though Fine was not going to speak, he went on. "She said you were lovers."

Abruptly Fine rose and circled his chair. "Yes," he said, "I love Kathy. But don't get the idea that I ever suggested I might divorce my wife to marry her." He perched on the edge of the table.

"Apparently she had that idea."

Fine shrugged. "Not with any encouragement from me. I even told her I would never marry anyone but a Jewish girl, and I meant it. Do you believe me?"

The rabbi thought for a moment. "Yes, I believe you."

"Does it surprise you?"

"No."

"Well, it surprises me." He threw himself back in the chair. "It doesn't make sense to me, but it's true; it's how I feel. Here I am, modern, enlightened, intellectual, and, in all modesty, even intelligent. My reason tells me that religion, prayer, faith

—the whole bit—is a lot of nonsense. I'm sorry, Rabbi, but that's how I feel. And yet I married a Jewish girl, and wouldn't marry one who wasn't. I suppose it's because it would upset my parents; and yet, I'm not particularly close to them. It's crazy, isn't it?"

"It's not so crazy," said the rabbi. "I know a Jew who is completely divorced from Judaism, but will not permit butter on his table at home when he is eating meat. Claims it upsets his stomach. And yet, always eats butter with his meat when he's in a restaurant."

"I'm afraid I don't get the connection. Yes, I suppose I do. You mean that in certain matters the most rational of us is irrational."

"Tell me, how do your folks feel about your being here?"

"They don't know. They're on one of these three week tours of Israel. I'm hoping to get out of this mess before they get back."

"And if you don't?"

The young man raised his hand to his forehead in a gesture of despair.

"Kathy—" prompted the rabbi. "You saw her that afternoon. That phone call you were waiting for, it was from her?"

"What about it?" he said belligerently.

"It might get you out of here. It could give you an alibi."

Fine leaned forward and spoke heatedly, "If she goes to the police with that story, or if you do, I'll deny it. I'll say she's just a crazy kid with a bad crush on me and with an overactive imagination. She'd have no way of corroborating her story; I took precautions not to be seen."

"But why?"

"Because it would ruin my marriage, probably end it," he said. "Don't you understand? I love my wife."

"You just admitted loving Kathy."

"So what? Monogamy is a social institution; it's not a natural law, not even of human psychology. I wouldn't go to bed with Kathy if I didn't love her. But that doesn't mean I don't love my wife. If you were ten years younger and not a rabbi, you might understand."

214

"I have been ten years younger, and I wasn't a rabbi at the time," he said good-naturedly, "and I have a good memory. I'd like to try to understand."

"All right," said Roger Fine. "My wife and I have a good marriage. We enjoy each other in bed. Right now, she's carrying my child, and I'm glad that it's with her that I'm going to have a child. But Kathy—Look, Edie is a nice, proper, middle-class Jewish girl. And that's a good type, but it has its limitations. With Kathy, we had this great yearning for each other, and when we came together there was total surrender of mind and soul and body, each to the other. It was good, so it cannot be wrong."

"I see."

"Do you?" Fine asked eagerly. "Do you really?"

"Of course. You want to have your cake and eat it, too."

"I'm sticking my neck out, you know," said Chief Lanigan, as he maneuvered the blue official car with its gold Barnard's Crossing police insignia into the heavy traffic of Route 128.

"Because it's in Swampdale rather than Barnard's Crossing?" asked the rabbi. "It's only across the line."

"Oh, Swampdale's no problem. Barney Rose there is a good friend of mine and wouldn't mind me coming into his territory to do some routine checking. No, I'm thinking of the Boston police. This is their case, and they might not take kindly to interfering."

"I see what you mean," said the rabbi. Then he brightened. "But strictly speaking, you're just checking out Kathy Dunlop's story. If you discover that she was not alone, that there was a man with her in the motel, a red-haired man with a limp, that could be Professor Fine who lives in Barnard's Crossing and that *would* fall under your jurisdiction."

"Yeah, yeah, David, maybe that kind of hair-splitting is acceptable to your rabbinical friends, but I'd hate to try it on Schroeder or Bradford Ames." He glanced at his companion. "Not that I'm really worried; just grousing. That's how cops make conversation."

"Well, in any case, I appreciate your taking the trouble."

"Oh, it's no trouble." Lanigan had a thought, and laughed. "You're sure you weren't worried the motel guy might think you were the girl's husband?"

"Well, that entered my mind, too," said the rabbi grinning. "Do you know anything about the place, its reputation?"

"It used to be chickens," said Lanigan with seeming irrelevance. "A guy worked for a salary all his life and saved up a little money and then decided he was tired of it, tired of the city, the dirt, and the noise. He and the missus would be hankering for a place in the country, and somebody would sell him the idea of a chicken farm. Just enough work to keep your mind from going wooly, fresh country air, and a regular income from eggs and poultry. Joe Gargan, who retired as lieutenant, was all hepped up about it. His last year on the force, he carried the literature with him whenever he'd come on duty. He'd tell me how you pay so much for feed and sell your eggs for so much and then you sell the birds themselves at so much a pound. There was no way you could miss. Except of course, sometimes feed costs went up and you couldn't make a profit. And sometimes disease would wipe out your stock. And then there were other expenses that you didn't figure on.

"Well, sir, chickens have had it. Now it's franchises, I understand. You pay down your life's savings and maybe go in hock for a lot more to operate a stand that sells somebody's hamburgers or hot dogs or ice cream. They tell you how you're working for yourself and they can prove it's bound to be successful."

He shook his head in wonder. "But for a while there, it was motels. All you had to do was make up the beds in the morning and put clean towels in the bathroom. A morning's work for a man and his wife, or for just the wife, while the man ran the office."

"The Excelsior is managed by a husband and wife?"

"Yeah. It's right by a small shopping center. You know how it is with these motels. If they're in a good location and get plenty of business, they'll operate nice and legal and respectable. But let business slack off and they tend to get a little careless, like renting rooms to hookers or college kids who are looking for a roll in the hay for a couple of hours."

"And how is business at the Excelsior?"

"So-so. Did she happen to say why she picked the place?"

"Only that it had been recommended by one of the girls in the dorm," said the rabbi dryly.

"Doesn't surprise me. Well, here we are."

A brass nameplate on a triangular block of mahogany identified ALFRED R. JACKSON, MGR. Jackson, dressed in sport shirt and golf sweater, came out to meet them and introduced himself. "Is there something I can do for you gentlemen?"

"Like to use your phone," said Lanigan.

"Sure, go ahead." He slid it over.

"Anything wrong?" he asked the rabbi, as the chief dialed.

Rabbi Small shook his head. Lanigan spoke a few words into the receiver and then hung up. "Just a routine inquiry," he said. "Can I see your register for the thirteenth of this month?"

"Anybody in particular?" asked Jackson as he went to the card file. "The thirteenth, that was a Friday?"

"That's right. Katherine or Kathleen Dunlop. She would have registered sometime that afternoon."

"Here's a Mrs. Kathy Dunlop. Mass. license plate 863–529. Came in at 1:52." He pulled the card and put it on the desk.

"That's not Mrs.," said the rabbi. "It's Ms."

"Oh yeah, that's right. Women's Lib." He laughed as though it were a good joke.

"Was she alone?" asked Lanigan.

"Gosh, I don't remember, Captain—er Chief. I remember the day all right on account it was Friday the thirteenth. I'm not superstitious, but you know how it is."

"She said there was a woman in charge," the rabbi remarked to Lanigan.

"How about it?" asked the chief.

"Oh, that would be my wife. Just a minute." He opened a door and called inside, "Martha, want to come out front a minute?"

They were joined by a woman in a housedress, her hair elaborately done up in plastic curlers. "I look a mess," she apologized. "Just getting ready to go out."

"These gentlemen are interested in a Kathy Dunlop who registered with us on Friday the thirteenth, early afternoon. You remember her? You checked her in."

"Yes, I do. A little bit of a thing. Nice girl."

"What makes you say that?" asked Lanigan.

"Well, I don't really know, of course, except that she was quiet and polite and—oh yes, she was wearing a cross, so I guess she didn't seem like some of these girls you see around nowadays. She told me she'd been driving straight through from the night before and needed some sleep, so I put her in Number 6 where she wouldn't be disturbed by people coming in later to register. And oh yes, she asked if there was a phone in the room, and I told her she'd either have to use the pay station across the way in the parking lot or the one here in the office." To her husband she said, "Don't you remember, Al? I said Friday the thirteenth was unlucky, and that was the day we had trouble with the switchboard."

Lanigan asked if she had used the phone in the office.

"Not that I remember. Besides, the one in the parking lot is nearer."

"What about visitors?"

"Well now, I don't spy on my guests," she said virtuously. "A guest rents a room, he can have people come to see him same as if it was his own home. I don't go around snooping."

"Did you see anyone with her? A red-haired man with a cane?" Lanigan prompted.

Mrs. Jackson shook her head positively.

"Who else was registered at the time?" asked the rabbi.

She looked inquiringly at her husband. "That couple from Texas?"

"No, they checked out at the regular check-out time. That's eleven o'clock. We must have been empty at the time," he said.

She amplified. "This time of year, people don't start checking in until late afternoon or early evening." She flipped through the cards in the file. "Here—4:20, 4:38, 5:02."

"What time did Miss Dunlop check out?" asked Lanigan.

The woman colored. "Why, I seem to remember that she stopped by in the evening to leave the key and say she was going out for a bite. I don't think—no—I'm sure of it; she didn't come back. You remember, Al, I said I thought she might have gone to a movie."

Lanigan asked Mrs. Jackson whether she had made up the girl's room the next morning, whether the bed had been slept in.

"I don't remember," she said, warily. "I'm sure it must've been or I would've remembered."

"One person or two?"

"How would I know that?"

"Oh, you'd know all right."

"I—I don't remember."

As they drove off, Lanigan said, "I'm sorry, David, but I'm afraid your friend Fine had no alibi. Neither the manager nor his wife saw him, there were no guests in the motel, and with the phone out of order no one could have called in and thus confirm he was there at a certain hour."

"There's the girl . . ."

Lanigan shook his head. "Not very good. No corroboration. And she's in love with him obviously, so it wouldn't be hard to believe she'd lie for him. Of course, Fine's lawyer might put her on the stand and hope she'd make a good impression on the jury. And she might, too, until the D.A. started tearing into her. He'd make her out to be a common whore, even worse for knowing he was a married man."

49

Lanigan and the rabbi entered the station house, and the desk sergeant called out, "Say, Chief. Grace just phoned from the neighbor's to say she's locked out. All right if I run down and let her in?"

"Okay," said Lanigan, "I'll cover the desk."

He glanced over the blotter. "How come you didn't log in the call?"

"Why, it's my wife, Chief. It's a personal call."

"A citizen phones to say she's locked out of her house and I dispatch a sergeant to help her. That's regular business. Every call has to be recorded, you know that. All right, get going."

Lanigan shook his head as he logged in the call. "Are you planning to go to see Mrs. Fine, David?"

The question caught the rabbi unprepared. "Why would I do that?" he asked.

Lanigan regarded him with interest. "Well, you saw her husband in jail, didn't you? All I know is if it was one of ours, the priest would go as a matter of course."

"But I'm not a priest. I don't have that sort of relationship with the people in my congregation. Besides," he said, "I had some trouble with her a while back."

"Oh?" said Lanigan.

"It was nothing serious," said the rabbi.

Driving home, he was far from convinced that he should see Mrs. Fine. For all he knew she was not even at home, she probably had gone back to her parents, and he certainly had no desire to face Mr. and Mrs. Chernow as well.

But he had to pass the Fine house and when he saw a light on he stopped.

Edie Fine opened to his ring. "Oh, it's you, Rabbi," she said, obviously surprised. "I—I was just on my way to my folks—"

"May I come in?"

"Well, all right, but I don't have too much time. I'm due there for dinner." She led the way into the living room. "I suppose you want to tell me you had nothing to do with Roger being— I mean, that business Friday night, I didn't put them up to it, you know."

"It's quite all right, Mrs. Fine. As a matter of fact, I saw your husband this morning. I found him not at all depressed."

"Well, I'm glad to hear that. Of course, I know it's all a horrid mistake, and it could happen to anyone, but it makes you wonder."

"What does it make you wonder, Mrs. Fine?"

"Why, about all sorts of things. Whether there's any justice in the world. About the police and the law courts and—if it pays to be decent—"

"Mrs. Fine!" He spoke sharply. "I am pleased to say that your husband appears to be bearing up well under this ordeal. I suppose that's because he is certain of his innocence. When I see him again, I should like to tell him you are bearing up well, too."

She stared at him, and then understanding came to her. She said in a quiet, controlled voice, "Yes, you tell him that. Thank you."

When he arrived home, instead of giving Miriam his usual, matter-of-fact, husbandly peck, he embraced her, kissing her on the lips with considerable authority.

"Well," she said in surprise, "what brought this on?"

"I have had a very unpleasant day," he said, "but I learned that I love you very much."

"Well, if you learned that, you must tell me all about it."

"I can't."

"Then at least let me fix you a drink."

"No, but I'd like a cup of coffee."

"So would I." And she went inside to put on the pot.

He unlaced his shoes and kicked them off. Then, punching a pillow into place, he stretched out on the divan. But the phone rang and he went to answer. It was the assistant district attorney.

"Yes, Mr. Ames. What can I do for you?"

"Sergeant Schroeder has just been to see me. He's quite annoyed with you. And I'm not sure that I'm entirely pleased with you myself."

"I'm sorry to hear that," said the rabbi. "Is it his feeling in general or is it something he thinks I did?"

Ames chuckled appreciatively. "He'd like me to order you picked up as a material witness. It's what you would probably call a sin of omission. A Kathy Dunlop came to see you with information bearing on this case. He thinks you should have reported it to the police."

"I see. So she went to you people with her story."

"She did."

"Well," said the rabbi, "I thought about it and decided that her uncorroborated story would not be of much use to the police, whereas reporting it might very seriously affect a matter in which I have some responsibility. I balanced one against the other and decided not to report it for a while."

"Indeed? And what matter is that, Rabbi?"

"The relationship between Mr. and Mrs. Fine. I performed the marriage, you know."

"You were afraid Schroeder might go see Mrs. Fine?" There was a pause. "All right, Rabbi, I'll buy that. Now how about your little trip to the Excelsior? That is purely police business."

"I can justify that, too."

"Save it, Rabbi. Why don't you join me after your class tomorrow morning in Hendryx's apartment. You can tell me all about it there. And Rabbi," he said, "it better be good."

He hung up as Miriam came into the room with a tray. "More trouble?" she asked in concern.

"Nothing serious. And nothing I have to worry about until tomorrow. Tonight I'm looking forward to a quiet evening at home."

She heard a car and went to the window.

"Oh, David, the police cruising car has just pulled into our driveway."

Sure enough, there was a peremptory knock on the door and Miriam went to answer. The policeman tipped his hat and said, "How do you do, Mrs. Small. I brought you your tickets to the Policeman's Ball."

"You deliver them in person now?" asked the rabbi.

"The chief thought it might be good for public relations. You know, get to know the people. We've got quite a program in public relations going down at the station."

"Well, I think that's a wonderful idea," said Miriam. "Why not do a good job of it and come in and have a cup of coffee."

"That's very nice of you, Mrs. Small, but my partner is outside."

"Well, bring him in, too."

"It's the latest wrinkle in police work," said the first officer, as he and his partner sat on the edge of their chairs, gingerly balancing coffee cups on their knees. "Public relations. It's all on account of these young people that go around calling the police pigs and other things. Then when you have to arrest one of them, they accuse you of police brutality. So the purpose of our campaign is to get the public to back their police, to know them. I suppose it makes sense, but personally I feel that the ones who aren't looking for trouble already know the police are there to protect them; the others are just sore because we try to prevent them from doing mischief."

"Is that your view, too?" asked Miriam of the other officer.

"Well, things might be different in the city, ma'am. But here in Barnard's Crossing everybody knows everyone on the force. So to me this public relations is like extra duty."

"That you'd just as soon do without, eh?" asked the rabbi.

"Oh, I don't mind," he said quickly. "We volunteered. It's nice meeting people like this, having a cup of coffee and chatting, not in the way of business you might say."

"Maybe they ought to try the same thing in the city," Miriam suggested.

The policeman shook his head. "It wouldn't work there. You take these young people, well, here we know all of them. I've umpired games for them when they were in Little League and Joe here has been coach and manager of a team for years.

They call us by our first names. But in the city, they don't know the police and the police don't know them. The same ones that are so nice and friendly to us here, when they get into the city they can become a bunch of raving maniacs when they come up against the police." He turned to his partner. "Remember how they carried on the day we had to drive Miss Hanbury back to college?"

"Yeah, the day the place was bombed. They were pretty hot, I can tell you."

"You drove back Dean Hanbury after the bombing?" asked the rabbi. "Why was that?"

"Well, she'd just got home," said Joe, "and phoned us to say she'd found one of her windows open. Lots of times people leave them open and then forget, so when they get home they call the police on account they think somebody might have broken in." He turned to Miriam. "Now don't let that keep you from calling us any time you think there's anything wrong, Mrs. Small. We don't mind. We're only too happy if it turns out you did it yourself and forgot. Well, anyway, we went right out to Miss Hanbury's house and I looked around, for footprints, maybe a mark of a jimmy on the sash, but I couldn't find anything."

"And while he was looking," his colleague continued, "a call came through on the radio about the explosion at the college. They wanted Miss Hanbury right back in Boston, and since she'd just driven out we offered to take her. And when we got to the school, there was this crowd of kids hanging around, ragging the officers who were guarding the building. They were jeering at them and laughing, even though the police were just doing their duty. Now if something like that happened here, we'd know every one of them and make a point of talking to their parents."

When they left, Miriam set about preparing dinner. As she worked, she talked—about the children, about conversations she had had in the supermarket that morning, her voice raised so that it would carry from the kitchen. But the rabbi was unresponsive.

When she finally came into the living room to tell him that

dinner was ready, he said, "I don't think I care for anything right now, Miriam."

"Is something wrong, David?"

"No, I'm just not hungry. I—I've got some work to do." And he got up and went to his study.

Later, much later, he was still there, not reading, not working, but abstracted, gazing off into space. When she asked if he were coming to bed, he did not answer but just shook his head in momentary annoyance.

50

The morning traffic was heavier than usual and the rabbi did not find a parking spot until a few minutes after nine. By the time he reached his office, it was ten minutes past. He was quite certain that his students had already left, but he hurried nevertheless on the chance that a few might have waited. To his surprise, when he reached the classroom he found the normal complement of students.

"There was a breakdown on the bridge," he explained by way of apology, "and traffic was single lane all the way."

"Oh, that's all right, Rabbi," said Harvey Shacter magnanimously. "We voted to wait until a quarter past."

"That was very considerate of all of you," said the rabbi. He smiled. "It shows perhaps you have begun to acquire the traditional Jewish attitude toward learning and study."

"You mean we got a special one?" asked Shacter.

"Of course," said his friend Luftig scornfully. "Get A's and make honors or Phi Bete."

"No, Mr. Luftig, that's not it," said the rabbi. "Quite the contrary, in fact. The rabbis held that learning should not be used as a spade to dig with, by which they meant that it should not be put to practical or material use. Learning and study are with us a religious duty, and hence not competitive. A's, honors, Phi Beta Kappa—these are the rewards of competition."

"So if you're not going to get any practical benefit, what's the sense?" asked Shacter.

"Because the desire for knowledge, knowledge for its own sake, is what distinguishes man from the lower animals. All animals have an interest in practical knowledge—where the best food supplies may be found, the best places to hide or bed down—but only man goes to the trouble of trying to learn something merely because he does not as yet know it. The mind of man yearns for knowledge as the body yearns for food. And that learning is for himself alone, just as is the food he eats."

"So you mean it's not kosher if a guy studies to be a doctor or a lawyer?" asked Shacter.

"He means he's not supposed to get money for it," said Mazelman.

"No, Mr. Mazelman, that's not what I mean. The learning one acquires to become a doctor or a lawyer, or a carpenter or a plumber for that matter, is of a different kind. It is practical learning for the purpose of society. And we favor that kind of learning, too. There is also a rabbinical saying that a father who does not teach his son a trade is making a thief of him. So you see, there are two kinds of learning: one for yourself and the one for society."

"What a doctor or a lawyer learns, isn't that for himself?" asked Lillian Dushkin.

"It feeds his mind, to be sure; everything one learns does that. But primarily he is training himself to serve society. A doctor does not learn about all kinds of sicknesses just to cure himself. Certain branches of medicine don't apply to himself at all, such as obstetrics—"

"They apply to women doctors."

"You're quite right, Ms. Draper," acknowledged the rabbi.

Luftig was struck by a thought. "If there are two kinds of learning, shouldn't there be two kinds of teaching, too?"

The rabbi considered this. "That's a good point, Mr. Luftig.

Professional study should be relevant. I don't see any sense in teaching medieval church law to the law student or the humours theory of disease to a medical student."

"Shouldn't all study be relevant?" asked Luftig.

"Why? Why should that matter in liberal arts study? There, anything that interests you—and it *could* be medieval church law or Latin epigraphy for that matter—is worth studying. Or to put it another way, in liberal arts study everything *is* relevant."

"Then how do you justify quizzes?" asked Mark Leventhal. "Aren't you breaking your own rules by giving us grades?"

"Yes, I suppose I am. But I have to follow the regulations of the school."

"What would you do if you had your way?" Leventhal persisted.

The rabbi thought a moment. "Well, since you receive credit toward an earned degree, I'd have to distinguish between those who made a proper effort and those who didn't. So I'd just have two marks—pass and fail. And I'd try to devise an examination that would indicate interest rather than just information."

"How could you do that?"

"I don't know offhand. I suppose you might have the choice of answering all the questions, or just a few, or even one at great length."

"Hey, that's a good idea."

"Right on. Why don't we do it that way?"

"Maybe the other teachers—"

"Hey Rabbi, you going to teach next semester, too?"

It was one of numerous questions, but the class fell silent after Shacter asked it, as though it had been in all their minds.

"I have not arranged to," said the rabbi.

"Maybe you could teach full-time," said Lillian Dushkin.

He realized that the questions indicated their approval of him as a teacher, and it was pleasant to hear. "Why would I want to do that, Miss Dushkin?" he asked.

"Well, it must be a lot easier than rabbi-ing."

"Yeah, but you make less," Shacter pointed out.

"Aw, he wouldn't care about that," Luftig countered.

"A rabbi is a teacher anyway," Leventhal pointed out. "That's what the word means."

It crossed his mind that earlier in the year he would have considered this free discussion of his future career impertinent, but he had come a long way since his first week of teaching. "You're quite right, Mr. Leventhal," he said. "And you're right, too, Miss Dushkin, teaching is easier. But I intend to go on being a rabbi and ministering to a congregation." He looked out the window at the apartment across the street and saw what he assumed were plainclothesmen moving purposefully between the Hendryx apartment and a car parked in front of the building. He turned to the class once again and smiling wryly, he said, "As for teaching next semester, I'm not sure I'll even be able to finish this one."

Later, when the class was over and he was returning to his office, Mark Leventhal fell in step beside him. "You know, Rabbi, my folks want me to go to Cincinnati when I get through here. They'd like for me to become a rabbi."

"Is that so? And you, how do you feel about it?"

"Well, I was planning to go to graduate school and then get a job teaching at some college."

They reached the office and the rabbi fished for his key. "Do you have a class, Mr. Leventhal?"

"Yeah, but I'd just as soon cut it."

"Come in, then." He motioned the young man to the chair and took the swivel chair behind the desk. "Are you looking for advice as to which career to pursue?" he asked.

"Oh well, you know, I'd like to hear how you feel about it, you doing both, kind of."

The rabbi nodded. "It's changed, of course," he said. "In the small ghetto towns of eastern Europe, which was the main center of Jewish culture, the rabbi was hired by the town, rather than by a synagogue. He was subsidized by the townspeople to spend most of his life in study, serving the community by sitting in judgment when the occasion required. He didn't conduct services or even preach sermons. He was required to address the community only twice a year, and usually it was not a sermon but a thesis on some religious or biblical question."

As he continued, he realized that he was talking as much to clarify his own thinking as to advise the young man. "He was usually highly respected by the congregation, if for no other reason than that he was the most learned man in the community in the only kind of learning they had—religious, biblical, Talmudic. But here in America, things are entirely different. He no longer sits in judgment, we go to the courts for that. And his special knowledge is no longer the only kind; it isn't even considered a very important kind by his congregation. Medicine, law, science, engineering—these are regarded as much more significant in the modern world and of course by his congregants."

"You mean he doesn't get the same respect he used to?"

The rabbi smiled. "You could say that. He's had to make his own job, and it's largely administrative and—well, political."

"Political?"

"That's right. And in two senses: he's usually the contact point between the congregation and the rest of the community; and he has to maintain himself in his position. Like any public figure, he always has an opposition to contend with." He remembered what Miriam had said. "But actually, although the job appears to have changed enormously, it's still the same job."

"How do you mean?"

"Basically, his job was to guide and teach the community. Well, that's still his job, only now his community is less plastic, less docile, less interested, and even less inclined to be guided. It's a much harder job than it used to be, Mr. Leventhal, and a much, much harder job than teaching in a college where your teaching is limited to a rigid framework of classes at specified times, quizzes, credits—"

"Well then, why would you choose the rabbinate over college teaching?" the young man demanded.

The rabbi smiled, for he now knew he had found his own

answer. "We say it's hard to be a Jew, and it's even harder to be a rabbi, I suppose, who is a kind of professional Jew. But haven't you noticed in your own life, Mr. Leventhal, the harder the task, the more satisfaction there is in doing it?"

51

Diffidently the rabbi rang the Hendryx bell. "Oh, it's you," Sergeant Schroeder said belligerently. "I've got some things to say to you."

"It will keep, Sergeant," said Bradford Ames. "Come in, Rabbi."

The room was ablaze with light from floodlamps mounted on collapsible stands, and several plainclothesmen were busy measuring, photographing, dusting for fingerprints. Ames explained that Hendryx's relatives from the West Coast were coming for his effects, so this was their last chance to give the place a final going over.

"How about the bureau? You want me to take some pictures of the drawers, Sergeant?" asked the photographer.

"Yeah, take each drawer. It'll give us a kind of inventory."

Ames motioned the rabbi to the bed. "Sit there. You'll be out of the way," he said. "I'm accepting your explanation on the Kathy Dunlop story, but I might as well tell you, your little investigation at the Excelsior Motel, well, that depends on what you came up with." He showed no anger, but his tone was distinctly cool.

The rabbi told them what he had learned—that no one at the Excelsior had seen Roger Fine and that the motel switchboard had been out of order that day. "So no one could have called him from outside."

Schroeder rubbed his hands. "Well, that's all right then. That's just fine."

Ames, too, smiled his satisfaction. In a more friendly voice, he explained, "You see, if it had been the other way, if there had been some chance of a possible alibi, then your inquiries could have fixed it in the person's mind, or even insinuated it there."

"I didn't really expect an alibi from Kathy's story," said the rabbi. "All she remembered was the time she called him at school. She did suggest that if Fine had just killed someone, however, he would scarcely be likely to visit her immediately after."

"And yet," said Ames, "there are cases reported in the literature of just that sort of thing. Adds a certain zest to the love-making as I understand."

"Well," said the rabbi, "the next day I checked with Fine in jail on the chance there was something Kathy had overlooked, but he didn't want it known he had been with her at all. He said even if that offered a possible alibi he wouldn't use it. To see for myself whether Miss Dunlop's story was true, I decided to check with the motel people."

"I can follow your reasoning," Ames admitted, "but that phase of the inquiry should have been left to the police."

"Hey Sarge," the photographer called out, "this bottom drawer is empty."

Ames went over and the rabbi joined him, feeling he was not actually required to remain seated on the bed. "Hendryx probably used that bottom drawer for his soiled laundry," Ames said. "It's what I do when I'm staying in a hotel."

"I don't think so, sir," said Schroeder. "There's a hamper in the bathroom."

"Then he probably didn't have enough stuff for that last drawer," said Ames.

"And yet the other drawers seem pretty full, even crowded," the rabbi offered.

"Is that so?" Ames chuckled. "It looks like we'll have to use that Talmud trick you told me about, and wait for—who was it, Elijah?—to come to solve that little problem."

"Talmudists didn't use it until they had exhausted all other possibilities," said the rabbi reproachfully.

"Well now, I did a little reading on the subject after I spoke to you," said Ames, "out of idle curiosity, you know, and according to this article in the encyclopedia, a good part of your Talmud is just a bunch of stories and old wives' tales and moralizing. But even the legal part, I gathered, was largely unsystematic arguing sometimes about the most improbable cases."

"The Talmud has a little of everything," the rabbi admitted, "but perhaps the most useful function it serves is the method it developed."

The technicians had finished and had packed up. Schroeder asked Ames whether he could give him a lift downtown.

"Just a minute, Sergeant. The rabbi is giving me a lesson in the Talmud." He chuckled. "And what was this method, Rabbi?"

"Basically," said the rabbi seriously, "it consisted of examining every aspect of a problem from every possible point of view, which is what I assume your encyclopedia meant when it suggested that some of the cases were highly improbable. They had plenty of time, those old Talmudists, and the more recent ones, too, and they didn't share the concern that you find in Common Law about the irrelevant, the immaterial, and the incompetent. Take this empty drawer, for example—"

"Yes, what would your Talmudists have said about an empty drawer in a bureau?"

The rabbi smiled. "Well, they would certainly have considered the two possibilities: A) that the drawer had never been filled; and B) that it had been filled and then emptied."

"I don't get it," said Schroeder. "Meaning no disrespect to this Talmud, whatever it is, what difference does it make whether it was filled and then emptied, or never filled. It's empty right now."

"Well, if it had never been used, wouldn't you wonder why?" said the rabbi. "Obviously it's not because he had nothing to put into it. Look where these sweaters have been piled on top of the undershirts."

"So maybe he was a guy who didn't like to bend down."

"But he had to bend down. His shoes were on the floor of the closet," the Rabbi observed.

"All right," said Ames impatiently. "Let's assume there was something in the drawer originally. Where does that lead us to?"

"To the next question: who emptied it? It was either Hendryx or someone else."

"Well, that sure is logical," said Schroeder sarcastically. "You could also say it was either me or someone else, or George Washington or someone else."

Ames grinned, but the rabbi continued as though there had been no interruption, "Or it could be both."

"It hardly seems that two people would be required to empty one bureau drawer," said Ames.

"I didn't mean they did it together," said the rabbi. "I was suggesting that Hendryx probably emptied the drawer to make room for something else. And that this something else was then removed."

"And removed by someone else? Is that what you're driving at?" asked Ames.

The rabbi nodded.

Light broke suddenly on the sergeant. "Hey, I get what he's driving at! Hendryx clears out that drawer to put something special in it, like papers or documents. Then he gets killed, and—now get this—Roger Fine comes here to get them, because naturally they're important to him—the confession and the exam papers. They're the only proof that he leaked the exam. So once he's here, he sees how easy it is to make it look like Hendryx returned to his apartment after the cleaning lady left, which would put Fine in the clear because he'd have an alibi, so he puts the pipe in the ashtray and lights a few matches."

The rabbi nodded approvingly. "That's very good, Sergeant, except that it couldn't be Roger Fine."

"Why not?"

"Because Fine has no alibi. Besides, Hendryx wouldn't have to clean out a drawer for the papers you mention. He'd probably put them in his desk."

"Then what *did* he put in the drawer?"

"I suppose the sort of things anyone puts in bureau drawers —clothing."

"You mean it was the murderer's clothing and he came to get it?" asked Ames. "But why? I still don't see it."

"Try she," suggested the rabbi. "*She* came to get it."

"A woman?" Ames thought about it for a moment. "Well, if she were—"

"Yeah, why not?" exclaimed Schroeder. "The guy was a bachelor, you'd expect him to shack up with a broad every now and then." He remembered Ames and stopped.

"It's all right, Sergeant," said Ames. "I know the facts of life."

"Well, what I mean, sir, is that if he had a woman drop in on him every now and then, naturally she'd stay the night."

"Naturally."

"And maybe she'd keep a nightgown here, and some pretties if she came often enough." He snapped his fingers. "Of course! Betty Macomber! They were secretly engaged. They don't wait nowadays. And come to think of it, she didn't seem so terribly cut up, not what you'd expect of a girl whose fiancé had just died."

"You said her father was not terribly upset either," remarked Ames.

"That's right. Hey, look—he's a golf nut," said Schroeder excitedly. "The kind that keeps his clubs right there in the office. Matter of fact, when I went up to see him, he was practicing putting on the rug."

"What's that got to do with it?" snapped Ames.

"Don't you see, sir, a golf club has a hook on the end like a cane."

"Hm." Ames nodded slowly. "Father and daughter. If he resented her marrying him—"

"Or say he found out she was sleeping with him," suggested Schroeder.

"Then he would kill him?" The rabbi looked his surprise. "Even though they were engaged? And come here to retrieve his daughter's nightgown so that her honor would not be besmirched?"

"It does sound silly the way you put it," Ames admitted.

The rabbi pressed on. "And does President Macomber have an alibi? Or his daughter?"

"No one in the case seems to," Schroeder admitted.

"Except Millicent Hanbury," said the rabbi.

"The dean?" Schroeder exclaimed. "Cummon!"

"An attractive woman," the rabbi pointed out. "Still quite young. And unmarried. It was you who first suggested her, Sergeant."

"I did?"

"When you first came to see me with Lanigan, you suggested she might be involved. We ridiculed the suggestion as I recall," the rabbi went on smoothly, "but it just shows that the intuitions of an experienced investigator are not to be lightly dismissed."

"Yeah, I did, didn't I?"

Ames chuckled. "This alibi you mention—"

"There were actually several," said the rabbi. "The meeting with the student committee at two-thirty—It was she who picked the time, I understand. Then walking out of the meeting was an excellent alibi because it was not immediately apparent. To ask someone for the time is automatically suspicious. But to leave a meeting and not return is to insure that after a while people will get restive and start looking at their watches. But the clincher was when she got back to Barnard's Crossing and called the police to report that she had found a window open. They could produce no evidence that it had been forced, of course, but the call had served its purpose— to record the time on the police blotter. Quite by accident I found out that the Barnard's Crossing Police Department is very strict about it."

"All police departments are," said Ames. "But the murder was committed earlier, probably around twenty-past two, and all those alibis are for later."

"That's why she had to make it look as though Hendryx was alive *after* she left. And the students would back up her alibi."

"But what about the medical examiner's autopsy?" Ames persisted. "She'd have to know that he would report the actual time of death."

"Ah, but that's because he examined the body shortly after death," said the rabbi. "And that was only because of the bombing. In the normal course of events, the body would not have been discovered until Monday morning, probably by me when I came in for class. That's some sixty hours later, and no medical examiner could have fixed the time within an hour or so, so long after the event. Besides, the evidence in his apartment would show that Hendryx was alive long after she had left the building."

Ames nodded. "And knowing we'd check his apartment, she stopped to retrieve her nightgown? Panties? Stockings? Yet how could they be identified as hers?"

"How about something a bit more personal?"

"More personal than panties?" asked Ames with a smile.

"I was thinking of a knitting bag," suggested the rabbi.

"Ah yes," said Ames. "I can see where she'd have to get that."

"Look," said Schroeder, "maybe I'm just a dumb cop, but you still haven't explained how she could have pulled that statue down on him without a struggle." He thought a moment. "Even if she once was a Phys. Ed. teacher."

Ames flashed the rabbi a questioning look.

"Let's go back to the Talmud again," the rabbi said. "It's the same business of considering all the possibilities. A statue on a shelf can tumble down as the result of a concussion, like a bomb's explosion. That was the point of view of the police when you arrested the students. Or it can be pulled down, which is the basis for your suspicion of Professor Fine and a moment ago, Sergeant, of the Macombers. But it can also be *pushed* off the shelf, and that's what I think happened."

"Pushed?" said Ames. "How could it have been pushed?"

The rabbi said quietly, "Our office phone feeds off the line in the dean's office; the wire comes through a hole in the wall above the top shelf near the ceiling. The statue was right in front of it. In fact, the phone man had to move it to make the hole."

"So there's a hole in the wall, and the phone wire goes through it," said Ames in annoyance. "What of it?"

"The wire comes through it, but there's still enough room for a thin but strong steel rod to be pushed through," said the rabbi.

"A thin steel—a knitting needle!" exclaimed Ames.

The rabbi nodded. "My guess is that when she heard me leave—and you can hear through those walls; the office shares a common partition—she moved the desk over to the wall and climbed up. Then she pushed the knitting needle through the hole and toppled the statue. She knew Hendryx's chair was directly under the statue. Sure enough, it tumbled down and killed him."

Ames was silent for a long moment. "And motive, Rabbi," he said at last. "Do you have some theory as to motive?"

"I have a theory," said the rabbi diffidently. "My guess is that she assumed she and Hendryx were going to be married, perhaps as soon as he was made head of the department. It was no secret that she was pushing for it but so far had been unsuccessful. Hendryx must have decided he'd have a better chance if the daughter of the president backed him, so he made a play for her and they became engaged. Friday morning, when President Macomber told the dean that Hendryx was at last getting his appointment, he probably told her why, since he'd know nothing of the prior relationship between his future son-in-law and the dean."

"It's a lovely theory, Rabbi," said Ames, "and it seems to cover everything, but you realize of course that you don't have a particle of proof."

"I'm not so sure it covers everything, at that," said Schroeder. "You say she moved her desk and then climbed up on it."

"I'm sure that's what happened," said the rabbi. "Any of the chairs would have been too low."

Schroeder shook his head slowly in flat negation. "The desk is a good three feet from the wall and it's screwed to the floor. She couldn't have moved it."

The rabbi frowned. Bradford Ames giggled nervously.

"Three feet, you say? Yes, I suppose it is." The rabbi's face brightened. "Then I might even be able to offer your proof, Sergeant." Rising from his seat, he stood about three feet away from the wall and leaned forward, his left arm outstretched, his hand pressed against the wall to support himself. He drew a pencil from his breastpocket, and jabbed it against the wall. "High up on the wall, there's a good chance the print is still there."

She looked up from her knitting as the three men entered her office. "You remember me, don't you, ma'am?" asked Schroeder politely.

"Oh yes, you're from the police."

"And this is Mr. Bradford Ames, assistant district attorney. He's directing the investigation."

"How do you do, Mr. Ames. And this man?" she asked.

"He's our fingerprint expert, Miss Hanbury," said Ames. "All right, Bill."

The man looked at the wall. "I'll need something to stand on," he said.

"Why don't you hop on the desk here," Ames suggested. "I'll put this paper down so you won't scratch it with your shoes."

She watched with interest as Bill mounted the desk, as he peered at the wall. "Yup, it's here," he said, "one print, full palm and all five fingers. Perfect."

She smiled as she bent over her knitting. "So you know."

"Yes, Miss Hanbury, we know."

52

Later, Ames joined the rabbi at the apartment.

"I could use a cup of coffee," said Ames. "Seems to me I noticed a jar of instant coffee in the kitchen."

And with the long practice of the bachelor, he scurried about the kitchen, boiling water, rinsing cups, setting the table.

They were both seated at the kitchen table, their steaming cups before them, before Ames said, "In spite of that Talmudic razzle-dazzle, you must have had some idea of where you were heading. And please spare me your facile explanation to the good sergeant that it was he who first put you in mind of Dean Hanbury. What was it actually?"

The rabbi set his cup down. "From the day I first met her, Millicent Hanbury has been in my mind. I suppose it's our general way of looking at things: the biblical injunction to be fruitful and multiply. To us, the unmarried woman, the spinster, is a tragic figure because she has not had the chance to complete her normal life cycle. In the *stetl*, the small ghetto towns of Russia and Poland where every girl was required to provide a dowry for her marriage, the poor girl, the orphan, was furnished a dowry by the community so that she would not be condemned to a life of spinsterhood. Even if she was ugly, they managed to pair her off with someone. There were no spinsters in the *stetl*."

"How about bachelors?"

"An occasional one." The rabbi smiled. "They were not considered so much tragic figures as failing in their duty, not pulling their weight, as it were."

"You, too?" In answer to the rabbi's questioning look, he explained, "I've got it from my family most of my life—not pulling my weight, not doing my duty. But it wasn't because I remained single; it was because I didn't become a bigshot lawyer. Not fulfilling my potential is the usual remark."

The rabbi smiled. "Well, in our modern system, where you marry for romantic love, it's pretty much a matter of luck whether you marry or not. But I venture to say that in the older system of the arranged marriage, you probably would not have remained a bachelor, and Miss Hanbury certainly would not have remained a spinster. She is too attractive. So I found myself wondering why she hadn't married. Was it for the sake of an academic career?" He broke off as a thought crossed his mind. "You know, the chances are that if you had

239

married, your wife would have seen to it that you became that bigshot lawyer."

Ames chuckled. "Then it's just as well that we don't have the arranged marriage."

The rabbi grinned in sympathy. "Well, shortly afterward I bumped into Chief Lanigan and he told me about Millicent Hanbury. She was a Hanbury, and Hanburys didn't associate with just anyone. But since she belonged to a poor branch of the family, she didn't even associate with those she considered her equals. She couldn't. It was a matter of pride in her family, her upbringing. And it left her emotionally crippled."

"I've known similar cases," said Ames.

"Yes, I imagine so. Well, along comes Hendryx who had left Barnard's Crossing in his early teens. And the Hendryxes were of the same social class as the Hanburys. She had known him, and it's quite possible that in spite of the difference in their ages she could have had a crush on him."

"Or *because* of the difference in their ages."

"True. And now he comes to her for a job. And he is not married. She not only gets him a job, but manages to maneuver him into the position of acting head of the department."

"He was a legitimate scholar?"

"Oh yes. Nothing outstanding, I gather, but he had a good degree and had even published some."

"Then why was he out of a job when he came to Windemere?" asked Ames. "We backtracked him and found he'd had several jobs in the last ten years or so."

"It could be a matter of personality," said the rabbi. "He was proud and supercilious, given to making snide, cutting remarks. In a lot of places, one's colleagues in the department decide on matters of tenure and promotion, and I'm sure these traits rubbed a lot of people the wrong way—as they did Fine. But I suspect that here at Windemere he at last decided to stay. He was no longer a young man. He was already in his forties, and unless you've made your mark it's not so easy to get a job at that age."

Ames nodded.

"I'm sure Miss Hanbury assumed they were going to be married. I just can't imagine her—what's the phrase, shacking up? —I can't imagine her just shacking up with a man. Her pride wouldn't let her accept so anomalous a situation."

Ames agreed. "When we questioned her, she said they were planning to get married as soon as Hendryx got tenure. Then she could leave her job, would have to, in fact, because they have a rule here against husband and wife both on the staff."

"Of course," said the rabbi. "And as long as his was a temporary appointment, hers was by far the better job. So if they got married before he got tenure, he'd be the one to go and she'd be supporting him. I'm sure she wouldn't care for that, and neither would he. So it was just a question of time."

"But he couldn't wait?"

"That's what I think," said the rabbi. "Hendryx decided to go for the president's daughter as the quicker and more certain route to his goal. And it worked. But Millicent Hanbury was proud, too proud to permit herself to be used and then discarded." He shook his head reflectively. "I wonder how he was able to manage it, courting one woman—"

"While diddling another?" Ames chuckled. "Oh, married men manage it often enough. It's even easier for a bachelor."

53

"I hope you don't mind my asking you to come this afternoon, Rabbi," said President Macomber, "but on Friday afternoons the building is practically deserted. We can talk in privacy and without interruption. But first, are you enjoying your teaching here?"

"Oh yes, I had twenty-five in my class this afternoon."

"Indeed," murmured Macomber.

The rabbi realized the president had no idea what he meant and hastened to explain.

"I'm sure it's the result of your teaching," said Macomber politely. He fiddled with a pencil and appeared embarrassed. Finally, he cleared his throat and said, "You shared an office with Professor Hendryx. You talked with him?"

"Yes, occasionally. Not too often, and usually not at great length."

"Tell me, Rabbi," he leaned back in his chair, "in your opinion was Professor Hendryx anti-semitic?"

The rabbi pursed his lips. "I wouldn't say so. He was prejudiced, all right. Most people are against one group or another. It's a natural reaction to the stranger, to the member of a minority. We Jews have suffered it more than most, I suppose, because we have been a minority in so many countries. But I don't call it anti-semitism if I am not liked, even if I'm not liked because I am a Jew. I don't consider it anti-semitism unless the prejudice is translated into action, political or legal or social. To work, a multiple society doesn't require that every segment of the population like every other segment. That's utopian. It works if every segment accords equality to every other segment, whether they like them or not. As for Professor Hendryx, he made disparaging remarks about Jews on occasion, but he also made similar remarks about Irish and Italians and Negroes. He was given to making bitter, sarcastic remarks on almost anyone and anything. I considered him a vexed, unhappy man."

Macomber nodded slowly. "I see."

"You seem disappointed."

The president laughed shortly. "In a way I am. It would make matters easier for me if Professor Hendryx *had* been anti-semitic." He was silent. Then, "With the end of the term approaching, we are quite disorganized. We do not have a dean, and the English department does not have a chairman. Normally, that last would be no great concern, but we're also short-handed there. And with Professor Fine leaving . . ."

"Does he have to leave?"

"Well, that's just the point." Macomber picked up a long

white envelope lying on his desk. "Before his death, Professor Hendryx made grave charges against Professor Fine to Dean Hanbury, charges which she brought to me and which led to my decision not to renew his contract. I venture to speak of this because Mr. Ames intimated that you were familiar with the circumstances." He looked questioningly at the rabbi.

The rabbi nodded.

"Well, I just can't ignore these charges, even though Dean Hanbury could be considered—er—discred'ted by the events that have since transpired. It's the sort of thing that a college president simply can't ignore. Not if he has a conscience."

"Let me understand, President Macomber, you would like to keep Fine on because you are short-handed—"

"And because I think he's a good teacher."

"But because you have reason to believe that he committed the sin of leaking an exam to a student, your conscience won't allow you to overlook it?"

"Ye–es, I'd say that's about right," said Macomber unhappily.

"But if I had said that Hendryx was anti-semitic, you would have considered that the charges had stemmed from bias and could dismiss them."

"Considering that I knew of the situation only through Dean Hanbury. I didn't talk to Hendryx."

"But now you feel she's been discredited."

"Yes, but there's this envelope, unfortunately. It contains proof of the charge," he said. "It's sealed as you see, with Fine's name written across it, but I know what's inside since I told Dean Hanbury just how I wanted it worded. I wrote it out for her to copy, in fact." He pulled open a drawer and drew out a folder. It contained a single sheet of notepaper. He passed it across the desk. "Go on, read it."

"It's not signed." The rabbi read, "No date." He looked up inquiringly.

"That's so we could add a recent date in the event Professor Fine went back on his promise," he explained.

The rabbi read on: "I hearby admit of my own free will that I arranged to show a copy of the final examination of the course English 74 to a student taking that course, thereby permitting said student to get a higher mark at the end of the summer term. I regret this action and promise that I will not be guilty of a similar offense during the remainder of my tenure here."

"The one in the envelope is of course signed by Professor Fine," said Macomber.

The rabbi was silent for a moment and then said, "The traditional function of a rabbi is to sit in judgment. Did you know that?"

Macomber smiled. "Bradford Ames said something to that effect when he discussed—er—things with me. Are you suggesting that if you were the judge you would view the charges differently?"

"If I were hearing the case, I would not admit this as evidence at all. It is contrary to Talmudic law."

Macomber smiled. "Since Roger Fine is a Jew, I suppose there would be a certain justice in judging him by Talmudic law. Judging a man by his peers, you might say. All right, how would you proceed?"

"I would first hear from his accusers."

"But that's impossible. They're both—"

"Precisely."

"But there's his own admission."

"But I could not admit it as evidence. By our law, 'No man may call himself a wrongdoer.' This is a fundamental principle with us in criminal law."

"Come to think of it, I guess it is in our Common Law, too," Macomber remarked.

"But there's a difference," said the rabbi. "In Common Law a man cannot be forced to testify against himself. In our law, he can't even if he wants to."

"I see, so if you were sitting in judgment on this case?"

"I would dismiss it," said the rabbi promptly.

Macomber smiled. "It's a way out, to be sure. And yet—"

"And yet you are dissatisfied."

"Well, yes I am."

"I am too," the rabbi admitted. "I suppose it's because we're involved not so much with law as with conscience. Yours and

244

mine. I believe I first referred to it as a sin rather than as a crime. This sin of leaking an exam—as a college president you regard it as unpardonable?"

"Well, no sin is unpardonable, I suppose," said Macomber.

"Then how would someone go about getting his sin pardoned?"

"I guess that's more in your province than mine, Rabbi. I suppose by confession—and repentance, and by promising not to repeat the offense."

The rabbi brightened. "Well, isn't that what Fine has done?"

"When? Now?"

"Right here in this paper. 'I admit of my own free will'—that's confession. 'I regret this action'—that's repentance. 'And promise that I will not be guilty of a similar offense'—that's the third element."

Macomber considered. Then he smiled. "Yes, I think that will do it. And that will take care of our problem with the English Department at the same time." He sat back in his chair and beamed. "Tell me, Rabbi. I don't suppose you'd like to try your hand at being a dean, would you?"